PANDEMONIUM

PANDEMONIUM

Towards a Retro-Organization Theory

GIBSON BURRELL

SAGE Publications
London • Thousand Oaks • New Delhi

First published 1997

All illustrations by Adam Young

 SAGE Publications Ltd
6 Bonhill Street
London EC2A 4PU

SAGE Publications Inc
2455 Teller Road
Thousand Oaks, California 91320

SAGE Publications India Pvt Ltd
32, M-Block Market
Greater Kailash – I
New Delhi 110 048

British Library Cataloguing in Publication data

A catalogue record for this book is
available from the British Library.

ISBN 0 8039 7776–X
ISBN 0 8039 7777–8 (pbk)

Library of Congress catalog card number 96-71480

Designed and typeset by M Rules
Printed in Great Britain by The Cromwell Press Ltd,
Broughton Gifford, Melksham, Wiltshire

This is a ludibrium to the memory of
Ruby Burrell (1913–1994)

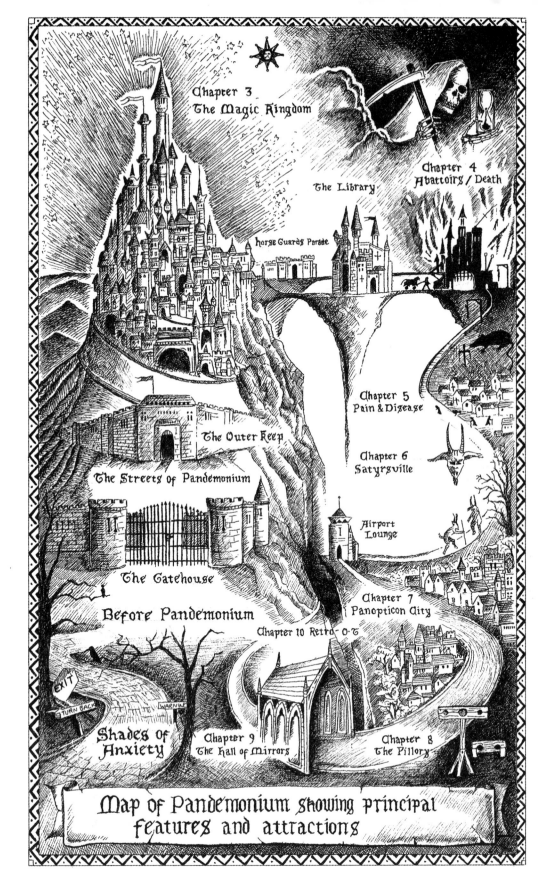

Map of Pandemonium showing principal features and attractions

Contents

The author and publisher wish to formally acknowledge the following:

Alain Boublil Overseas Ltd for permission to use 'Master of the House' from *Les Misérables*, a musical by Alain Boublil and Claude-Michel Schonberg, lyrics by Herbert Kretzmer

Penguin Books Ltd for permission to use lines from *The Bacchae* in *The Bacchae and Other Plays* by Euripides, translated by Philip Vellacott (Penguin Classics 1954, revised edition 1972) copyright © Philip Vellacott, 1954, 1972

Orion Publishing Group for permission to reprint The Combat by R.S. Thomas in *Collected Poems 1945–1990*, Phoenix, London, 1995, page 291

The Guardian Newspaper for permission to use an (enhanced) version of the Wheel of Fortune diagram from an article by Finbar Sheely entitled 'The Humours and the Seasons' which appeared in *Guardian Education*, 5 July 1994

The Tasmanian Museum and Art Gallery, Hobart, Australia for permission to reproduce Governor Arthur's Orders, 1829

The Ordnance Survey for the map of part of Ashington, Northumberland, from LandRanger no. 81 (1:25 000 Pathfinder map), reproduced with the permission of The Controller of HMSO © Crown Copyright, Licence no. MC85718M

The following letter was published, in response to a review of *Pandemonium* in the journal *Organization* 5(3) 1998:

The review of *Pandemonium* published in the last issue of this journal was a testament to the notion that the biographical details of an author are crucial to any understanding of the meaning that should or could be attached to his or her writing. This is a travesty. We must escape from the discredited and dated idea that any author has authority over the 'real meaning' of any text simply because they wrote it. Authors often know little of the causes of their motivation in sitting down and putting pen to paper or fingers to keyboard. What does it matter why someone writes a page? Surely it is what is on the page which is important and how it might be interpreted by any and every reader?

Let us not ask why *Pandemonium* was written. By all means let us ask *how* it was written for there is a blatant failure to develop an argument, the 'dual carriageway' structure is perverse and the supposed attempt to reverse or even escape linearity is not at all unproblematic. The reasons why such contrivances were used may be deemed of some minor significance but, and this is a large but, surely to goodness we can attempt to read the text as it is, in full and harmless ignorance of the author's state of mind in 1995–6.

The following is an extract of a review of *Pandemonium* which appeared in *Organization* 5(2) 1998:

This book appears to many to be the febrile product – indeed some might say the inchoate ramblings – of a disturbed mind. At the beginning of the year in which it was written, Burrell had his 48th birthday and it is said, by those that knew him, that his fears about premature senile dementia and cirrhosis of the liver intensified. About this time, his professorial colleagues had presented him with an unpleasant question. Did he wish to pursue the tasks of a full-time administrator as Chair of the Faculty of Social Studies at Warwick or keep up the pretence of being a proper academic? He tried both. *Pandemonium* represents a last gasp effort to establish his credentials in the latter arena but as we shall see, it unfortunately fails. It is not written much in the first person. Yet for those who knew him, the book is redolent with his personal fears and nightmares – the mid-life crisis which is so well reflected in the quote from Amis with which the book begins. An even better insight into his mind might have been provided by another section of *Time's Arrow*. 'The work looks like hell to me. . . . Blood and bodies and death and power. I suppose you can see the connexion. They are reconciling themselves to their own mortality. They are doing what we all have to do down here on earth; they are getting ready to die' (Amis 1991: 87). As it turned out, it would have been *this* section which would have been prophetically right. . . .

When people move – when they travel – they look where they've come from, not where they are going. Is this what humans always do? [It] doesn't appear to make much immediate sense. For example, you have five reverse gears and only one forward, which is marked R for reverse. When we drive we don't look where we're going. We look where we came from.

(Martin Amis, *Time's Arrow*, 1991: 30)

A Rough Guide to Pandemonium

> The primary images of the baroque were . . . the ruin, the labyrinth and
> the library: all of these phenomena are based upon deception, complex-
> ity and artificiality.
>
> (Bryan S. Turner in Buci-Glucksmann 1994: 23)

Why, poor traveller, should you tour Pandemonium's meandering
streets? What follows here is very much a rough guide and is intended
to show you that Pandemonium can be visited cheaply and safely if
you so wish. If you want to stay there semi-permanently, which is
likely to be much more exciting, threatening and therefore liable to
make you old, well before your time, then please do so. But that kind
of commitment is not to be made lightly nor yet. Until you have sam-
pled the local customs, fare and night life then it would be premature
to ask you to give up your career, lifestyle and even soul. Think of what
follows as the tourist video where camera angles keep out the power
station at the end of the runway, only the most tanned bodies are
shown in shot and the beaches are never too crowded. Not a single
turd blots the azure blue of the ocean. This part of the chapter, by
popular request, is the selling video for Pandemonium.

But of course it is not a video. It is a book. But I do want it to look
and feel different from normal books – particularly that kind of stulti-
fying text which is labelled as the 'set book'·for an academic course.
Why? The reason is simple. I do not believe that the normal textual format can fully express the range of ideas of a critical and questioning
kind which I wish to address here. A key way of organizing our lives,
we have to acknowledge, is the way in which information is provided
to us by others (Jennings 1985: 5). Normally the symbolic ordering of
our lives takes place textually on the page or the screen but it is laid
out in very, very particular ways. These constrain our thought and
our ability to envisage a set of other possibilities. This book is meant to
escape from the normal conventions of textual presentation which
pass for common sense within Western social science.

But you won't have noticed that yet. Because I am postponing the

1

gratification of releasing myself into the deep-piled luxury of other more adventurous forms of presentation until we actually enter the confines of Pandemonium itself.

Writing in an esoteric way might take many forms. First, of course, I could have chosen not to write at all. Indeed there are those of my close colleagues who think this has been a well established strategy of mine for years. But communication with large numbers of unknown people is difficult without writing and I do feel passionately that there are things which need to be said about the modern, organized world. In so many ways, one is forced to write in ways predetermined by spelling, syntax and normal conventions of the language we call English. But what is possible at the margins? Well, in a second strategy, I could have written a text which, like Derrida in *Margins of Philosophy*, inserts a commentary on the text alongside the text itself but which is not designed to be read at the same time. It is marginalized, but relevant. *Pandemonium* could also have been written in a messy, aphoristic style much like Wittgenstein's *Philosophical Investigations* or Nietzsche's later work. But unfortunately I am not a Derrida, a Wittgenstein or a Nietzsche.

Third, the publishers of *Pandemonium* might well have been asked by me to provide at no extra cost, you, the reader, with a 'spinner' upon which numbers would be printed from which to select pages to be read in random order. Cheaper than instructor's notes and requiring more thought, perhaps. Morsels of *Pandemonium* could then be hand-picked by the reader rather than the author by letting the spinner decide the order and measure of what is to be perused. Perhaps you do this as you practise your readership skills anyway. I know of several people who read the references in a text first to see if they are cited. If they are not then their interest rapidly wanes. Some read the first section and then the last page. Others buy books never to read them at all. You may know already, if you are one of those who plunge your fingers into the recesses of books right from the beginning, that *Pandemonium* does look different in its layout. It adopts a fourth approach which contains elements of the second and third. The text is designed to be disruptive, randomizing and reliant upon the reader's creativity. It takes a proximal rather than a distal view (Cooper and Law 1995).

If you are more restrained and linear in your approaches to the spinal columns of books then you should now be told that *Pandemonium* is written, after the first 35 pages, as a divided highway or dual carriageway in which text across the top half of the page moving from left to right 'meets' text moving from right to left across the bottom half of the page. Pages have a central reservation which it is always dangerous to cross. I realize, of course, that this structure, which is modelled on the inner ring road of Pandemonium itself, is still hemmed in by conventions of linearity and order. It only escapes from our conventional understandings a little. But the highway is a winding one, as you will see from the map on the frontispiece and turns back under and over itself in many places. In this way duplicity is maintained.

In the act of reading this 'introduction' to *Pandemonium* perhaps you think it apparent that there is firmly fixed in my mind the notion of a beginning to the text. However, Paul Reiser argues that since everyone flicks open to the middle of any text he feels the necessity to place his beginning of *Couplehood* on page 146. So perhaps this rough guide is not the entry to the City Of All The Devils but is merely a cul-de-sac within the central maze of the Palace Gardens.

For

the structure of this book is deliberately designed to be a little challenging. It is 'Fiction, fragmentation, collage and eclecticism all suffused with a sense of ephemerality and chaos' (Harvey 1990: 98).

Non-existent

journal reviews of *Pandemonium*, written before it was published or even penned, are placed up front and the extensive bibliography is to be found in the 'middle'. The 'end' of the book is merely the middle. And you have a dangerous if creative role to play in finding 'humuments' (Phillips 1987). Tom Phillips, in his classic book, *A Humument*, claims:

> I took a forgotten Victorian novel found by chance. I plundered, mined and undermined its text to make it yield the ghosts of other possible stories, scenes, poems, erotic incidents and surrealist catastrophes which seemed to lurk within its wall of words. (Phillips 1987: dust jacket)

Within the book, Phillips highlights words, connects them in order across and down the page by using coloured shapes and out of the larger text suddenly appear smaller stories and incidents. By juxtaposing the contra-moving text in Pandemonium's streets and highways, new connections and stories are made visible *within* as opposed to *from* the book itself. You have a key role to play in finding these humuments, for I will only point to a few particularly disruptive ones. Similarly I have been affected by my reading of Rosicrucian literature where attempts were made in the seventeenth century to hide meaning within pieces of literature so that the full textual content is accessible only to a small group of hard-working initiates. Thus, as in some famed Beatles' tracks on vinyl, there are hidden meanings located within this text of which even I am aware. Jan Zwicky's *Lyric Philosophy* (1992) was so beautifully produced and so staccato in its construction that when I first saw it it appealed to my limited aesthetics. A thin version of that book is what I hope *Pandemonium* feels like.

3

Pandemonium's pages have also been influenced by Amis's book *Time's Arrow* with its portrayal of the reversal of time. Here an attempt is made to run the text backwards to some extent in order to disrupt the normal flow of common sense which informs the vast majority of all our reading. So, if you indulge yourself in crossing the central reservation when instructed not to do so you will end up by being more inventive than the author. *Pandemonium* is intended to be adventurous. I wished it could have been more so.

So now, what about the relevance of *Pandemonium* to that body of knowledge unlaughingly called contemporary organization theory? Well, to put it crudely, folks, the unedited video, decidedly not for public viewing, shows that we're swimming in deep shit. The pressures to carry out work of an empiricist kind, to make this research relevant to a managerial audience and to play for good and instant feedback from teaching our clients, places tremendous pressures towards conservatism on lecturing staff. But conservatism also comes from ourselves. Every middle-aged person presumably thinks that standards are in decline because of their own physical suffering, locked as they are within a 'body which is doomed to decay and dissolution and which cannot even do without pain and anxiety as warning signals' (Freud 1958: 14). Yet there really *is* little to be optimistic about in the field. All around, the postmodern fears have us in their grip, whether we are aware of this or not. Bauman (1995), in inventive ways which seem to deny the onset of age's debilitating effects, has identified these deep concerns. He sees us humans as in the grip of the fear of the end and death itself. He maintains that all human strategies ultimately involve the tinkering around with that which can be altered whilst the mother of threats – death – is unassailable. He articulates some 'lesser' fears which, despite the adjective, are no less frightening. Even if they do remain at the level of the tinkerable, one's worries about the development of the panopticon, of being reduced to a mere sensation-gatherer, of seeing one's body as private property and therefore of being responsible for keeping it fit and perfecting oneself in so many other ways, incapacitate us on a regular basis. Bauman finds a generalized fear in what he sees as the movement towards tasting and away from touching the Other. Here, he argues, the emphasis is on flavourful uniqueness, on savouring specific and unshared close proximity with the Other before it disappears into self, rather than the sharing with and restoring of the Other which touching suggests. We are no longer touched by social situations. We consume them (Morgan 1986).

Each of these fears and other forebodings is addressed in the meanderings of medieval Pandemonium. But not in the wide boulevards of mainstream and malestream organization theory. There is hardly any material in organizational behaviour on the Baumanesque fears which haunt our lives. These issues are waved aside for they are seen as being in the province of cultural studies or postmodernism and therefore not of managerial interest. Well, in my view, organization theory is a branch of social theory and it is important that this should not be lost from view. The absence of these issues has worried me for a very long time and in the exhibition and viewing halls of Pandemonium there is an attempt to bring them to an audience which has been largely deprived of a considered exposure to these frightening but very human concerns. Thus, for those who wish to know, *Pandemonium* is about those branches of social theory which take the Enlightenment to be a source of misgivings and worry rather than the beginnings of civilization as we know it. For, as they educated themselves in self-government, the European bourgeoisie (Habermas 1989: 50–2) succeeded in excluding the non-literate, the non-affluent and the non-male. Some historians once understood the Enlightenment as the work of about twenty men (Jacob 1991: 215), the so-called party of humanity. However, today, we realize that there was another Enlightenment which evolved alongside the other. In this parallel development there was a very popular social movement which attempted to eradicate the past and with it the Middle Ages. We must realize, of course, that as individuals we must view history from a specific point fixed firmly in time and space. How do we know even what the medieval period was, for it is obvious that no one alive at the time would call their epoch by that name? How will we ever come to know the period as those who inhabited it did? Well, the short answer is, 'We cannot.' But since it is in the past, *Pandemonium* allows us to locate, as a diviner does, traces of the present. I am not interested in reconstructing the past in some more or less 'accurate' way (Burrell 1992a: 78). What is sought here is a way of invigorating my discipline and I will make history bend and groan if necessary in attempting to carry out that task.

In recognizing the centrality of the Enlightenment to the modern world, this book argues that organization theory is in need of rejuvenation through the medium of dawn-picked extracts of the pre-modern. *Pandemonium* revels in the pre-modern period in European thought and seeks in the pre-scientific era, ideas and themes of relevance for today (Turner 1991: 26–30). It looks to the predominant occupational grouping of this epoch as the source of notions and forms of knowledge. It looks to the peasantry rather than managerial groups or those associated collectivities of blue-collar workers. It does not privilege the peasants' existence but merely signals their relevance to contemporary understandings.

It is a work of depression and melancholia. *Pandemonium* is typical of *fin-de-siècle* thinking in its celebration of boredom, ennui, alienation and anomie (Alexander 1995). Indeed, an attempt is made to celebrate these very (different) characteristics. An effort is also made to utilize the distinction between the *Apollonian* and the *Dionysian* traditions in social theory in order to show how a concentration upon the Apollonian in my own field has led to some terrible consequences. But *Pandemonium* is not a celebration of the Dionysian, for this strand in thought is very phallocentric and the distinction itself neglects those elements of thinking which are not driven by the logic of the phallus. We need genuinely non-gendered concepts from which to undertake the tasks ahead and overall approaches which manage to avoid the classic or Cartesian dualisms. Organization theory is so limited, too, in the genre available to it that the book attempts to utilize a variety of different literary styles and fashions in order to demonstrate yet again that constraints are always acting upon us, particularly in the range of expressive modes that we may 'legitimately' draw upon. It attempts to draw upon the Nietzschean tradition and that of the Marquis de Sade. I want to escape from some academic forms of discourse, especially those which emphasize objectivity and distancing of the self from the subject matter. *Pandemonium* is my own little bit of Hell and, as you will soon see, also a piece of a personal Heaven. I don't want to hide behind the impersonal authorial mask. I would urge you in the strongest possible terms to reject all those who seek to do so and revel in your *own* self-aware journey through reality – in all its diabolical nature.

One final point. Rough Guides are meant to help those in possession of such texts to navigate safely through strange exotic lands, to be able to survive the experience and to ease the travellers' return home. Unfortunately, or fortunately, this hitch-hiker's guide which prefaces a brief reading tour of some hours and four centuries, is designed much more to provide the serious reader with some *dis-ease*.

Mustapha Mond, it will be remembered, says to the Savage in *Brave New World* (Huxley 1932: 197):

> 'you're claiming the right to be unhappy. . . . Not to mention the right to grow old and ugly and impotent; the right to have syphilis and cancer; the right to have too little to eat; the right to be lousy; the right to live in constant apprehension of what may happen tomorrow; the right to catch typhoid; the right to be tortured by unspeakable pains of every kind.'
> There was a long silence.
> 'I claim them all.'

And so do I.

CHAPTER 1

Pandemonium Awaits

The mind is its own place, and in it self
Can make a Heav'n of Hell, a Hell of Heav'n

(Milton, *Paradise Lost*, Bk I, ll. 254–5)

As 'your instructor in lunacy' (Euripides 1973: 203) let me say that
science, philosophy and art are all interconnected. By opening yourself
up to *Pandemonium* you have entered upon a mechanical structure, a
world of print, where ancient, organically based chemicals have been
impressed upon dead, crushed xylem. Any form of natural structure is
a morphology of death. Epoch upon epoch, bone upon bone, sediment
upon sediment, humus upon humus, rotting flesh upon rotting flesh,
structure forms from decay in spontaneous generation.

In at least one sense, *Pandemonium* is completely dead. It consists
of dead ink on dead wood expressing dead thoughts, from dead individuals. Yet it struggles from its first page to achieve as ill-structured
an existence as is possible in order to retain some remnant of life. At its
infantile best *Pandemonium* is merely necrotic. To retain some sign of
vitality it seeks to be as miasmic as possible; it has pretences to represent an intrusion into our organized world of one other world of
possibilities where life still exists, pantingly ill-prepared for its own
morphogenesis. And where is this other world? The future, of course.
I seek to download the future into the past to revitalize some particles
of the present.

The design of the text is meant to be the mechanism by which this is
achieved. If successful this manuscript will be terminally ill, but not
yet dead. For it seeks to avoid genres – to exist fleetingly, if fittingly,
outside of a genre. It is not a textbook, nor a research monograph; still
less is it an autobiography, or a science fiction novel; it is not a tour
guide nor a horror comic. It searches to be, in part, a patchy reflection
of expressions of all of these. It is repetitious, yet unconnected. It
flows forwards, backwards, up and down the pages yet seeks to be
staccato in composition. It is ill-designed in order to appear to be (a

simulation of) an inter-textual collage.

Pandemonium is like a small, local museum in some Victorian, British town where 'The orderly soul of the . . . student will quake at the sight of a Chinese lady's boot encircled by a necklace made of shark's teeth, or a helmet of one of Cromwell's soldiers grouped with some Roman remains. Another corner may reveal an Egyptian mummy placed in a medieval chest and in more than one instance the curious visitor might be startled to find the cups won by a crack cricketer of the county in the collection' (Greenwood 1888: 4).

WARNING: LINEARITY KILLS

It is mid-January and the rays of the Southern Sun beat down relentlessly on Zincless heads. We Aquarians watch the 50-foot waves in regular unpredictability smash against the shore of Ocean Beach. They have travelled an 8,000 mile 'send' without the interfering interruption of landfall. Behind us, ranges the South West Wilderness where, a century and a half ago, a full and complete act of genocide was committed. Coming towards us, blown on the Roaring Forties, is a piece of paper on which is inscribed a warning about murder and execution. It looks like this representation opposite.

To 'us', this may mean something. We start at the top of the page and 'instinctively' read to the right and down. When the final image in the top row has been seen we know to look to the first, left-hand side of the second row. This processing switch is of huge interpretive significance and is culturally given. We continue processing the images until the next switch is called for, apparently by the text itself until finally the bottom right-hand box is reached with the symbolic denouement of the pictorial narrative. The cartoon of life and death of a people has been told in an uncontentious, linear, developmental form.

Easy isn't it? Unless, of course, you are unfamiliar with those Western conventions of writing and reading which permeate the logic of the narrative. You, dear reader, are using these unchallenged conventions at this precise moment. The British administration of the island upon which the South Western Wilderness stands even today, made some attempt to prevent the extermination of the Aboriginal people using the linear rationality we see above. The drawing is meant to suggest that white men murdering Aboriginals would be executed for their crime – in the same way as Aboriginals would be executed for the murder of any white person. Since the Tasmanians did not endeavour to speak English, the device of a cartoon-like poster was adopted. This linear narrative, naturally enough, was not specifically responsible for the

9

Governor Arthur's orders, 1828.
Collection: Tasmanian Museum and Art Gallery

genocide. But nor did it prevent it. It was a hapless, culturally specific attempt at communication which came to nothing. Look at the drawing again. Not only is it assumptive of linearity. It presumes leadership, clothing, domesticated animals, particular child-rearing patterns and so on. It assumes the correctness of British nineteenth-century culture.

The Aboriginal hunters and gatherers of Tasmania had a level of technological development which was in decline. They had lost the art of making fire and depended upon fire sticks. They had also turned their back on fishing, and fish hooks lay unused. These peoples, 'primitives' to their observers, confronted bureaucrats who were not entirely malevolent but whose assumption of linear thinking prevented them from communicating with an ancient people. Behind their drawn-out attempts at maintaining 'law and order' lay a belief that they represented a higher stage of human and societal development than the indigenous population. The Tasmanians looked for all the world to be people in terminal decline – or so it was said. They represented, to the experts of the British Museum, the missing link between simians and humans. An evolutionary linearity in assumed racial superiority thus played its part. So too did the linear thinking locked up in the British settlers' conceptualization of blood lines and their wish for their own direct families to own and ultimately inherit that particular tract of land. These beliefs were contextualized within the anthropological framework that these tribes were clearly primitive and developmentally inferior, way behind the industrial capitalism being attempted in modern Launceston and Hobart. In its crudest sense then, the entire original population of a large island was wiped out in the name of linearity and lineage (see, however, Clarke 1983: 51).

The clear paralleling of bureaucracy to lineage and linearity is no accident. One finds the twin features juxtaposed time and time again. Whether it is in the architecture of the Pyramids and their particular geometry associated with the necropoli of hydraulic societies, or in the horizon-seeking railway tracks of the late nineteenth century or in the information super-highway of the twenty-first century, organization has come to be associated with the straight line. Organizational principles, much more often than not, manifestly involve the linear by depending upon it for structural design, to communicate through its utilization and then in turn come to promulgate its use to reproduce organizational power. Thus we depend upon 'vertical' control, 'horizontal' communication, 'lines' of command, 'transmission' of information, time-'tables' and 'spans' of control. As the Open University series on The Enlightenment shows, the British Royal Navy developed linear forms of command at a very early stage in order to cover large tracts of the surface of the earth. Action at such distances involves the principle of linearity in many forms and not only the conceptualization of lines of latitude and longitude. The unsafe navigation of a vessel in space and time is closely paralleled by the dangerous navigation for officers and men of their own social sphere.

In the labyrinthine, unilluminated depths of *Pandemonium* we seek alternative principles of organization. We retreat from linearity, go back far into the wilderness of the south-west of Tasmania, out of the rays of the Enlightenment sun, hide from the encroaching waves of those borne on all too navigable waters and away from the diseased gaze of European rationality (Sennett 1996: 121).

European, or Western Rationality, as we all know (*sic*), is linked inextricably to its organizational representation within bureaucratic structures. Bureaucracy of course means rule by those within offices. But the Bureaux themselves are called such because of the wooden desks in them. And since the desk is the place at which one writes, bureaucracy, in its classic form, depends upon the inscription of symbols on a receptive medium. Today, this is done electronically across many parts of the Earth's surface. Elsewhere and in other times it was and is done in handwritten form. Bureaux thus had inkwells and their necessary accompaniment, burels. These were lengths of coarse woollen cloth laid on the desktop to soak up any spilt ink and prevent its spread. 'Bureaucracy', as a term, thus comes from the use of burel, a tweed-like material which lay upon the desks of the scribe. So too does my family name. The Burrell family lineage – its inheritance – is directly related to the inscription of words upon a desk – but not by salaried representatives of the metropolitan scribe. Rather, it is as the tenders of sheep that the family has its occupational origins. However, metropolitan scribes and sheep-tenders have rarely been close socially and their identity of interest is, to say the least, widely masked. Indeed, their relationship is oft-times very hostile (Sennett 1996: 36).

11

Reflective of this hostility, *Pandemonium* contains many tensions. It is part vignette and contains elements of autobiography. It is meant to be both retrogressive and experimental. It is both old and new. It is a *mundus* – a pre-linear hell hole (Sennett 1996: 108). It is about the hostility between countryside and the city, between peasant and metropolitan, between the bucolic and the urbane, between writer and manager. Essentially, it focuses on the history of the diabolical present. It is, under it all, about the Godforsaken and the twisted.

And who are these exemplary people inhabiting the back streets and underpasses of Pandemonium? They are those who are the day to day victims in war, whether hot, cold, cultural or gender – often innocently. They are those who live and die in hellish conditions. They are often rendered invisible, to be written off as merely 'collateral damage' in military terminology, as 'labour surplus to requirements' in management terminology and as wholly outside the mainstream disciplinary interests in organization theory. Victims are often voiceless, faceless and therefore meaningless. Civilization means little to them, but after all they mean very little to civilization.

Consider the Romans. By which, of course, we mean Roman men. They considered themselves only to have sworn an oath if they held their testicles in their hands at the moment of swearing. The evidence of women and eunuchs could not be believed under the law, for they were not capable of being fully trusted. It was only 'real' men, in swearing upon their potency, who were therefore expected to tell the truth. The links here between male sexual activity and the law, indeed between men's sexual activity and the *truth*, is fascinating. The possession of the truth was much more assured if one possessed testicles. The truth could not be expected from, nor known by, those not blessed with these 'squashy pieces of tissue'. The Roman world was phallocentric. Clearly there are links here to the notion of phal*logo*centrism (Cixous and Clement 1986) where the dominant logic of the period – indeed most periods including the present – is the loud voice of the talking phallus. The access to logic and command of knowledge is given largely to the possessors of the phallus and its lower accessories. Solemnity, truth, revelation and justice are only available to the straight whole man. (As Heidegger (1978: 308) says 'Man fails to see himself as the one spoken to'.) These men who held the truth, the family line and themselves so tightly in their hands felt themselves to be *The* Romans. But what of other Romans? How can we have avoided and ignored those pronounced within the phallogocentric voice to be twisted and the Godforsaken for so long?

12

Organization theory as 'suppressing fire'

Let us talk of ballistics. Organization theory has put down so much 'suppressing fire' over the decades that so many of those who inhabit relevant parts of our lives have kept their heads down to such an extent that we are not even aware of their existence. What conventional organization theory has done is to suppress whole categories of human beings and force them to keep their heads down. It has done this with regard to women in 'malestream organization theory' (Hearn and Parkin 1985). Women are often ignored in the literature and in the Academy, so that a separate 'section' is usually called for, where it stands peripheralized at best and at worst totally ejected from the predominant, phallocentric perspective (Calas and Smircich 1993: 229). 'Keeping your head down' does not only mean avoiding incoming fire, of course. It also places your head in the classic position of subservience – the kowtow – with the individual avoiding eye contact and showing the body language of submission.

What organization theory has also done is to ignore those who permanently have their heads down – the peasantry. We have looked only at those who have looked at us. Eye contact is established with those who knowingly stand and wait and even more with those who walk forward towards us in a knowing way. As a discipline we have looked only at those who walk and those who stand, not at those who keep their heads down. We have not considered that what we do acts as a form of suppressing fire. We force, usually unwittingly, whole sections of the global population to kowtow before we begin our analysis of those who remain upright. For, once on their knees, with heads down these groups are anonymous. The individual is in the classic position of avoiding eye contact and showing the body language of submission. Faceless. Depersonalized. When your head is down, resistance is much more difficult. If you dare to *speak*, of course, it is even more threatening to the powerful.

We must remember, however, that those of whom *we* speak may not be able to speak for themselves. According to the Routledge *Atlas of the World's Languages* (1994) almost a third of the world's languages are now spoken by less than a thousand people. Up to 3,000 of the 6,000 currently spoken languages will have disappeared by AD 2100 and another 2,000 may well disappear in the following century. In Australia, 135 of the 200 surviving Aboriginal languages are spoken by fewer than ten people. Thirty-six of these languages are only spoken by one person! In Latvia, only nine people speak Livonian, whereas 300 years ago it was spoken by tens of thousands of Latvians. Elsewhere in Europe, there are seven languages with fewer than 15,000 speakers including Tsokanian in southern Greece which is only spoken by 300 shepherds. In Papua New Guinea there are 155 languages spoken by fewer than 300 people, whilst in the Americas the figure is over 100 which are hardly spoken at all. At the time of Columbus, there were at least 7,000 world languages but this has been reduced by 15 per cent due to colonial expansion. In another 500 years there could be only 10 per cent of the *current* number. Only between 300 and 600 of the world's current languages are 'safe'. Whilst genocide and empire building, no doubt, will continue to play their part, we must now look on the role of television, the megapolises of the Third World, the destruction of natural habitats and the intolerance of nationalism as added factors. Not only do the people whom Pandemonium seeks to encounter within its confines not have a voice with which to be heard, they are even in danger of losing the language with which to formulate the pre-vocalized thought. This is Newspeak on a global scale. In the wake of the imperial ballista comes the language of the Empire and the privileging of the metropolitan.

As a second-year undergraduate I was taught organizational sociology by Nicos Mouzelis. When I was told that in the 1970s – and beyond – that he had turned his attention to theorizing the 'peasantry', I could not understand this 'retrogressive' step. It is a step which I now

13

intend to take, tentatively, myself. According to Cohen 'discussions of . . . the way in which the world of industry is parasitical upon, or interdependent with, the world of domestic and peasant labour, do not appear in traditional . . . research' (1991: 3). 'Labour' has come to mean middle-aged, male, trade union bureaucrats in the capitalist West (Cohen 1991: 2). But consideration of the 'proletarianization' of the developing world has been at the cost of the continued analysis of peasanthood. Clearly massive changes in rural lifestyles have been wrought by the capitalist world system since the sixteenth century but it would be foolish, as many Marxists have done, to see the peasantry as conservative and passive in the face of activist proletarians. Nor are the peasantry across the world today necessarily in decline numerically. Even if they are forced to become peasant workers or 'the peasantariat' they retain much if not all of their deep-seated social and political characteristics. They remain 'peasants who travel'. As Shanin (1971) argues: 'Labour migrants carry aspects of peasanthood not only in the traces of the past in the present, but also in terms of actual relations and contacts, both real and imaginary.' Of course, the term should not be supposed to represent an amorphous mass. Whilst none are wage labourers some of them are 'wage labour equivalents' (Bernstein 1977: 73). Many millions of peasants have moved thousands of miles: Africans to the US, Italians to Brazil, Indians to South Africa, the Irish to Australia. Yet some, like my own paternal family, have not moved their home above a day's walk for the last 500 years. In their case, first as peasants, then as peasantariat working the same landowner's property but from beneath the soil and then as fully fledged wage labourers three miles out under the North Sea. Organization theory cared much more for them once they embraced wage labour (a false embrace since they did not have any choice). As peasants and peasantariat they are hidden from view, kowtowing in the fields of the Northumbrian countryside when, above or below ground, organizational sociology knew them not – nor cared less. For, after all, to be a peasant is not to know bureaucracy, nor hierarchical organization, nor industry. These appear only with proleteranization, surely?

All this talk of imperial suppression makes me anxious for my discipline. Could it be that one hidden theoretical object which organization theory has not yet addressed as its explanandum is the 'peasantry'? Might it be that in the absence of any disciplinary concentration upon this numerically massive group we miss 'a history of the hidden'; a history of those who live like troglodytes below our eye level? But what *does* lie within our perspective?

Trips to the edge of darkness such as this need to fulfil an educational function as well as one of entertainment. So I will try not to detain you too long in the field before Pandemonium's ramparts.

Along the lines of organization theory

In the 1960s the field of organizational analysis was deceptively simple and involved assumptions about the centrality of modernity, the institutional superiority of bureaucratic structures and the need for measurement of Weber's ideal type construct. The rise of contingency theory had done nothing to question these assumptions, for theory was still to be tested by collecting data, usually of a quantitative kind, utilizing standard positivistic methods in the search for managerially relevant conclusions. The writers on organizations of this period, in which the growth of the welfare and warfare state had created a movement towards corporatism, saw their role as being that of scientization of the field and adding administrative science to the list of managerially relevant fields like operational science and economics. Their subject matter – the organization – was gaining an importance from major societal changes to do with bureaucratization. In their discussion of the work of Max Weber, his original philosophical and political tensions are almost totally ignored. Moreover, their analysis of organizations could be held up as in no need of Marx or leftist ideas. Right Weberianism provided the perfect defence of bureaucratic rule and the importance of the administrative function (Mouzelis 1975). The relevance of Left Weberianism was ignored along with the concept of *Verstehen*. No sooner had a modified Weber been presented as the patron saint of organizational analysis than the vandals began to daub the holy figure with the graffiti of political and methodological disaffection. Thus, almost from the outset, a unified organization theory began to dissolve in front of our eyes. Administrative science then is no stranger to fractured lines of analysis. The Weber who was politically of the Left and intellectually idealist had been ignored in much of the classic work. As soon as *this* Weber had been resurrected, then the project of organization theory, almost at its moment of conception, became fought over. Organization theory, from that day on, was 'contested terrain'.

15

Such a view of organizational analysis suggests that contestation over political, epistemological and methodological grounds was present even in the heyday of the Aston Studies, and through the launch of *Administrative Science Quarterly* and the rise of contingency theory. Its coherence had to be asserted rather than demonstrated to audiences of the day which were not yet aware. Bruno Latour (1988) has shown us that for a field of science to be successful, an actor network tends to be developed and whether the area does or does not develop to full fruition in practice depends upon hard work and political nous amongst its leading lights. Thus one can forgive the first organization theorists some of their myopia for it served a highly important political purpose. However, the notion of a golden age is always suspect, for when we look back we can see not only a much smaller field but a mythical one in which the powerful agreed to ignore fundamental problems in addressing fundamental issues.

The myth that usefully springs to mind here is found not in Greek mythology but in the Bible. Like all myths its significance is capable of multi-layered analysis, but one effort which the reader might find helpful is to be found in George Steiner's *After Babel: Aspects of Language and Translation* (1975).

In Genesis, the story is told that God became unhappy with humanity in the shape of the builders of the temple at Babel (Babylon). Their temple is so high and their aims so transparent as to rival God in his power that God decides to spread them to the four corners of the Earth in a diaspora which leaves builder unable to speak unto builder. The diaspora of the builders is motivated by God's desire to ensure their deliberate division into many warring encampments. The speaking of many languages comes only *after* the abandonment of the work on the same edifice (Wittgenstein 1973). What is important is the shared project, not the shared language. The babel of voices comes from the cessation of the shared task, and not vice versa. What organization studies lacks today is a shared language and a shared project. How then does this fit in with the much used notion of 'the project of modernity' and the role of organization studies within it? The answer is that modernity in its late or postmodern phases *questions* bureaucratic organization and its legitimacy almost as much as it was interrogated in those far-off pre-modern times before industrialization. With the explanandum of our activities in retreat is it any wonder that our explanans, too, suffers from a lack of confidence? Pfeffer (1994) in a recent piece of provocation, has argued that organization theory needs to be much more disciplined, centralized and controlled by a small elite grouping if it is to have any future at all in the groves of academe. Although he does not use the metaphor of Babel there is a clear idea of a disparate, fragmented field ripe for hostile take-over from those without, who allegedly are better organized and more centrally commanded. Please consider three elements within the structure of the field. The first is the nature of the fragmentation of our discipline into schools of thought and a corresponding lack of universally recognized élite in control; the second is the resultant lack of shared explanans (an agreed theoretical framework) and the third is the cause of both – the shifting nature of the administrative enterprise itself. Of course these are interconnected but let us concentrate upon one at a time.

The builders of organization theory do not live in a single city. The discipline is global in its sites of production. For example, the transatlantic nature of much of organization theory has long been recognized. The importation into the USA of Weber's intellectual

16

remains is but one form of traffic. The reverse importation back into Europe of organizational principles developed on the railways of the Eastern Seaboard itself merely reflected the importation of French ideas on discipline and linearity into West Point Academy somewhat earlier (Hoskin and MacVe 1986). Yet in each import and export, small changes are necessarily made to customize the intellectual product for particular markets. Something is added. Something else is removed. Thus the European concerns with property, with serfdom, with the absence of land for the masses, with aristocracy and monarchy, with the sheer weight of tradition, are not as vibrant and alive in the USA from the outset. What is seen in the arena of administration when we look carefully is the confrontation of the new world by the old. How can they possibly have the same views about how to administer the people within their domain? Hence, just as Weber is partially lost in both translation and in transatlantic, the builders of organization theory rely upon and use different assumptions about the nature of the social and psychological world – depending upon which side of the North Atlantic they happen to be standing at the relevant moment. However, lest the accusation of hemisphericentrism be levelled against your instructor in lunacy allow me to quickly point out that much current work of interest is being carried out in the southern hemisphere and around a larger ocean than the Atlantic. The Atlantic no longer represents the undisputed geopolitical centre of organization theory it once did, for it was upon one night in May 1985 when air traffic above the Pacific was denser for the first time than over the Atlantic. This shift in global trade is also quite recognizable in organization theory and its intellectual exchanges.

Just as the builders came to 'fall out' over the terms and methods to be used in the construction of the tower, so too in organization theory is there very little agreement over the *types* of conceptualizations to be used, never mind the actual conceptualization itself. The moments of force for dissolution are there in the area right from the start. It would be foolish to imagine the existence of some coherent structure which came to the point of incipient collapse. All that happened in the late 1960s was that the reality of fragmentation grew clearer when it became glaringly obvious that one particular group of contingency theorists had, hitherto, shouted down the other voices on the far side of the structure. The idea that one voice could drown out the rest is an attractive one to the pulmonarily gifted but it is a dream which can never be realized fully. There will, thank goodness, always be the voices of dissent and the clamour of alternatives vying for aural space. What we had in the 1960s was merely the period of hushed opposition before the volume of babble rose. Different explanations of differently conceived problems quickly came to prominence as the numbers of academics employed in the arena of organization theory increased.

The demographic changes in the academic population are significant but should not be seen as the cause of fragmentation. They merely made it more visible.

In the same way as the demographics of the academic population affected the nature of the fragmentary dynamics within organization theory, so too did the changes occurring within the population of organizations in which our interest had centred. Privatization, franchising, the break-up of the large corporations into quasi-independent entities, the attacks upon bureaucracy, the attacks upon the middle manager and so on all meant that the explanandum (that which has to be explained) itself was changing. The mode of organization was altering to the extent that markets and networks were starting to take the place of those bureaucracies of which Weber had been a major theorist. Whilst very few thought, or more accurately think, that bureaucracy is 'dead' clearly it is in retreat to some extent across the developed world. The diaspora of theoreticians has been matched by the diaspora of the isomophic organizational form. There is no easy silhouetting here, for there is no close identity between those, for example, who study the voluntary sector and those who use a particular managerial stance. The lines of fissure do not match up. The fragmentation is much worse than that (Cooper and Burrell 1988).

Linearity kills again

Given all these lines of fissure and the desperate need, under modernity, for academics to claim an understanding of the world, it is little wonder that the theoreticians have attempted to 'fix' the organizational world and by reducing its dynamics to a static classificatory system thereby to imprison it. We must now look to the ways in which the stabilizers have attempted to offer momentary glimpses of a world in flux. In this they have forced organizational analysis on to a procrustean bed on which it groans and squirms because it is not the right size to fit the cramping framework into which it is being pressed. Yet the forcing goes on. Each of the terms to be addressed below forces the subject into an understandable and simplifying framework. This, after all, is what science does. But we must realize that what every concept does is to exclude as well as include, to ignore as well as concentrate upon, to consign to obscurity as well as into the limelight. Concepts stretch the point.

Key to the issue is the centrality of science in our ways of looking at administration and organizational behaviour. Science begins by placing the perpetually dynamic into a field of stasis. *Ceteris paribus* clauses, the experiment and the laboratory all are ways of stabilizing the real world's perpetual flow. There is the terrible example of a 4,900-year-old bristle cone pine tree in Wyoming being cut down by an impatient yet curious researcher because his tree corer would not work:

> We wanted to visit the bristle cone pines. They are the oldest living things on earth. . . . Seems a researcher was trying to count the tree rings and establish a maximum age for the bristle cone. And he was having trouble with his cone drill. So he took a chainsaw to what was thought to be the oldest tree on the mountain. And it worked. (quoted in Zwicky 1992: 146)

This was in the Wheeler Peak area of Nevada in 1965. The tree, WPN–114, grew on the north-east face at an altitude of 10,750 feet and was measured, after its death, as having begun growing about 4,900 years ago (ibid.). It was said that refinement of the scientific hypothesis concerning the age limit of the bristle cone pines could only be possible with 'more extensive sampling' of the oldest trees up there high upon the mountain. Similarly, Zwicky (1992) also shows how an ornithologist justifies 'obtaining and preserving a specimen' (i.e. killing a bird) because it 'forms the foundation of theoretical advances in the design and management of biological reserves' (ibid.: 146). In other words, killing things is good for the scientific understanding of 'biological reserves' and 'biolographic history'. Indeed it is essential. As the Romantics knew only too well, to understand life more fully we must extinguish it.

19

The creation of stasis, the better to hold the scientific victim steady so that it might be better anatomically examined, is a long one. We *must* look at the range of conceptualizations within organization theory as ways of enforcing anatomizing stasis upon the dynamics of organizational life. They are notions of and for stasis through which the mobile, the dynamic, the restless are forced to offer themselves up unto the gaze of the observer. Concepts are the ultimate form of the panopticon (Foucault 1977b). By classifying and marking their victims, concepts perform an imprisoning act of considerable sophistication. But much more than incarceration takes place. Once immobilized, the body of thought becomes subject to inscription. Concepts inscribe their marks upon the body of the literature and in the process of marking with cuts and incisions, they leave a trail of lesions behind which all can follow. The deeper cuts are those which make the biggest impression upon those that read off the significance of the author's remarks for themselves. But these impressive cuts ultimately spell death and immobility. At the very least the subject is wounded by the deepest and most incisive inscriptions (Dale and Burrell 1995).

All models and theories are incised lesions on the body of organizational life. Analysis of almost any kind requires the death or at least the mutilation of that which is analysed. To identify anything as an explanandum is to offer it up for execution. To alight upon anything as an explanans is to provide at the very least a fearsome weapon of mutilation. Thus words, especially in the form of conceptualizations, serve to imprison, immobilize, and injure that which they seek to address.

The avoidance of linearity? Foucault's pendulum

Foucault, it is authoritatively said, was one of the first French citizens to die of AIDS. He lived a life of considerable risk and was very keen to avoid immobilization through labelling. His untimely death in 1984 did nothing to stem the burgeoning interest in his articulation of his intellectual *approaches*. Note that the plural term has to be used here, for it is clear that Foucault's hatred of being labelled, boxed in and categorized affected his own body and his own body of work. He sought to evade fixed terms as best he could and changed his own intellectual position constantly. His movement from what is called the 'archaeological' to the 'genealogical' orientation will be discussed below but it must be recognized that we, ourselves, are always fixing in time and space, within relatively crude classifications. Ideas from an intellectual the stature of Foucault are essentially dynamic and are even more difficult to fully appreciate and express for they transgress many of our assumptions. Yet his work is directly relevant to organization studies for he concentrates, in his later writing particularly, on issues in which our discipline is traditionally interested. At first sight, however, such are the difficulties in comprehending his ideas that their relevance for all of social science and not just organization theory needs careful articulation. To do so requires more space than is available here so the reader is referred to Dreyfus and Rabinow's lucid text on Foucault's work (1982). Certain key points, nevertheless, need some attention here.

Whilst the metaphor of the careful uncovering of history and historical artefacts has influenced many social scientists with the appeal of its sedimentary imagery, Foucault does not, in his early work, adopt a crude structuralism in his discussion of archaeology. For him, discourse analysis is that method which 'the archaeologist' performs upon the past, seeing within history the precise codes of knowledge which have lain there awaiting our discovery. Any archaeologist of knowledge must distanciate themselves from the past and seek to be objective but they realize very quickly and very clearly that our present period itself contains discourses. Our codes of understanding today are therefore discourses too, subject to the same rules of articulation as those located in the past. Our contemporary discourses are subject to the same inflexibilities and problems as any theories emanating from the Middle Ages. Discourse is put as far away from its social setting as possible in this early work of Foucault and, acting as the archaeologist, he attempted to discover the rules which govern its own self-regulation. To do this, he enlisted the help of a rather short-lived notion – that of the 'episteme'. The episteme unites the set of discursive practices which exist at any one time so that in any given epoch one will find that a particular episteme predominates. Modernity then becomes characterized by the episteme, put crudely and genderedly, in which Man invents himself. This episteme required a catastrophic upheaval, an 'archaeological mutation', which signalled that the Classical Age had come to an end before it could struggle into existence itself. Since it first struggled for life it has succeeded in coming to dominate the epoch.

In his book *The Archaeology of Knowledge*, Foucault takes his method to new-found depths of analysis. In the text he is interested in 'serious speech acts', mindful that the context in which this sort of discursive practice takes place is crucial for understanding profound differences in meaning. Ludwig Wittgenstein had obviously noted this tendency too and this interpretation had an important effect upon Thomas Kuhn. But Foucault is relatively silent on the whole issue of paradigms as 'language-games'. Dreyfus and Rabinow (1982: 60) conclude that this silence is because he misunderstood the notion and its Kuhnian intent. The silence may also have been a result of his unwillingness to confront ideas from outside a particular realm of his *own* discourse. He was to say later in life that he had not read Habermas's work on discourse when this, too, would seem to have been a useful exercise. Certainly, he was not ignorant of the existence of such literature.

Once he had dispensed with the archaeological method, Foucault turned to genealogy. Dreyfus and Rabinow ask, rhetorically, what is genealogy? The answer, they say, is:

> genealogy opposes itself to traditional historical method: its aim is to 'record the singularity of events outside of any monotonous finality'. For the genealogist there are no fixed essences, no underlying laws, no metaphysical finalities. Genealogy seeks out discontinuities where others have found continuous development. It finds recurrences and play where others found progress and seriousness. It records the past of mankind to unmask the solemn hymns of progress. Genealogy avoids the search for depth. Instead it seeks the surfaces of events, small details, minor shifts and subtle contours. (1982: 106)

Thus the search for the modernist goals of hidden meaning, for truth, for the meanings of the unconscious rests on a failure to recognize that these are shams. Foucault says that we should shun these sorts of activities for there are no essences which we can uncover. Thus, Plato is the arch-enemy to the genealogist, whereas, of course, Nietzsche is the central, heroic figure. The foundations of morality are not to be found in ideal truth but in *pudenda origo*. History is about lies not truth. It is about a struggle for domination acted out in a play of wills. But there is no one who is responsible for the emergence of any event; for the genealogist there is no individual nor any collectivity who can move history. For we all live in the interstices created by this play of dominations. And all that we see is all that there is.

This is important because it firmly suggests that the relativism of human conceptualizations of truth, beauty and virtue need to be recognized. These are ever-changing notions and are not located in something essential. Even the human body is not to be understood as something with an essence which has stood the test of time over millennia. Just the opposite. It is a notion which has undergone many changes. And the human body was to be one of Foucault's major concerns. In *Discipline and Punish* (1977b), Foucault reversed the priority of archaeology to genealogy by privileging the latter. The genealogist is portrayed as a diagnostician who concentrates on the relationship between power, knowledge and the body. At this point, Foucault turns organization theory around by focusing on the body as the locale where minute social practices meet the large-scale organization of power. The organization of the body and its pleasure becomes a prime area for theoretical and practically orientated debate. Whilst not taking Merleau-Ponty's notion of *le corps propre* – the lived body as opposed to the physical body – to heart, Foucault (1977b: 25) does explore the way in which 'the body is also directly involved in a political field. . . . Power relations have an immediate hold upon it; they invest it, mark it, train it, torture it, force it to carry out tasks, to perform ceremonies, to emit signs.'

This wonderful passage prefigures his interest in the political technology of the body which, it is claimed, has the greatest significance for Western society (Shilling 1993: 75–82). But we should not assume that this analysis suggests that it is *the state* which is the key to understanding power-knowledge and the body. In fact, Foucault does not believe that the state plays a major role in this at all. Rather it is in institutions, like prisons, asylums, schools, factories and barracks that one finds the loci of power. The metaphor of the prison is central here for all these types of institution are claimed to be imprisoning, and in a famous section of *Discipline and Punish* Foucault articulates the importance of Bentham's panopticon as marking the search for the 'ultimate managerial tool'. Here the bodies of inmates are subject to the disciplinary technologies of close surveillance, the gaze and the process of 'normalization'. What Foucault does is to open up the analysis of organizations to new notions in which the body plays a central role as a target for a plethora of disciplinary technologies located within organizational forms which all bear an uncanny resemblance to prisons. Power comes from the knowledge of the body which develops in the minds and comes into the hands of 'the judges of normality'.

These are organizationally based professionals who are key parts of the 'somatic society' (Turner 1992: 12).

Whilst the concern for metaphors drove the teaching of courses in many programmes, the Foucauldian legacy – for by 1984 this is all we had – drove considerable amounts of research (for example Hollway 1991, Townley 1994, Rose 1989). Of course, it would be foolish to say that many academics embraced this particular French philosopher with any relish, for his work is difficult to pin down and is theoretically challenging. Yet within organization studies, attempts have been made to elevate surveillance to a primary focus of attention and, almost weekly, new analyses of panopticism appear which show the relevance of Foucault to the mid-1990s through his concentration on power-knowledge. It is possible to say that the genealogical approach is much more in tune with postmodernism whereas, perhaps, the archaeological method stands much more in tune with modernism. Foucault turned his back on discourse analysis quite early on, saying that: 'I confused it too much with systematicity, the theoretical form, or something like a paradigm'.

For us to label his later work 'postmodern' would be fair perhaps but we must note again that he explicitly rejected this epithet, preferring instead to claim that any classification scheme, any labelling device, was itself part of a field of power-knowledge in which the speaker as well as the one who was spoken about became subject to disciplining. He is difficult to classify as a thinker because almost any work that he did was self-consciously opposed to the piece which preceded it. Movement allowed the evasion of capture.

Derrida too is one of a number of French writers in the last fifteen years who have attempted to shift social theory away from the certainties of the 1960s. For him, social life is made up of texts which are constantly read in very different ways so that our understandings are continually being broken down and reassembled. Just as Foucault seeks to avoid imprisonment for his ideas, Derrida argues that at least a *double* reading of any text is possible. Fixity is no longer tenable. Derrida's notion of deconstructionism has proved to be a powerful stimulus to postmodern forms of thought. It asserts a rather different way of thinking about and 'reading texts'. Whilst under modernism it was believed that the medium and the message were tightly interconnected, Derrida sees these as 'continually breaking apart and re-attaching in new combinations'. Texts are the way in which writers and readers come to understand the world and each new level of understanding produces new texts which are added to the textual weave. Inter-textual weaving comes to have a life of its own, for we write things of which we know naught and our words cannot convey what we mean. Language works through us, not the other way round. So, for the deconstructionist, one text dissolves into another, one text is located within another, one text is built upon another. Thus the objective of deconstructionism is to break the power of the author to claim the primacy of a particular narrative or to impose meanings upon the reader. All fixed systems of representation become seen as merely illusory and as capable of at least a *double* reading (Cooper 1989: 492–501).

The key form of discourse in postmodernism is the collage or montage. The inherent heterogeneity of this form of cultural work means that both producers and consumers of the artefact participate in its meaning generation. This is profoundly democratic, based as it is upon popular conceptualizations of the product within the audience, but of course the very incoherence of many conceptualizations does allow for mass-market manipulation. The montage is vulnerable to recombinatory meanings which are never fixed and never stable but may often be exploitative and imprisoning. It seeks to escape the optimism of linearity.

Well whatever *these* forms of knowledge produce, it is unlikely to look the same as the performativity conscious (Lyotard 1983) artefacts of the twentieth century. In the classic tension between the *Geistwissenschaften* and the *Naturwissenschaften*, surely it is not simply a matter of one achieving re-ascendancy over the other? Of course it is not that simple. But in that antinomy there is an exceptionally good place to attempt to build organization theory for the new millennium. It is from deep within *pre-modernity*, where we will also find a good time with which to begin an innovative approach to the future of our discipline in terms both of what we look at and how we look at it. Our explanans and our explanandum are in dire need of a refreshing trip to pastures new. Backwards and downwards, away from the field.

Pastures new or shades of anxiety?

What you have read thus far has been a brief survey of a field benighted by its own self-neglect. We must, perforce, re-locate. Hidden deep within the wintry campus is a large metallic door upon which is inscribed in Gothic lettering the word 'ANXIETY'. Reluctantly you allow yourself to be seduced into entering it, only to find that you are descending the spiral steps of a concrete bunker. The smell is vaguely disquieting and you notice that, as you gingerly feel your way down the staircase, it has been constructed for left-handed defenders. From this moment you know that what is to follow must be entirely sinister. You find yourself to be one member of a very small party of paying guests who, once assembled, are suddenly addressed by the author from a lectern down below. His tone is justificatory and you cannot fail to notice the angst in his voice. It is as if he is aware of being too personal, too defensive, too egocentric.

'Thank you very much for coming. This bunker was constructed fifteen years ago with capital provided by a book called *Sociological
Paradigms and Organizational Analysis*. Since its building I have
rarely ventured forth into the campus except for an occasional foray. I
have been aware of bright painted wagons, heavily loaded yet moving
rapidly, progressing towards Pandemonium, and have been vaguely
interested in what they contained, why they were heading in that
direction and why their numbers were increasing. But it is only
recently that I perceived that all these bandwagons had upon their
sides David Harvey's anxiety-provoking question [*from the stage an
overhead projector is switched on*] "who are we and to what
space/place do we belong?" (Harvey 1990: 427). Today, various forms
of time-space compression allows us to enter Pandemonium in search
of an answer to this existentialist conundrum.'

The author now leaves the four equally sized rooms he has been
stalking, camera in hand, and, pointing to the south, says: 'If you are an
organization theorist you will, I hope, be at home in Pandemonium.
The age of the tourist is over and we need somewhere to rest our
aching bones. Should you wish to follow me to and thence *into* this
nether world all you have to do is to keep turning the pages – both
ways.'

The author absent-mindedly looks around for something material
with which to demonstrate his approach – a visual aid like a video
tape or a photographic representation. None is to be found in any of
the four rooms. Even the work of Ivars Peterson in *The Mathematical
Tourist* (1988) and *Islands of Truth* (1990) are too rationalistic for his
purposes. So too is that of Czarniawska-Joerges and de Monthoux
(1996). He continues:

'This journey you are about to undertake is not about the organization of production – although that figures within our travels. Nor is it
about "organizations", exclusively, where this undertheorized term
signifies collectivities of human beings, labouring under control to
achieve specified goals. It is not solely concerned even with those
large bureaucratic structures which exercise much influence over our
day to day lives. Rather,' he says, adopting the paternalistic tones of a
journal editor, 'we must be concerned with the production of *organization*. Bureaucracy within organizations is only one form of
organization, albeit a key and defining morphism. Human life is organized in other ways, through networks, markets, gift relationships and
straightforward affection. Human life is shaped by emotions such as
hatred, fear, loathing, disgust and passion. *Pandemonium* is about
human life and its organization and not about 'organizations and
human life'. The latter is contained within the former and certainly
needs to be exhibited during our visit to Pandemonium. But so too
does the former.' He takes a deep breath, as if his survival depended

25

upon it. Now he becomes patronizing; indeed, abusive: 'If, dear reader, you are only interested in "organizational behaviour" as is currently taught in most Anglophone business schools, then your personalized Exit is below. You should go no further.' For your own sake.

26

[There is the sound of an opening door and a slow shuffle of ascending slippers]

'They' have gone. Only 'we' remain. You too can see 'them' climbing the stairs out of the bunker, re-entering eagerly and noisily back on to the campus through the heavy lead-lined door marked 'ANXIETY'. In their hands, they protectively carry something almost indiscernible. Just as the door shuts behind them you see it is in every case, a 'Safeway' plastic career bag.

The author looks back at the remnants of the remainder of the group, but he sighingly says to no one in particular 'Why does one tend to call the collection of organizational behaviour students who've just left, 'your royalties'?' He swivels as the unseen window of the bunker loses its outer shutters and the artificial light, expensively provided by the university, dims. As one overhead disappears another appears – yet but dimly. You strain to read it because the writing is so small. Indeed you have the distinct impression that you are not *meant* to read it.

IN THE DISTANCE

STANDS

PANDEMONIUM

Tiny beginnings. In the beginning was the end and in the end was the beginning. Writing is a linear activity in which – in the Western tradition – we begin at the top left of the page and move downwards and rightwards in the text to the conclusion of the argument. This is profoundly limiting for it encourages simple presentations, clarity of exposition, linearity of argument and reliance on logic. As we have seen, it is also implicated in genocide. There is a tremendous temptation within the confines of academic discourse to develop a narrative, build up an argument and come to a conclusion. Indeed, if these are not present, criticisms of a fairly intense kind are heaped upon authors. Critics of a high modernist persuasion do not look kindly upon non-standard approaches which eschew the normal academic conventions.

Pandemonium is, I suspect, more challenging to the reader/listener, asks more work of him/her and requires more investment of time/energy than most of the modest experiments I have tried elsewhere in seeking the escape from linearity. That is why the exit from this text was shown early to those who feel more content with 'Heathrow Organization Theory' and its practitioners (e.g. Handy 1994). This text is by far and away the largest non-standard piece that I have attempted. It stands fundamentally opposed to Handy pocket theory with all its superficiality, ease of travel, liberal humanist stance, technobabble language and fundamentally conservative political leanings. To all that consultancy-speak, *Pandemonium* is 'anathema'.

Rather, it relies upon and is characterized by an approach adopted here which is called, pretentiously perhaps, *retro-organization theory*. Evidence for and origins of such a perspective are not presented in one place throughout *Pandemonium*. You will find foundational supports for such a theory littered in many places throughout the city. The characteristics of retro-organization theory are something like the following. This is a form of analysis which seeks to underplay the importance of developing an argument in a linear, logical way. There is a rejection of beginning at the beginning and claiming that the conclusion which falls at the end (of course) represents progress and enlightenment. Retro-organization theory is written in forms which question progress and logic – without, let it be said hastily, being so abrasive as to produce a book which cannot be 'read' at all. It values pre-modern history, particularly pre-Enlightenment history, in so far as this area of study can help us understand the modern and the postmodern but it also plunders history for insight and data, not mindful of chronology, anachronisms, the respect for meta-narrative or story. It seeks to bring to an end 100 years of 'progress'. For it assumes synchronicity. Just as Renaissance art often shows Christ before Pilate in one part of a painting yet being crucified simultaneously in another, we too assume that events which are 'apart' in time and space can be

27

juxtaposed. Causality, therefore, need not be Newtonian but metonymic (Althusser 1969). Retro-organization theory self-consciously pushes back the study of organizations 400 years to a pre-modern period when, as we shall see, not only is Christ everywhere but devils walk the Earth. Whilst I am not a diabolist, this sort of material has a relevance to the contemporary world which has been suppressed. *Pandemonium* will surface sights, sounds and smells from a forgotten age and all of them are likely to be unpleasant. Like this one, for example.

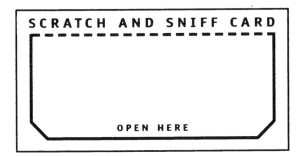

For some colleagues, 'retro' will also mean a return to the benighted ages when the luminosity of the Enlightenment had not yet fallen upon organization theory to grace and warm it. For them, what follows will be barbaric madness, not knowledge. I have to tell them that this inversion is precisely my motivation in putting pen to paper. 'Three-minute culture' as a conceptual device suggests shortened concentration times in a reading and viewing public. This book will move through time and space alighting quickly then moving on from 'story' to 'story', anecdote to anecdote, piece of trivia to piece of trivia. Present and future, here and there, all intermingle within its walls. We can and will 'channel hop' constantly.

The seductive trap I would enjoin you to avoid, however, is that of seeing *Pandemonium* as representing an argument, or a thesis or a story. It is a *ludibrium* – a playful toying with ideas – more than anything else and contains hidden meanings of which I am not aware. You are invited not to treat it seriously but to look for enjoyment and pain where you can find it within the back streets of this imagination. *Pandemonium* can be reconstructed as well as deconstructed by the reader in numerous ways. Each page contains many humuments which take the form of patternings of words or single letters across the page where meanings lie dormant until revealed by the reader. These humuments may contradict the force of the argument on the page from which their existence derives. Most humuments, it has to be said, are probably much more interesting than the text itself.

Thus purged of theory and some self-aggrandizement, a dis-embodied voice of the author says mechanically but in a middle European accent:

'We are now before the gatehouse of Pandemonium'

'Dear guest, You are in Torment – or at least the south-eastern part of it.' You stand in the cold, outside the forbidding escutcheons of the massive gatehouse of the city of Pandemonium. High in the rain clouds the author stands in a pulpit. You look up, trying to keep the rain from your eyes. He speaks to you directly, using, is it Kafka's voice?

'I have to speak to you first from a distance. Otherwise I am too eas-ily influenced and tend to forget my duty.' In his own voice the author tells you that you now stand before the City of Pandemonium, a place of wild disorder and chaos. It is the Miltonian metropolis of all the devils – the high capital of Satan and his Hadean peers. His speech is halting but given his location upon such ramparts this is not surpris-ing. He continues:

'Whenever I "have" time I think of organizations and organizing. It's my job. The notion of Pandemonium has been a recurrent theme in this activity, reflecting not only the inchoate nature of thought but the fragmentary tendencies within that which is thought about. The trip around this castle started off as an attempt to expurgate these devils of misrule and by facing them, end them. The nightmare image of orga-nizations as being places of chaos, death, decay, disease and distress within a contextualizing world which was no better and no different was to be willingly confronted. There was hope, such hope. My thought would be better organized, more resistant to fear, more robust, more reconciled. But this hope has not materialized. In acting as your guide, I have come to *live* in Pandemonium. Milton's *Paradise Lost* allows us to recognize the place where we now stand as: 'Pandemonium, the high capital of Satan and his peers' wherein 'with ruin upon ruin, rout upon rout, confusion worse confounded', one is forced to say 'so farewell hope, and with hope farewell fear, farewell remorse; all good to me is lost'.

The author's voice is quiet at this point and you need to listen care-fully above the howl of the wind blowing straight on to the great door of the city to hear what is said next. 'In preparing for my task I have read de Sade, Nietzsche, Kafka and Sartre. I have read about Buchenwald, Beria's gulags, The Harrow, Goebbels's propaganda. Across many pages I have had to face torture, imprisonment, death. If writing is a machine for the suppression of time it is also a mechanism for the transmission of experience and, let us be clear, of pain. Therefore much of what I read was contaminatory. From viewing Pandemonium from afar and from the outside, one quickly becomes the tourist. On entry through the gate marked "ARBEIT MACHT FREI" one begins to think "It's Friday so it must be the literature on torture." Soon thereafter, the weekend's holiday has become an extended stay. Eventually, one has become a full-blown member of the community of Pandemonium. And with the attraction of complete revulsion one finds – as *you* will find and as Milton found – it is a damn sight more interesting than Paradise.' As the author speaks he taps a piece of mistletoe wood and there is an almost imperceptible noise of large machinery starting into life and the gates beginning to open. 'You stand, dear guest, at the door of Pandemonium. Within lies "Demoniac frenzy, moping melancholy and moon-struck madness". At one time I would have tried to act as a warning. DO NOT ENTER HERE I would have said, not really meaning it. After all, you have probably already paid your admission price and the barker always seeks to titillate, inveigle, seduce. To warn against is to invite.' By now the door is ajar and the first glimpses of the inner courtyard are opening up into your field of vision. The voice seems closer and you do not have to strain to hear. 'Note well,' says the speaker no longer author, no longer barker, no longer priest in the pulpit, but now clearly the keeper of the gate-house, 'as you enter Pandemonium remember Kafka's doorkeeper in *The Trial* (1953) who bellows in the ear of the man who has waited by the door for many years. "No one but you could gain admittance through this door, since this door was intended only for you. I am now going to shut it."'

30

The gatehouse

Once through the door, and the portal closed behind you, the guide addresses you thus:

'The textual layout of this book is based upon the traffic flows of contemporary Pandemonium. In Milton's time, we are told, the visitor "shall tempt with wandering feet the dark unbottom'd infinite abyss and through the palpable obscure find out his [her] uncouth way", but today Pandemonium has become modernized and modernist. Through yesterday, today and tomorrow, though not necessarily in that order, increased traffic flows have necessitated a different system. Like all traffic management schemes it has been deliberately designed to create as much chaos as is diabolically possible.'

The majority of the bookish journey you may now wish to undertake is a divided highway in which the meridian or central reservation separates reading which is moving in one direction from reading which is moving in the other. If you, as visitor to this version of Pandemonium, attempt to cross the reservation and the separated traffic flows you will find that accidents, often messy and sometimes inconvenient, may well happen. Since at this precise moment you are in a pedestrianized queuing area – the gatehouse – you are being led through the text in the classic modern way. Disneyfied McDonaldization has got as far at the portcullis of the gatehouse of Pandemonium.

You find yourself ushered into something resembling an underground car park. Gibson addresses you thus:

'So, welcome to a world of time-space compression. How are we to move around Pandemonium?' On the 'time' issue we need to recognize the *repetition* of ideas, problem identification, problem solutions and approaches to human issues. Take for example a recent idea being developed to allow cars within the modern city to follow pre-set electronic ways at a constant speed. These would obviate the need for the driver to be constantly aware of close context and would co-ordinate a large number of movements for hundreds of travelling individuals. Cars would be connected together, electronically, in particularly dense parts of urban arrangements. Someone from Transport 2000, a pro-public transport group, opined in response to this proposal that she was in favour of the idea and suggested a name for the system. Why not call them *trains*? Trains, of course, are relatively new ideas themselves. In almost every society in which railway systems developed, trains were carriers of culture and carriers of disease (as in the old joke of the 1980s: 'the only culture round here is in the yoghurt' there is some identity between them). Trains are also carriers of linearity. As Camille Paglia (1990) has attempted to show, unidirectedness is predominantly a male characteristic brought about by the possession of a penis and the basic need to avoid infantile soiling in ejaculation and urination. But as we have already seen, Hoskin and MacVe (1986) demonstrated that the growth in the US railway system in the nineteenth century acted as a transmitter of West Point's military forms of thinking about organization into the very heart of the USA. The Academy took ideas from France about discipline (Foucault 1977b), shipped them across the Atlantic and transhipped them westwards in the form of 'railway systems of thought'.

31

Railway systems of thought include an emphasis on linearity, on timetabling, on gradations of staff, on the portability of all human life, especially on the concept of railway 'lines', and on cheapness of movement in regulated, predictable ways. The regular marching of soldiers leads to the regular movement of trains and passengers and freight (Taylor 1979). Given all this, Pandemonium is not keen on trains. As in Los Angeles, the train systems were bought up and closed down on the same day by some satanic joint venture. But since here, as in all cities, the average traffic speed is declining and is well below 6 miles per hour (outside the rush-hour when it drops even further) then you, dear guest, could just as easily walk. We do not recommend recourse to foot, however. The streets of Pandemonium are ill-lit, the power supply often fails and the pavements seem warm and are uneven. There are absolutely no signs saying 'Beneath the pavement, the beach'.

'It is advised that you follow the road system but, as is expected, when you wish to confuse yourself more than the text is designed to do, feel free to travel however and wherever you like. All this text can do,' the guide lies, 'is to point one way through the labyrinth. But since labyrinths are often of one's own making you may enjoy forming bricolages and mosaics from the *Pandemonium* you will find there as well as here. If you do leave your car, beware. Do not march purposively. Saunter, stare, peruse, perambulate. Do not act as a tourist on any account. If you do, you will find police approaching you, laughing, saying "Give it up, Give it up"' (Kafka 1961).

You will be pleasantly surprised by the fact that, architecturally, the Pandemonium you are supposed to intour more resembles an inner ring road than an infernal labyrinth. The original labyrinth was seen as lying at the gates of Hades protected by Cerebus, the three-headed monster. But for the Greeks of classical antiquity, the absence of straight lines and the failure of the linear to dominate was hellish indeed. Immersed in their enmity for the Cretans, the Greeks' advocacy of the linear argument, rational discourse and the pursuit of logic led them to dislike the dark corners, the non-linear, the hidden recesses of the mind recognized by their southern neighbours. For the Cretans, however, the labyrinth was the architectural expression of the hidden side of human nature which they wished to recognize in all its potency. The abhorrence of linearity allowed surveillance to be undeveloped. It permitted secrecy, privacy and inwardness.

Where you are about to enter owes more to the Cretans and their love of the spiral as a geometrical shape. The pathway you are invited to follow is not a spiral but you can attempt to make it so. Whilst the labyrinth of *Pandemonium* is usually accessed via the relatively straightforward means of the road system of this text, should you leave the road at any time the labyrinth with all its fearful monsters for the modernist may well beckon seductively. Thus whilst we are entering a labyrinth it is accessed via a road system but this can all too easily be left at will.

Light appears up ahead. You leave the underground car park. It is sunny. In a vapour trail, high above you the following words are discernible.

THE RULES OF MOVEMENT

Prague's crowds can be avoided if you know how. A sort of tourist 'super-highway' stretches from the National Museum, down Wenceslas Square, through the Old Town Square, across Charles Bridge up to Malostranke Namesti and on to Prague Castle. But stray from that route even by 50 feet in many places and you find yourselves alone, back in Prague of 20 years ago – or even 40 years ago, or even two or three centuries ago. (Rocks 1994: 80)

To maximize the chances of disorganization it is important for you to know the rules before being admitted further. First, you are about to become 'a mind on legs' (Bennett 1995: 6), for Pandemonium is also a place for those who wish to undertake a directed itinerary of organized walking. Second, there is to be 'No swearing, no spitting, no brawling, no eating or drinking, no dirty footwear, no gambling' (Bennett 1995: 27). For these activities would show how embodied and visceral you really are. Third, you will discover that Pandemonium is a medieval city, so the first two rules cannot and will not apply. Unless otherwise instructed do not read complete pages. When in the 'upper traffic flow' only read down to the central reservation and then move on to the next page. The meridian will be clearly marked and you can see that the counter-moving text has a doppler affected-print difference to its composition. Continue to the 'end' of the book and then start the journey backwards reading in the opposite direction. This does *not* mean that you should start at the end of sentences on the right-hand side of pages and 'begin' there. Reading '.cte dne eht' is not appropriate. Even devils would not be that malicious. When in the lower traffic flow read the right-hand page first but in the normal left to right way. Then move to the left-hand page and do the same. Then turn the page backwards heading towards the gatehouse and exit moving towards the lower numbered pages all the time. Confused? Good!

If you need direction look for the arrows (symbols in Renaissance art of disease, particularly the plague). You will see one at the bottom of this page instructing you that you are in a pedestrianised area and to continue normally. The gatehouse is not the only such area within Pandemonium. You will find several others where both traffic flows (upper and lower) meet, mingle and mangle. For example, there is The Public Library, Horse Guards Parade, The Airport Lounge, Gibbet Hill Road and The Management Science Factory where you can take your time and browse around the features located there. Access to these traffic-free areas of Pandemonium is sometimes controlled by traffic lights and sometimes by textual roundabouts.

From now on, however, you must be prepared for two streams of textual material moving in opposite directions. You'll be confused at first but that is all to the good. If you do look down make sure you get out of the habit very quickly. It's a skilled driver or pedestrian around Pandemonium who can spot the humuments and jokes without crashing in the first chapter or so. Open the door. Belt fastened? Ready? Off you go. . . .

33

Abandon Hope All Ye Who Enter Here

CHAPTER 2

Into Pandemonium

Pandemonium, the Palace of Satan rises,
suddenly built out of the Deep

(Milton, *Paradise Lost*, Bk I,
The Argument)

𝔉𝔍𝔑𝔍𝔖

The streets of Pandemonium

Pandemonium is that most unnatural of all things – a city still with the countryside deep within it.

The streets of the city around you contain the countryside, not in the usual sense of that where nature is exhibited and controlled in parks and formal gardens but in the sense of a living in the midst of and immersed within nature. Of course, therefore, disease is rife. The close proximity of bodies in houses, streets and markets is a breeding ground for those small-scale animals who know nothing of disinfectants, cleanliness and the value of good drains except that they profit from the absence of such circumstances. Their life is made possible by the streets of the city. The notion of a bath is anathema to one and all. It is common to bathe only on the first day of spring or on one's wedding day. Flea bags hang around the necks of every woman and man, who each seek to sacrifice this part of their anatomy, in order to save the rest.

The circumfence

We are used to having a birthday each year and as it arrives we commemorate, sometimes happily, sometimes not, the fact of another year of life. Indeed, this manuscript was finished on 31 January 1996 – my birthday. Little do we realize that each year we also have a death day – one day each year which will be the anniversary of the day on which we die. Were we to know which day this was, would we celebrate or mourn its coming? And when we do know; what of that?

The houses contain wooden floors which are covered in rushes from nearby marshy ground or with threshes from the fields. A piece of wood – the threshold – contains these floor coverings within the room until they are thrown out when they appear to all concerned to be too dirty. Mice and a variety of insects inhabit this natural floor covering. The legs of such furniture as is available rot in the damp conditions under the threshes and periodically the legs are sawn off to keep the table or bed steady. There is usually only one bed, to which the parents unquestionably have sole access. Children sleep in the same room as their parents. Access to the upstairs where this upper storey exists is often by a rope ladder. The very small children known as cubs rather than kids live in holes in the chimney wall which are therefore labelled widely as cubby holes. Dogs and cats will live alongside the family, twenty-four hours a day; their task is to keep down the level of vermin. Excrement flows through the streets. It is thrown out of windows in the morning from brimming chamber pots. The overhang prevents passers by from catching too much of the contents but the shout of 'guardez-l'eau' is still to be heard. The stench is always there but in the summer it becomes unbearable. The well-to-do of Pandemonium leave the city in this period and follow the Royal Progress into the rest of Hell.

37

THE COMBAT
by R.S. THOMAS

You have no name
We have wrestled with you all
day, and now night approaches,
the darkness from which we emerged
seeking: and anonymous
you withdraw, leaving us nursing
our bruises, our dislocations.
For the future of language,
there is no redress. The physicists
tell us your size, the chemists
the ingredients of your
thinking. But who you are does not appear, nor why
on the innocent marshes
of vocabulary you should choose
to engage us, belabouring us
with your silence. We die, we die
with the knowledge that your resistance
is endless at the frontier of the great poem.

(*Collected Poems*, Phoenix, 1995)

This seasonal escape serves the happy function of carrying the plague into all areas of the kingdom as well as its more manifest purpose in allowing the majority of escapees to avoid the worst of the summer months and the increased dangers of catching many a disease.

Yet, Pandemonium is a happy place. The presence always of death means that life is lived to the full. Feasting, carnivals and intoxication are the way of life and are constantly reinforced in the day to day existence of the populace (Stallybrass and White 1986). Death is everywhere and the charnel houses are constantly full but this is seen as natural and as part of the rhythm of existence. Children grow up with little sense of self-control. The mirror, that most important tool in the growth of self-control, is not available to the masses and so we expect to find that collectivist orientations still predominate. Sex and sexual activity are taken for granted and are discussed openly in front of children. Indeed couples live all aspects of their lives in front of the children.

The concept of childhood itself is unlikely to find much recognition in Pandemonium. The whole street will see the marriage bed of newly weds and watch the consummation of the wedding. This is not surprising since the family will always be able to see and hear their parents making love from the comfort of their cubby holes. The Anglophone 'I' – a huge capitalized thing so significant of a strong individualism – has not yet developed. It still has not developed in France and Germany with their understated 'je' and 'ich' perhaps but in Pandemonium there is little sense of the cult of narcissism (Lasch 1979) affecting anything but a very small section of the population.

doing we ensure the concreticity of its existence for those to follow. Certainly, 'L'Enfer, c'est les Autres.'

Hell, also, my friends, is oneself.

But, of course, all of this still involves writing and reading. The experience of reading and writing is one which I would hope one day to transcend – or even just avoid. It is painful and difficult for me to undertake these tasks on a regular basis. The words inscribe and mutilate those with whom they come into contact. *Pandemonium*, in being published, has caused trees to die. Can any book claim that it enhances life more than it destroys the living? Certainly not this one. And, anyway, I don't feel enhanced. Just knackered.

CHAPTER 10   *Retro-Organization Theory*

In Pandemonium there is no fully developed 'I', nor is there any common accent or language itself. It resembles, quite naturally, the Tower of Babel, the Tower of Babylon.

In the back streets and ginnels of Pandemonium, there is a multiplicity of languages and a certain impression that the building work has not been fully completed. It is literally a shambles. It resembles the city of the Bladerunner. The street argot is a polyglot concoction which allows communication of sorts but there is, amongst the inhabitants, always that feeling of uncertainty and of talking past one another which is so typical of human interaction. This is exacerbated by the tendency of certain occupational groups to use their own private languages to escape from surveillance. Cockney rhyming slang, for example, was originally an attempt to communicate without the police of the time – the watch – understanding what was being said by those whom they were attempting to control. It is difficult to see why it was vital to illegal economic activity to remain secret about 'having problems with your Chalfonts' – but even in Pandemonium the citizens might not wish to broadcast this particular medical condition.

→

←

the oral tradition. Yet this choice is not asked of us. Like Janus, we must face both ways and see the need to recognize the existence of both Dionysus and Apollo, the Zoroastrians and the Magians, sexual passion and contemplative ratiocination. This is not to call for some superordinate synthesis for both cannot (pre)dominate simultaneously. But not to recognize the existence of the 'diabolical', the visceral, the goatish, is to create a shadowy half-world in which rationality tries, always unsuccessfully, to push out the passionate. Pandemonium is a place where the rational has refused to recognize the existence of Sybarites and Babylonians. It is a place where the devils have been excluded – not where they seek after life. Pandemonium is not a place where we visit and can on exiting, leave. Pandemonium is where we are now. We can leave it, not by embracing the Apollonian and the ritual of the religious order of bell, book and candle but by recognizing that the nether world of organization is created just as much by the search for order as it is by the embrace of narcotic pleasure. And in so

CHAPTER 10   *Retro-Organization Theory*

There was an equivalent traders' 'back slang' which also continues to exist in certain occupations where words of a hurtful and abusive nature are spoken backwards in front of customers to enhance control of them or resistance to them by the staff serving in shops. Often these are explicitly sexual and demeaning to women, such as 'kool ta eht esra no taht'. So too in Pandemonium. As in the contemporary Mafia, the words of the country dweller are used to hide what the city dwellers think of as criminal activity.

Within this rural city, traders still speak private languages, there develops a language through which immigrants and residents can discourse, and a language of the underclass seeking to escape surveillance. The language on and of the streets is vital, dynamic, liberating, enslaving, conservative, radical, hopeful yet full of references to death. In the face of death, apothecaries are common. They sell comfort, whether psychological or pharmaceutical, at some cost. Their remedies are full of the kinds of material drawn from the surrounding natural world of which Shakespeare speaks in *Macbeth*.

> Fillet of a fenny snake
> In the cauldron boil and bake;
> Eye of newt and toe of frog
> Wool of bat and tongue of dog
> Adder's fork and blind-worm's sting
> Lizard's leg and howlet's wing . . .
> (Second witch, *Macbeth*, IV.i.12–17)

It is also a place in which Radhakrishnan's (1994: 305) observation is very valid:

> The peoples of the world are currently unevenly situated between two historiographic discourses: discourses of the 'post' and the 'trans' whose objective seems to be to read historical meaning in terms of travel, displacement, deracination and the transcendence of origins; and discourses motivated by the need to return to pre-colonial, pre-modern and pre-nationalist traditions of indigeny.

Pandemonium is both a chimaera and a place in which 'post' and 'trans' meet the 'pre'. They are not mutually exclusive. They lie at the top and bottom of many pages – though not in any order necessarily. So does this mean that *Pandemonium* is suffused only with the written tradition? Are my grandmother's words lost for ever? I hope not.

If one had to make a choice – which one doesn't – then organization theory and organizational analysis will almost certainly end up in the embrace of the classical and written traditions. Your guide through Pandemonium, on the other hand, if forced to choose, would embrace

We shall return, perchance to dream, to Shakespeare's place in Pandemonium, but note here that the natural world contains all that is necessary for human survival within the magic kingdom.

Let us enter another magical kingdom as developed in the work of Terry Pratchett, one of the medieval period's greatest exponents.

legends which has provided the principal codes of recognition, of self-identification, in modernism'.

But, he argues, the twentieth century has witnessed the end of this myth of modernism. 'The gentle bull has become the minotaur of blood', for 'nothing in the accomplishments of a Goethe or a Schubert prevented a single moment of Auschwitz'. The latter, he argues, represented the deliberate constructions of Hell on earth when the old Hell beneath us no longer carried any conviction. It is highly symbolic, says Steiner, that nothing of artistic merit has come from the landings on the Moon – 'a breathtaking act'. The fear for the 'future', indeed the tenuousness of that concept itself, is typical of a *fin-de-siècle* period. Postmodern writers have said that narratives are dead and so Steiner wishes for a new narrator – a teller of tales. It is as if he wishes to remind us of Flaubert's *Madame Bovary* where we are told:

> Language is like a cracked kettle on which we beat out tunes for bears to dance to, while all the time we long to move the stars to pity. (cited in Barnes 1985: 51)

But it may not be in the macrocosm that aliens exist. It is in the microcosm at the level of genetic engineering where our dreams – and our nightmares – confront *Homo sapiens* in our brief domination of an insignificant planet. Flaubert moved between a concern with the celestial and the bestial. He saw himself primarily as a bear (Barnes 1985: 51) but other animals interested him too. Flaubert loved fairs and particularly the freaks shown to the public in sideshows. A five-legged sheep with a tail in the shape of a trumpet caught his admiration as did the notion of an ostrich trying to rape a donkey. He said of himself, 'I attract mad people and animals'. He also wished that he had been born a woman and when a doctor called him 'an hysterical old woman' he judged the observation 'profound'. He was a kind of chimaera himself.

→ *The Streets of Ankh-Morpork*
The novels of Terry Pratchett contain humour, fantasy and a creative
fertility which has proved attractive to many readers. Often, these fans
of Pratchett are portrayed as first-year undergraduate engineering students who will soon grow out of their fascination with the Discworld
and the grotesques who inhabit it. Along the length of the Rim of this
flat world, which is supported on the back of four huge elephants, live
particularly unusual and deformed creatures. They are prevented from
falling over the edge of the great waterfall which marks the end of this
world by the 'Circumfence'. But often smaller life-forms slip through
the netting of the fence and go over the Rim into oblivion – or is it?

> 'What else is down there? I mean, if you jumped off, what would you
> see? . . .'
> 'My home is down there, perhaps,' he said slowly . . .
> 'A real world. Sometimes I come out here and look but somehow I can
> never bring myself to take that extra little step . . .'
> 'There's another world down there?' said Twoflower, peering over.
> 'Where exactly?'
> The troll waved an arm vaguely. 'Somewhere,' he said 'That's all I
> know.' (Pratchett 1983: 193)

42

But the most alien chimaera that Western civilization can imagine
seems so often to look like Ridley Scott's film *Alien* (1979), for that
alien was a copy of medieval images of the Devil. The cloven hooves,
the reptilian tail, the human body and the goat's head all suggest that
the tridentine mass of reptile, goat and human is the defining chimaera of the last 500 years of Western thought. There is a fortune to be
made in the first laboratory which produces an enfleshed satanic form.
In Arthur C. Clarke's *Childhood's End* (1983) the satanic form is that
which the extraterrestials have as their body morphology and, knowing the fear this is likely to engender in humans, they originally hide
from the Earth's population. It is explained in the novel that human
fear of the reptile/goat/human comes not from a *memory* of old terrors
but from a *premonition* of what impact the aliens will have in bringing
about the end to human childhood. For Clarke, the chimaera is not an
old terror but a future terror. George Steiner gave a lecture at the 1994
Salzburg Festival in which he argued that the name of 'Europe' begins
in the myth of the insemination of Europa by Zeus who takes the form
of a bull to carry her off the island of Crete. The metaphor of this loss
of virginity to a horned creature and insemination by a god, Steiner
argues, is a primordial one. *La Belle et la bête*. He maintains that the
twentieth century has as its major texts of modernity many forms
← of plays upon the Greek myths. He says 'it is the repertoire of Greek

To take the step over the Edge requires great bravery or foolhardiness for we know not what we will encounter there. The troll who lives on the Circumfence thought about taking that final step often but never did. As for all of us, the security offered by the known, the world contained by the Rim, is profoundly attractive. Sitting on the fence too has something to offer but what can a trip over the edge provide?

As Pratchett tells us, the magicians crossed the Bridge of Size on their way from the Wizard's Pleasance to the Unseen University expressing their interest in what structuralist principles underlay their world. This discussion led ultimately to their building of an exploratory vessel. Thus, they 'built a gantry and pulley arrangement at the tip of the most precipitous crag and lowered several observers over the Edge in a quartz-windowed brass vessel to peer through the mist veils' (Pratchett 1983: 23).

Under the rim

But Shakespeare's world, particularly in the later years of his life, was much more threatening than that conceptualized by Pratchett in his elaborations upon issues within Discworld. For example, when King Lear enters the equivalent of the brass vessel to peer beneath the veils into human nature, he cries 'O! that way madness lies; let me shun that; No more of that' (*King Lear*, III.iv.21).

43

engineering approaches envisaged by Aldous Huxley in *Brave New World*. The possibility of a chimaera produced through genetic engineering is clearly with us. Crichton's *Jurassic Park* describes in some detail the achievement of dinosaur DNA from the amber pieces in which 'Jurassic' mosquitoes have become imprisoned. If they had fed upon the blood of dinosaurs just before their entrapment then there would indeed have been foreign DNA within their bodies. Whilst this might be theoretically possible, today's genetic engineering looks at more feasible projects. The regular production of hybrids of lion-tigers (ligers or tigons) is relatively easy although these hybrids, like mules, cannot then reproduce themselves. But, since we are told that chimpanzees and *Homo sapiens* share 98 per cent of the same genes, primate hybrids are much more likely to be attempted by ambitious genetic engineers. Think of the spare parts which would be available to medicine from the farming of higher-primate/human hybrids. If they could be trained, unrewarding work in deep space and nuclear power plants would be open to them. Thus the nightmare (?) images of *Planet of the Apes* and *Brave New World* would come about through the use of chimaeras.

When the King does decide, or is forced into contemplating what the underside of humanity represents, he encounters waste products, dirty work, the obscene, the stinking, the valueless. Here is where germs breed, flies multiply, odours intensify and all that is rotten finds its home. Lear's speech is populated by animals of such variety and numbers and the blasted heath is so inhospitable, even to members of the animal kingdom, that the play becomes seen clearly as a tragedy about the expulsion of the old, from the comfort of the social, back to raw nature.

Pandemonium, which lies ahead of you, *is* that underside of human life. Pandemonium is built upon the underside of typical organizational lives today and yesterday and probably tomorrow. The streets of Pandemonium provide much evidence at every corner of 'the terrors of the Earth'. Whereas Prospero can claim to control these through the powerful magic of his book and wand, Lear's renunciation of the throne, an equally powerful symbol on the face of it, has left him to the fate of the vast majority of the human race.

> As flies to wanton boys are we to the gods
> They kill us for their sport. (*King Lear*, IV.i.36)

But these gods inhabit the microcosm of the human psyche as well as the macrocosm of Heaven and Hell. At the end of the play, the characters are totally exhausted from unspeakable suffering from within as well as from 'without'.

44

was possible to conceptualize chimaeras as horrendous malformations of the gods' of God's 'natural order'. The Gothic novels of Mary Shelley and others envisage a world wherein science makes possible the assemblage of such a beast. Frankenstein's monster is made up of several and severed parts of human beings which, once assembled, take on a human but more importantly holistic form. The monster has a soul. The chimaera is powerful but mistreated and misunderstood. Leaving aside a feminist interpretation of the 'monster' misunderstood by its male creator, Shelley's novel adopts a mechanical engineering approach to the chimaera in which an assembly of manageable parts is undertaken to await vitalization through electricity.

Today, genetic engineering has moved beyond the mechanical engineering scenario of *Frankenstein* and through the phase of chemical

Yet, in *Lear*, contradictions between good and evil are very well highlighted. So too are those between a determinism and a more voluntaristic approach to the recognition and explanation of human suffering. For not only are we as 'flies' but 'the gods are just and of our pleasant vices make instruments to plague us'.

Shakespeare here adopts a classically neutral moral position to the evils which stalk the heath and thence the world at large. In *King Lear* then, the playwright explores the philosophical antinomies which face all of us, asking us how we might explain the evils of the world.

In the Restoration and in several periods since, there have been 'happy-ending versions' of *Lear* (*à la* Hollywood's audience-pleasing treatment of the conclusion to *Fatal Attraction* in which Glenn Close's character is violently murdered rather than committing suicide as happened in the first, unpopular version). Both the eighteenth and the nineteenth centuries saw an ending in which Goneril and Regan are poisoned and the Fool is entirely omitted; Lear regains the throne and Edgar marries Cordelia! Dr Johnson encouraged this version (Billington 1994: 4) and it was widely accepted as the 'authentic' version until the beginning of *this* century.

Eric Bentley in *The Life of the Drama* (1966) claims:

> What the Restoration did to Shakespeare was to accommodate him to a philosophy. The happy ending to *Lear* makes sense. Sense is exactly what it makes. Shakespeare's play does not make sense; it is an image of the nonsensical life we live, the nonsensical death we die.

45

Magians, Babylonians and Sybarites. Whilst they cannot agree on what lay behind creation they oppose the defenders of rurally based *oral* instruction.

Chimaera's role

In Greek mythology, which began as an oral tradition, the chimaera was a fire-breathing monster with a lion's head and a goat's body. As a term it has since come to mean a wild or foolish fancy. *Pandemonium* is a chimaera in this sense and the devils who inhabit it may be thought to be fanciful and foolish inventions. The juxtaposition, indeed the mating, of genetically incompatible material has been the object of this text. By having two counter-moving flows to the text it is possible, as in the children's game of placing incompatible heads upon very distinctive bodies, to create horrible patterns of incongruity. Each page to *Pandemonium* then is a chimaera. And so is the text as a whole.

But the metaphorical associations do not end there. For the Greeks and the Romans and the North Europeans in their classical phase, it

One can find an amoral, pitiless, nihilistic world in *Lear* or, by looking carefully, a world where good shows itself rarely. Ultimately, the play and the text are insoluble, which is probably the secret of its success as a major tragedy in world drama. Lear would have been at home in Pandemonium for it, like the blasted heath, is also full of drama and tragedy. For our purposes here, *Pandemonium* is about the dangerous and the unhygienic. On every corner there are examples of the relatively hidden world of death, decay, disease, lust, pain and discomfort which lies under the rim of modern organizations and modern organized life.

As an experience it is also meant to be about the processes by which those who write about what life-forms exist under the rim become besmirched themselves. One has in mind here the works of the Marquis de Sade on one hand and Nietzsche on the other. These were authors who drew our attention to what others wished us to forget and paid for it in terms of their reputations. Whilst, of course, they did not address the issue of bureaucratic organization in anything like a systematic way, there are elements in what they both had to say which should impact upon the contemporary analysis of organizational reality.

In the work of de Sade we confront Pandemonium in the form of an explicit discussion of sexuality and the role of pain in pleasure. But this easy association of de Sade with Sadism simply will not do, for in his writings there is a complex discussion of human motivation, drives and hedonistic proclivities which mean that a reduction of his ideas to what we now call Sadism is an oversimplification of a very crude kind. So crude, in fact, as to suggest to us that this crass equation

large-scale orgies and of believing in astrology and witchcraft – in short, of following the devas. Darius, the great ruler of Persia claimed to be a Zoroastrian but he helped the Jews rebuild Jerusalem and the Babylonians to repair the temple of Bel Marduk. Whenever Cyrus Spitama is threatened in the book, he throws the anathema – the formal denunciation of the opposed doctrine – at the perpetrator. He has been a pupil of Pythagoras who was also, in part, a Magi and in part a believer in Egyptian ritual. To break out of the constant cycle of death and rebirth, Pythagoras advocated self-denial, ritual purification through diet and the study of music, number and mathematics. The flesh, in other words, was seen as our tomb. And in this Pythagoras was totally opposed to the peoples of Sybrias – the Sybarites – who were devotees of luxury and the sensual vices and advocates of enjoyment of the body. There is then, in Vidal's overly simplistic terms, a line of thinking going back well before the 5th century BC in which the great holy thinkers – the rationalists – are opposed by the diabolical

must have been politically motivated by those who wished to see de Sade's reputation fall into an irredeemable state.

Similarly, the writings of Friedrich Nietzsche have become associated in the minds of many in the advanced Western world with despair, delusion and the kind of ideas one is likely to come up with if one is infected with terminal syphilis. His notions of the 'Superman' and 'the will to power' both have resonances with the development of the Nazi Party in later generations. A recent exhibition on 'Art and Power' at the Hayward Gallery in London (1996) made much of the dominating physical presence of the male body as it was portrayed in Nazi art in the period 1935–45. The notion of the *Übermensch* is very strongly represented here. The ideas that Nietzsche developed can be ignored by many thinkers because of the supposed links they have to a besmirched and of course militarily defeated political ideology. With the relationship between his ideas and his syphilis, and his ideas and Nazism, very firmly established in the minds of some commentators, it becomes easy to see Nietzsche as someone who is merely telling tales from Pandemonium. His reputation, like that of de Sade, has suffered from his willingness to take the quartz-windowed brass vessel and peer into the mist beneath the rim.

What has to be presented in and through the streets of Pandemonium is a set of arguments and images based upon the work of de Sade and Nietzsche in which the visceral, the carnal, the bodily, the unclean can come to be the focus of attention. We have to peer under the rim and look at what lies there, under the edge of an organizational reality which we are told is often clean, inviting and natural. We must avoid sanitization and the Handy flea bags with which we are regularly presented.

In fact, what is much more natural in the urban countryside that is Pandemonium is the accretion of human politics, fear, loathing,

A sentiment, if you have read this far, with which, you will ajudge, I am in total and obvious sympathy. Cyrus Spitama was the grandson of Zoroaster, the Wise Lord. The Zoroastrians were made up of, yet opposed by, the Magi. The Magians believed in rituals of exposing the dead to the open elements (as did the Lancastrian Doctor, Buck Ruxton). They were Devil worshippers, they drank a sacred brew called haoma and worshipped fire. Zoroaster had envisaged a twin brother to the Wise Lord, named Ahriman, who was unremittingly evil and lived in the House of the Lie. The mag(ic)ians were followers of Ahriman and committed in his name to Devil worship. Zoroaster did his best to convince most mag(ic)ians to adopt monotheism and to abandon their practices of hacking up living oxen, of carrying out

CHAPTER 10 *Retro-Organization Theory*

disgust and pain which has built up into so many layers that we can only begin to scrape the surface before readers find themselves with the smell of disease in their nostrils. According to Nietzsche, we swim in a sea of disorder, chaos, destruction, individual alienation and despair. 'Beneath the surface of modern life, dominated by knowledge and science, it is clear that he saw vital energies that were wild, primitive and completely merciless.'

Nietzsche himself asked the following question:

> do you want a name for this world? A solution to all its riddles? A light for you, too, you best-concealed, strongest, most intrepid, most midnightly men? – The world is the will to power – and nothing besides! And you yourselves are also the will to power – and nothing else besides! (Nietzsche 1968: 1087)

Here Nietzsche is quite obviously equating the influence of the Enlightenment with the centrality of light and vision and how what had previously been hidden in darkness comes into human view. Both Cooper and Law, however, have pointed out a number of times (e.g. 1995) that the Enlightenment can also be taken to mean (in English at least) a reduction in weight so that things become lighter and thus more

48

Come back again, soon

In the first few pages of this trip we were reminded of David Harvey's question: 'who are we and to what space/place do we belong?'

Cyrus Spitama, Gore Vidal's central character in *Creation*, says at the very end of Book 5, 'I know exactly who and what I am – a corpse-in-waiting' (1981: 416). Vidal's lighter touch is not evident in this text which imagines an individual who could have known, in the space of seventy-five years, Socrates, Zoroaster, the Buddha and Confucius. It is 'a sort of crash course in comparative religion and ethical systems' (ibid.: viii). In the book, Vidal claims that four separate literate societies abandoned their ancient oral system in favour of writing everything down at more or less the same point in time. Using the fictional Cyrus Spitama's journey to Babylon, India and Cathay, he attempts to compare and contrast their systems in the context of a lack of enthusiasm for monotheism. His writing on Zoroaster is particularly interesting. Vidal tells the reader in the Introduction to the book of meeting M. I. Finley and of asking him about one of the latter's colleagues who had written on Zoroaster.

> 'Was he reliable?'
> 'The best in the field. . . . Of course he makes most of it up, like the rest of us.' (Vidal 1981: vii)

CHAPTER 10   *Retro-Organization Theory*

easily transportable. This is an important point to which we may even return. For Nietzsche, however, the visual metaphor was the crucial element in what he has to say here, for it is the 'benighted midnightly men' whom he is addressing. The mists which encase the world can be penetrated to reveal the will to power and the will to power alone. (And those who are interested in such penetration will be men, obviously.)

He was very unhappy with the notion of a thinking, feeling subject who could or would think logically or causally. The subject, rather, is self-deceptive, lacking in consciousness, wilful, vengeful and as we have seen, is driven by a repressed, nihilistic will to power. Ideologies and religion which emphasize the subject are merely 'ruses by which decadence has attempted to stifle the innocent spontaneity of strength'. Along with a number of other writers, Nietzsche is often seen here as proclaiming the death of the subject. Umberto Eco has recently expressed this most forcefully in *The Name of the Rose* where he states: 'In the pages to follow I shall not indulge in descriptions of persons . . . as nothing is more fleeting than external form, which withers and alters like the flowers of the field at the appearance of autumn' (Eco 1987: 4).

In J.G. Ballard's work we see 'the surgeon of the Apocalypse' argue that the Apocalypse, our own total destruction, is what humanity actually desires, rather than fears (Fortunati 1993: 88). It has become our goal. So endism is rampant. But as Kumar (1995) so eloquently shows, such doomsaying is unusual even for a *fin de siècle* for there is no sense here of the Apocalypse leading to some utopian outcome at the end of it. In the last century even the authors of the extravagant fantasies of destruction saw some remedy available to their 'cleansing disillusionment'. Could the Panglossian good society be far behind if the era of disasters was about to befall us? And as this millennium comes to an end, *the* millennium, the dawning of the Age of Aquarius, is seen as possible. The sentiment is this: 'The idea of the end of the world is simply a negative utopia' (Enzensberger 1973: 74).

Krishan Kumar (1995: 207–8; Kumar and Bann 1993: 77–80) rejects Fukuyama's triumphalism in the notion that history has ended. He rejects, too, the ending of the grand meta-narratives that one finds in postmodernism for it is an end without an end. It is, says Derrida, 'an apocalypse without hope'. It is a period in which melancholia triumphs. In D.H. Lawrence's words: 'the winter stretches ahead where all vision is lost and all memory dies out'. What Kumar wants, still, is some sense of forward direction to a shining beacon which is the future. But there is none. There is melancholia and a sense of false rainbows which end in nothing.

CHAPTER 10   *Retro-Organization Theory*

Moreover, Nietzsche has had tremendous influence on the post-modern understanding of truth, for he ridiculed the love and pursuit of knowledge and emphasized myth over truth. For him, anyone who claimed to know the truth was highly suspect. Rosenau (1992) has recently claimed that Nietzsche was the forerunner of today's sceptical postmodernists in that the constellation of positions they tend to adopt is very reminiscent of what we can see in his writings. In his efforts to shock middle-class German sensibilities, Nietzsche showed that those Greek values which were highly prized in the pursuit of a neo-classical tomorrow were in fact the product of Dionysian intoxication with interpersonal violence. The two principal institutions of Hellenic society, he argued, were competitive games and love of rhetoric in political discourse, which he went on to claim relied for their cultural centrality upon hidden violence. Civilization, as Germany understood it, was a rational mask hiding the deeper and altogether more important reality of sex and violence.

The work of the Marquis de Sade on the other hand is not so much postmodern as modernist. What he was concerned with was a serious knowledge of the world and of 'man'. He has been described as having a systematically pessimistic philosophy in which the universe is nothing but violence and cruelty. In *Aline et Valcour*, for example, there is praise for and a celebration of atheism, blasphemy, egoism, cruelty, theft and murder, adultery, incest and sodomy. Gilbert Lely (1962:

WARNING: LINEARITY KILLS

William Rees-Mogg wrote in 1992 that:

> If we are lucky, mankind as it is has about 50 years left. Most of the graphs of human development, population, ecology, technology, nuclear proliferation and the spread of disease are on an explosive curve. The lines shoot off the graph somewhere in the middle of the next century. (quoted in Bull 1995: 204)

Notice here that history comes to a shuddering halt through lines on a graph and not as it is so vividly expressed in the Book of Revelations.

391) claims that 'were it not for [the fact] that the notoriety of the author's four letter name made academic criticism blind to it, this novel which throughout, despite the daring nature of the feelings described, never ceases to be decent, would long since have been listed among those works of imagination of universal significance which like *Don Quixote*, the *Decameron* and *Gulliver*, have opened new realms to man's imagination.'

The novel occupied de Sade in the Bastille from 1785 until 1788. It was published in eight volumes in 1795 after its original publisher had been arrested and executed. The *120 Days of Sodom* was written in late 1785, also in the Bastille, and hidden in the walls of his cell to lie there, unfinished. De Sade describes it to the reader as 'the most impure tale that was ever told' and indeed for some authors and critics, these two books show that Sade was 'the corruptor of the European mind' (Thomas 1978: 184) and mention of his name was seen and is seen in some quarters as unforgivable.

Nevertheless, his work is claimed by some to be central to Western understanding. Baudelaire, for example, maintained that 'One must always return to Sade to observe mankind in its natural state and to understand the quality of evil' (in Lely 1962: 393).

As Pandemonium will attempt to show, the lived-in world of past,

means 'the poor are always with us'. Of course, as individual humans die and new ones are born from their parents' DNA, 'the selfish gene' may be at work ensuring its survival through newness and change over time. But from the outside, the spiral may be moving but *not* progressing. One does not give up utopianism lightly but one's confidence in millenarianism ebbs with age. The period of history upon which I have drawn cannot conceivably be seen as a 'Golden Age' using conventional measures and methods of evaluation. The first Elizabethan period cannot compare to the second. Or can it? Anyway, my fixation is not offered in the spirit of it being a 'Golden Age'. It is a period across Europe of massive interest in the lives of countryfolk – partly because they were revolting – partly because their power and relevance was dwindling. It is a period of pre-modernism before the Age of Reason reaches its zenith. And since the Age of Faith was in decline those who held on to Christianity or happier pagan religious beliefs were also likely to prove troublesome. Yet, the spiral of time ensures conceptually that the 'Age of Reason' goes into decline and the rise of 'blind' faith comes yet again to dominate. Note that it very well may be faith in science, because science itself requires much more faith and less reason than hitherto. Science *is* faith today (Law 1991).

CHAPTER 10   *Retro-Organization Theory*

present and future organizations is indeed full of lust, despair, death and mayhem. Yet we continue to deny this. In much of management theory and the analysis of organizations there is a turning away from dealing with such issues. The managerial props which are often used in conventional denials of this de Sadean picture are very 'Handy' but they sacrifice any understanding of what lies and lives beneath the rim. As Kundera has argued, there is an aesthetic ideal which is well established in the Western world where 'shit is denied and everyone acts as though it did not exist. This aesthetic ideal is called kitsch' (1986: 248).

Kitsch is a German word, born in the middle of the sentimental nineteenth century, and from German it succeeded in entering all Western languages. Repeated and extended use, however, has obliterated its original metaphysical meaning. For Kundera: 'kitsch is the absolute denial of shit, in both the literal and figurative senses of the word; kitsch excludes everything from its purview which is unacceptable in human existence' (ibid).

In this sense at least then, organization studies tends to be kitsch because it ignores or, worse still, consciously hides that which is thought to be unacceptable in polite company. There is little mention of sex, yet organizations are redolent with it; little mention of violence, yet organizations are stinking with it; little mention of pain, yet organizations rely upon it; little mention of the will to power, yet organizations would not exist without it. Consider any of the major textbooks, let alone the Handy (1994) libraries of 'Thought for the Day', and you will see almost none of the underside of organizational life.

By way of another example, the majority of texts one opens in the management area eschew the concept of failure as having any value whatsoever. It is all too obvious that to mention failure is to be

Do not cross the central reservation

means am I seeking here to go back four centuries 'to put the clock back'. Retro-organization theory is not that naive. But we can go back to when the clock was different. That is another thing entirely.

Retro-organization theory and time

Elsewhere, I have written on the issue of time and how it might be conceptualized (Burrell 1992a). I favour the spiral conception described by Filicove and Filipec (1986) and found in at least Buddhist and Cretan approaches to temporality. Spiral orientations allow one to dispense with utopianism – for, in many senses, and not only the biblical, it

associated with dirty work (Douglas 1987; Ackroyd and Crowdy 1992). And to be dirty in one's work through one's speech is to be besmirched with the shit of saying the wrong things. To be pure and avoid the profane, we have to hide the reality of the objects we study. There is this aesthetic ideal which positively charges the masking of death and disease. The funeral director or the mortician masks the faces of the dead using sutures and rouge to cosmeticize the reality of tissue decay and necrotic collapse. The management writer equally cosmeticizes the necrotic collapse of organizational structures one day with the rouge of excellence and mastering change (Peters 1990; Moss Kanter 1990), the next with BPR and TQM.

It has been estimated that of all the US business organizations which existed in 1885 the percentage which survived in one form or another for 100 years is merely 1 half of one per cent. Corporations fail – and as a category they fail continually. Yet we prattle on about success, both individual and organizational, when the truth for the vast majority of people in their employment is that they will be associated with personal and institutional collapse. MBA students recoil from such messages, for the financial investment they have made in seeking the qualification and the stories they are told by recruiters encourage them in droves to seek the holy grail of individual success and career. They too are seeking to deny shit and the shittiness of organizational paths for their own progression. They too seek after kitsch.

Suddenly a pungent odour offends your nostrils. Your shoes are covered in shit. You realize that you are standing beneath a *garde-robe*. The guide beckons you within.

53

Yet in this respect we should remember that D-Day in 1944 changed almost all our futures. Willmott, in his book *The Great Crusade* (1992) said: 'the American dimension to the Normandy landing represented the first invasion of Europe from the outside world for 590 years'. That is, since Sulesmand Pasha entered the Balkans in 1394. This mid-twentieth-century date 'marked the end of the period of European supremacy in the world that has existed for four centuries'. D-Day also represented an end to the supremacy of the tradition of the peasant and its supplantation by a tradition of proletarianism drawn from the Far West (Keegan 1989).

For our purpose here, however, what is crucial is what the peasantry brought with them to America and not so much what happened to them on arrival. And we must recognize that this is a reversal of the dominant approach which regards the key issue as being immigration. For us, the issue is *emigration* and what that involved. By no

Into the Outer Keep

The author says 'Here we are in the Outer Keep. Around the walls you will notice the impresa of the educated and powerful classes of Europe in the sixteenth and seventeenth centuries'.

Notice, too, that below you the traffic is now flowing back to the gatehouse from its long journey around Pandemonium. You are just beginning this trip but they, the readers ahead of you, are almost finished now. They are not looking at the impresa – or if they are, they may well be lost. Around 1600, judges, lawyers, artists and the literati in general were keen to understand classical literature and bring its relevance into their own lives for their own purposes. A key text for this task was Ripa's *Iconologia* which was published not in Latin but in Italian, and in great detail presented what was to form the basis for moral allegory for the next 200 years of human thought in Europe. The subject of this book was classical mythology. The way in which painting, sculpture, bridal chests, trays of food for women at childbirth, tapestry and wall decorations all used these allegorical devices from the publication in 1593 of *Iconologia* is crucial to the understanding of what you will see in Pandemonium. For here within the confines of the city, we are surrounded by the period late in the sixteenth century and early in the seventeenth century when the Renaissance has happened and the Counter-Reformation is about to begin.

54

(community v. association) for the peasant entering New York, for example, is very rarely portrayed in novels and movies. In *The Godfather Part 2* the immigrant from Corleone in Sicily is portrayed as blending in with city life in a way which underestimates the problems that were likely to be encountered. The amount of time the Mafia required in order to deal with the urbanized, *Gesellschaft* world of the city was extensive because 'the omertà caused by poverty, suspicion of the law and a hatred of the courts [was] badly affected by the concept of the American melting pot' (MacKenzie 1967: 249).

Whilst the USA had a tradition of accepting the peasantry on to its shores, it never had an indigenous self-formed peasantry. As soon as the peasantry did touch Ellis Island attempts began to industrialize it, transforming it in this century from a largely non-Anglophone peasantry to a largely Anglophone proletariat. In the previous centuries, it had been converted partly from one based on immigrant peasants to one of share-croppers (or possibly free farmers) but this was within a culture very reflective of an absence of an established Church, of rationalism and of a commitment to economic progress and change. Thus we must note the USA's exceptionalism on this and move on.

Around us, the Enlightenment has not yet taken place and the liga-
ments of modernism are still to be drawn up. The impresa on the
walls of this courtyard are the mythical symbols we will need to
understand the period in which we find ourselves. Our mythography
needs to be developed before we proceed any further. Not to do so is to
invite confusion at the outset. For between the Renaissance and the
Enlightenment we can begin to grasp thought which is not yet modern,
not yet fully contaminated by 'science', not yet completely seduced by
the search for certainty. Logic in this world is by no means superior.
Logic is portrayed as 'involutus' or curled up, meaning that it does not
show itself fully to humans and is better conceptualized as sophistry.
The impresa on the walls speak to us of an age in which anything is
possible – and when it does exist it is usually monstrous (Hall 1974).

Beyond the next curtain wall lies a world upon which we all too
often seek not to look. From the images of the period placed upon the
walls of Pandemonium and now staring us in the face, we can perceive
that we are about to turn our backs upon the Apollonian world of
rationality, organization and bureaucracy. We are about to leave Reason
behind, forgo the rudder of intentionality, shun the stringed instruments of self-control and logic. We are soon to turn our backs on light,
the sun, the world of civilization, brains and Theseus. The impresa,
like the left-handed staircases, speak of loss.

running from freedom to slavery's non-freedom, serfdom represents an
intermediate unfreedom. The abolition of slavery did not create serfs in
the USA. Rather, it created the freedom to starve, a freedom which those
given manumission across the globe recognize only too well. In other
words, manumission did not, in the USA, regress the black immigrants
into serfdom. It moved them in line with the North to enjoy the freedom
of capitalist exploitation. Thus, a retro-organization theory seeking to
explore a pre-modernist society would not – indeed could not – include
the USA in its historical survey. It might include, if it were truly ambitious, the North American indigenous population – but these were not
the peasantry which much of Europe once understood and which Asia
and South America still understand today. This is the sense in which I
argue retro-organization theory is pre-American in origin.

Whilst the Inquisition may never have crossed the Rio Grande in any
virulent form, it is not my argument that retro-organization theory is
irrelevant to the USA. Far from it. Its relevance comes from the large
numbers of peasant immigrants landing on the Eastern Seaboard and
beyond, who brought their intellectual structures with them. The mag-
nitude of the confrontation of *Gemeinschaft* and *Gesellschaft*

CHAPTER 10 *Retro-Organization Theory*

We will not be able to find Anteros, Cupid's twin brother who is controllable and nice, nor Democritus the laughing philosopher, nor Sancho Panza who is so much more worldly-wise than his master. There will be an absence of Jehovah and his servant Elijah, no putto or amoretto much beloved in Counter-Reformation art, nor the book-burning St Paul nor the dragon slayer St Michael, nor Heaven itself. Instead, behind the bricks in the wall, lies the real world of organizational life as viewed from a pre-Enlightenment perspective. There is passion, disease caused by arrows, the syrinx and the thyrsus, masks and the hourglass, lots of sacrifices. There is darkness, blindness and drunken sleep. The barbarians, in the shape of centaurs and beasts with cloven hooves, are in control. There is a worship of sorts to the cult of Baal, the celebration of the story of Jezebel thrown out of a window by two eunuchs, the myths of the perpetual torments of Ixion, Sisyphus, Tantalus and Tityus. There is room for Medea, Pasiphae, and Priapus in the labyrinth at the gates of Hell. There is, all in all, the story of the overthrow of reason for the sake of animal passion.

In the combat of Ratio and Libido, Apollo, Diana and Mercury fight on the side of reason. While on the other side, in celebration of the passions, are arranged the forces of Cupid, Venus, Vulcan and Bacchus.

56

First, retro-organization theory has focused on European history as much as on the American experience. This is not by accident. The position taken with regard to OT on the streets on Pandemonium is that a pro-European stance needs to be developed for the sake of the area as a whole. This is not to say explicitly, nor to hint, nor to imply in the slightest way that an anti-American stance is being taken. If anything, retro-organization theory is *pre-American*. I do not mean that the indigenous peoples of the American continent in the pre-Columbian period are not worthy of study – but they did tend to be hunter-gatherers rather than peasantry. It is only with the Europeans in the English, Welsh, Scottish, French, Spanish and Irish varieties that something approaching large-scale agriculture began. And it began – or at least grew significantly – outside of the tradition of the peasant as formed in Europe in 1570–1630. Indeed, that is what it was largely designed to do.

Rurally based witch-hunts in the Americas did take place, but they were localized and the absence of established religion, the presence of possessive individualism and a predilection for science all worked towards an agricultural labour force, often African in origin – which had no tradition of peasantry or germane rural lifestyles. They were either slaves or free men and women (see Martin 1977). There was no tradition imported nor established of serfs (those who serve). In the spectrum

Bacchus (or, in Greek, Dionysus) is the God of wine but was originally a fertility god worshipped in the form of a bull or goat. The rites
of worship involved frenzied orgies when the animal was eaten raw by
the predominantly female followers. The female devotees of Bacchus
were called the Maenads or Baccante and were portrayed in pre-
Enlightenment paintings as beating that most lustful of instruments,
the tambourine. Bacchus is often shown as a naked youth, holding a
wand tipped with a pine cone and entwined with ivy. He is often seen
to be drunk and is transported by goats and centaurs. His entourage
consists of satyrs, snakes and the minor god, Pan. Goat heads and
cloven hooves predominate as do the syrinxes, a well-known phallic
symbol of Pan himself. Often, Pan and Bacchus are to be found in
Arcadia, a pastoral idyll where the disease-ridden towns and cities of
the period are strikingly absent. Arcadia is inhabited by nymphs and
satyrs, the latter usually chasing the former for sexual purposes. The
key story of the period for those impressed with mythology may well
be that of Pasiphae, who had designed to her own specifications a
wooden cow in which she could place herself in order to mate with a
bull. The result of this act of impregnation was the half-human, half-
bull creature, the Minotaur. This story was widely interpreted and
portrayed in the late Renaissance period as a tale of reason succumb-
ing to animal lust.

57

Rural life and retro-organization theory

Retro-organization theory seeks to reassert the role of the peasantry in
contemporary life – across the globe. This will come as no surprise to
rural sociologists or Third World specialists. Yet for organizational
theory, I imagine it will be a surprise. There is no claim that this group
brings moral superiority, new ideas or innovative thinking. They are
not likely to be 'world-historical figures' of the kind the Hegelians
have sought in such as Napoleon, the working class, and Marx himself.
And now the peasantry? No.

They are ignored, however, at our peril. The other elements of retro-
organization theory have been raised at various points. Let me attempt
to form a bricolage of these various elements at this point in the
journey.

The converse story where passion is defeated by Reason is equally well represented in the story of the Rape of Hippodamia. Here, the centaurs led by Eurytus meet the peace-loving Lapiths in a battle at the wedding feast of Hippodamia. Largely due to the influence of Theseus, the centaurs are beaten eventually, but blood and brains, those twin features of passion and reason, are spilt everywhere before the triumph of rationality is assured. The battle forms the theme for a key part of the so-called Elgin Marbles and was very popular with baroque artists in the period in which we are interested and within which Pandemonium sleeps.

So, in the tension between the story of the Rape of Hippodamia and the appetites of Pasiphae it is clear that Reason wins out in the former and passion in the latter. Within Pandemonium it is the left side of passion, the side of the goats, in which the populace appears to show its most appealing moments. Here, within the inhabitants, it is Jezebel, Priapus and Medea who are seen to dwell within the labyrinth and not the forces of problem solving and dragon slaying. It is snakes and the cloven hoof which lie just off the main thoroughfares of Pandemonium. The streets of the city are the place of the passionate.

The story of the Bacchae has come to the twentieth century from the Renaissance artists and thence to us from Euripides, born in 484 BC in Athens. At the age of 73 he left the political activity, artistic creation and intellectual brilliance of 'fifth-century Hellas' and went to the court of the King of Macedon.

in some capacity or another. Gambretta (1993) says that the Sicilian situation in the eighteenth century was one of a countryside where there were many absentee landlords and thus a vacuum of power was created. The Cosa Nostra grew up to offer protection to those who felt a contract might not be honoured. This took place in conditions of 'endogamous distrust'. The Mafia took on the role of a 'clearing house', but one made up of families who sometimes did collide because of endogamous distrust. They meet still in the *Commissione* which regulates murder and control over the territory. Members expect to die young and human life thus has little intrinsic value to many 'foot-soldiers'. Even the Capo di Capo, currently Toto' Rina, claims to be a poor shepherd rather than reveal his 'real' position. The language of rural life remains central to the Mafia.

CHAPTER 10 *Retro-Organization Theory*

Here, in this rural mountainous area, he wrote *The Bacchae*, his greatest and last(?) work (Euripides 1973). It is a product then of Euripides' retirement. It is also an *agon*, a tragedy based on a struggle or issue in which the psychology of violence is deeply explored and a conclusion reached that there are no external sources of morality. The Greek male of his time was very ready to blame women for everything untoward and Euripides constantly – though ironically – reminds his readers of this. For him, women are victims of rapacious men and this is shown distinctly in *The Bacchae*. Women, traditionally vilified for their crimes – Clytemnestra, Medea and Phaedra, for example – most unusually, are treated sympathetically as human beings. It is men who are contemptible.

The theme of *The Bacchae* is the infamous Dionysiac cult written about within the context of a concern for human character in relation to the natural environment. As we have already seen, the notion of two opposing sides to human nature is by now familiar within the Greek world. For Euripides, the rational and civilized side of our lives is fundamental to city life in particular, for it provides stability, law, conventions of sex and property and facilitates the organizing of war. The other side he recognizes depends on the life of the senses without the ability or desire to describe let alone analyse it. It is a side to human life which is all too conscious of its unity with the animal world and the supernatural power that comes from this.

prosper in a world ('in *our* world' say the Mafiosi) which is not a bureaucratic 'paramount reality'. Like cockney rhyming slang, Mafia ways allow subservient, subordinate groups to live a counter-cultural lifestyle. And since this lifestyle is deemed illegal by the state, its rituals and ceremony are designed to protect it from state suppression. For example, in the early 1920s, Cesare Mori, Mussolini's Chief of Police, began a campaign of flogging, maiming, flaying and castrating hundreds of Mafia suspects. But he concluded that the Mafia was as much a philosophy as an organization and therefore attempts to wipe it out were probably doomed to failure (MacKenzie 1967: 254).

To live this philosophy, in 1993, the three consanguine groups mentioned killed around 2,000 individuals. Together they have about 17,000 'regulars' and up to half a million people who are 'connected'

For Euripides, 'worship' of the gods did not mean adoration nor even approval but simple recognition that they existed. A Christian or Judaeo-Christian version of worship in which a total faith in the omniscience and beneficence of a God was professed was not one he would have recognized. Thus Dionysus is not condemned or 'worshipped'. He is understood, rather, as a source of deep human experience and need. If we *suppress* his influence or seek to repress it, it is then that the full power of destruction and disintegration are invoked. Pentheus, the victim of Dionysus in the saga, is betrayed by his *own* fear and violence.

Dionysus is the spirit of life and all that liberates it from pain, tedium and ugliness. He is associated with wine, music, dancing and the excitement of group emotion. 'Worship' is a form of recognition and understanding rather than a request for divine intervention and is done collectively in a company distinguished by its dress, secret rites and the consciousness-liberating feelings of surrender to the supernatural. The life of Reason perhaps is at the cost of the simple joys of mind and body at one with nature within the Arcadian fields.

with a rope around the neck. Whilst this appears to be carried out for its cruelty, it does allow bodies, alive or dead, to fit into car boots.

Whilst formal links to the Freemasonry lodges are not allowed, it has been shown recently that *Mafiosi* belong to lodges along with lawyers, *carabineri* and drugs officials. Since lodges also have a code of silence, for Mafia families this twin loyalty problem is an unwanted complication. Nevertheless there are some commonalities in orientation. First, there is the presence of hierarchical levels reminiscent of the old guilds more than modern-day bureaucracies. Then, as we have seen, the code of silence predominates, with threats of death associated with revealing any secrets of the group. Women are excluded and elaborate ritualistic checks are made to ensure this works effectively. Initiation rites are long, complex and heavily mythologized. In short, such organizational forms do not represent legal-rational bureaucratic structures. Indeed, they may well be designed to survive and to

In *The Bacchae* (Euripides 1973: 215–18) the Herdsman describes the characteristic Dionysiac experience. A large band of worshippers enjoys a picnic in the sunny mountains leaving behind all metropolitan cares. They sing and dance in an organized, orderly manner. But suddenly they begin running, find themselves endowed with and impelled towards mass violence. They are merged with nature and have become animalistic. They act with murderous ferocity tearing cattle and goats into pieces, eating them raw. Once the ecstasy has passed, they wash and return to peaceful perambulation.

The imagery here is of *the hunt* and in it and through it the manifestation of the god to his worshippers. Dionysus has splendour, strength and freedom but is as pitiless as a bird of prey and is impervious to human sensitivity. He is the archetype of that world of experience which has led to the concept of 'black magic'. It is this anti-rationalistic stance which leads the hapless Pentheus to say

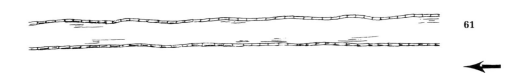

61

In Naples in 1994 a 'school of murder' was discovered where Camorra members, who were being initiated, could learn how to assemble and clean weapons, develop their killing abilities and how to counteract bodyguards. It was also estimated that the Cosa Nostra, Camorra and Andranghetta have an annual turnover in Italy of £11 billion which makes them the fifth biggest industry. Violence is endemic. When sanctioned by the local *capo* or, for important assassinations, by the Council of Families, anyone can be killed. If the code of silence is broken (even to admit the Mafia exists is punishable by death) then not only does the individual lose his or her life but so may every member of the family. Vats of sulphuric acid are a favourite way of disposing of bodies and 'the goat' is a typical form of exacting punishment. This is where victims are tied up with arms behind back and legs tied to arms

CHAPTER 10   *Retro-Organization Theory*

Keep your hands off! Go to your Bacchic rites and don't
Wipe off your crazy folly on me. But I will punish
This man who has been your instructor in lunacy.
Go, someone quickly to his seat of augury, smash it with crowbars,
topple the walls, throw all his things.
In wild confusion, turn the whole place upside down,
Fling out his holy fripperies to the hurricane winds!
This sacrilege will sting him more than anything else.
The rest of you – go, comb the country and track down
that effeminate foreigner, who plagues our women with
This new disease, fouls the whole land with lechery;
And once you catch him, tie him up and bring him here
To me: I'll deal with him. He shall be stoned to death.
He'll wish he'd never brought his Bacchic rites to
Thebes.

(Euripides 1973: 203)

And as this chapter forms in my mind I must admit that this speech conjures up an image of it being spoken in those few studies and rooms of conventional organization theorists whenever a copy of *Pandemonium* is read. But being dealt with by the powerful and well-heeled followers of Pentheus may well be a fate one should tolerate. Because for the Apollonian, the followers of the vision of Pentheus, there is created a world which is even more strange than the Baccanalian image of snakes and the cloven hoof.

62

very, very carefully to be full of meaning. Silence is respected above all. Entry into the Mafia for foot-soldiers may well take the form of being asked to murder someone. If this is done without question and efficiently, acceptance into the ranks is forthcoming. Corleone has a population of 11,000 and yet the number of murders in the post-Second World War period rivals the New York area – 1,000 times bigger. There were 159 murders in the period 1944–8 alone. Time is measured in parts of Sicily by the murders which are committed. When asked when did this (x or y) occur, the typical answer is 'about the time A or B was killed'. Linear time here is measured by murders not coffee spoons. The dehumanization of the victims of the act of murder is accepted and encouraged. It is called 'killing a goat'. Mafia proverbs also identify the element of manliness, silence and violence for a purpose. Strict codes of honour are still in force, which means that slights of the smallest kind may well end in feuds which last generations – sometimes centuries (Zanini 1994).

CHAPTER 10 *Retro-Organization Theory*

These images of the leather sole and the cloven hoof are not without their significance, for the social division between rural and urban became very important in the late sixteenth and early seventeenth centuries. In the middle of the period of which we speak, around the year 1613, we find the very height of the witch-hunts across Europe. In Cohn's *Europe's Inner Demons* (1976), an argument is presented which states that Europe in the late Middle Ages resonated with antiquity to the extent that both had a fantasy that there existed in the midst of their society a smaller clandestine group addicted to practices which were felt to be wholly abominable and anti-human. This anti-human stance was witnessed by their approach to the body. The witches whom the authorities sought out were accused of ritual murder, cannibalistic feasts, every form of erotic behaviour and the worshipping of a strange divinity in the form of an animal. This is a very old tradition. The Bacchanalia of 186 BC, for example, was a large-scale orgy in which: 'when wine had inflamed their minds and night and the mingling of males with females, youth with age, had destroyed every sentiment of modesty, all varieties of corruption first began to be practised' (Livy in Cohn 1976: 10).

The Consul in charge of suppressing this outbreak of the cult of Dionysus, however, saw it as having the objective of 'control of the state' by becoming a 'united body' of resistors to the ruling élite. The fact that their bodies 'united' was seen as deeply problematical and threatening. Vast numbers of the cult were imprisoned or executed. In the same way, and for the same reasons, the early Christians were accused of 'Oedipean mating', 'Thystean feasting' (i.e. eating their own children) and the Agape (a love-feast held in connection with the

63

The 'Cosa Nostra' is linked to the Camorra in the Neapolitan region of Italy (Lepper undated: Chapter 27) and the A'ndranghetta in the Calabrian area and in each case it is plain that the organization has grown up in opposition to the northern and Roman domination of their locality. Unsurprisingly, therefore, the Mafia adopts an organizational form which is deliberately quite unlike the state – to some extent. Initiation often takes the form of an oath sworn in blood which recognizes that withdrawal from the Mafia is impossible. The cards of saints are initially torn up. The code of *omertà* – literally manliness – stresses how men behave under stress. They say little – sometimes nothing. In an effort to dominate each situation, words are chosen

Lord's Supper) was maintained to be an excuse merely for excessive drinking and feasting. The importance attached to the Eucharist in which the body of Christ is eaten and his blood is drunk did nothing to stem such stories of cannibalism and feasting. Moreover, it was said that Christians worshipped nothing more than the genitals of their god. Karl Marx was convinced that these tales had much substance. He believed that the Romans had tolerated all religious sects – except the Christian – for this reason.

However, according to Cohn, once in a position of domination, Christianity itself treats all pagan forms of worship in precisely the same way as it had been treated. Witches are accused of the selfsame abominations as all other groups who refuse the rule of the state. A witch was a human being, usually a woman, but sometimes a man or even a child who was bound to the Devil by a contract to act as his servant. Usually he appeared to humans in human form but sometimes as an animal. The satanists tended to be in a condition at the edge of human endurance but once they had accepted the diabolical bargain they were left with the mark of the beast on the left side of their body. Witches seldom won wealth or erotic satisfaction. What they received was the skill to carry out the 'maleficium' – the ability to put a successful curse on their neighbours.

64

The Mafia in Italy

The origins of the term 'Mafia' are very unclear. There are at least four basic myths of origin. Some believe it comes from Arabic and is a word meaning 'refuge' (MacKenzie 1967: 242), others hint at a term from Ancient Greece. One suggestion is that it is connected to one Joseph Mazzini who authorized theft, arson and poisoning. In Italian this is *Mazzini autorizza furti, incendi, avvelenamenti* or by its initials, MAFIA (Lepper, undated: 212). A connection between Pythagoras and an early form of the Mafia has been identified, although it is not well substantiated in the literature. The key thing of importance is the isolation of Sicily from continental mainlands and the fact that it has been subject to an almost continuous wave of invasions over the centuries.

They specialized in killing babies and small infants. Their greatest pleasure was to kill, cook and eat an unbaptized baby. This flesh also allowed them to fly. They met at sabbats which were held at night in churchyards, under gallows or at the summit of mountains. The sabbat was presided over by Satan in the form of a monstrous being, half-man and half-goat. He had enormous horns, a goat's beard and a goat's legs. Sitting on his high chair he would accept the offerings of love and obedience from the faithful. This would take the form of them kissing his anus and he responding with particularly noxious farts! Food of an unappetizing kind would be served and then an orgiastic dance would take place with the followers facing outwards dancing around a witch with a candle placed in his or her anus. An orgy would begin in which incest and sodomy were encouraged. At the height of the orgy the Devil would copulate with every participant, whether they were man, woman or child. This was painful and decidedly unsatisfying for human beings (Russell 1961). His semen was always ice cold. Satan would end the sabbat by sending his followers back to do their worst against their Christian neighbours (Cohn 1976: 101–2).

This vision of witchcraft was held right across Europe in the period of 1580–1630. It was well accepted that this is what happened when country folk got together in lonely isolated locales in an organized, united and therefore threatening, way.

Do not cross the central reservation

Knowledge of the organization was compartmentalized to prevent one cell which had been penetrated providing information on other active service units. Throughout the 1970s, 1980s and 1990s the high command of the IRA and its political wing changed strategy on many occasions. However, in County Fermanagh the structure of the active service units ranged against the British army and then the SAS remained, it would seem, constant. Clandestine organizations whose members face death for their activities seem to adopt the cellular system in order to protect themselves from the superior logistical and numerical strength of the state forces ranged against them. Within the countryside this cohesion is much easier than it is within the city. The oath swearing which accompanies this, allowing members to say they are 'up' to being within an illegal and therefore dangerous organization, is typical of many agrarian-based resistance groups.

CHAPTER 10 *Retro-Organization Theory*

An understanding of the significance of the use of the body in pro-
scribed ways is essential if one is to come to a view on the importance
attached to erotic activity outside the 'normal range'. Witchcraft was a
subordinate reaction to a church and society which were totally identified. To rebel against authority was to rebel against the Church and
involved, therefore, a rebellion in some way against current understandings of Christ himself. It was this nihilistic paganism to which
witches were seen as attached. And, in the classic sociological irony,
by attempting to suppress such views it was the Inquisition which did
most to further the cause of the nihilistic paganists.

Ginzburg's book *I Benandanti* (1983) shows how this process is very
clear in northern Italy in the relevant period. Armed peasants in the
district of Friuli fought pitched battles with 'members of the local
witch cult' who engaged in fertility rites, eroticism, banqueting and so
on. After 1610, a generation of Inquisitorial trials took place at the
end of which the locals regarded *themselves* as Devil-worshipping
witches, whereas they had not beforehand.

66

The development of the IRA itself after the Easter Rising was very
much as a guerrilla force and it came to command control over large
areas in the South. But whilst Ulster remained loyal to the 'Crown', for
the guerrillas had not been able to command much agrarian support in
the North, the political solution adopted by Lloyd George had been par-
tition. In the 1960s, as political events in the North gathered apace, the
IRA returned to its cellular existence in order to prevent British agents
from infiltrating its ranks. Whilst in Derry and Belfast this proved hard
to sustain because of the large number of Northern Irish who had close
British connections, in County Fermanagh it was much more difficult
for security forces to break into the rurally based cells. The IRA in so-
called 'Bandit Country' was highly successful, forcing the British to
supply their garrisons by helicopter because by day and night the
countryside, to all intents and purposes, was in Republican hands.
Cells, usually referred to as active service units, consisted of four individuals in two pairings. They had tremendous freedom of action within
the structure of the IRA once a strategy had been developed.

The subjugation of rural life is the theme which Cohn (1976) challenges in his book. He stands out against the thesis that the witch-hunts in the late 1500s and early 1600s took place because the Church wished to suppress the widespread practices of rural groups such as fertility rites, orgies to welcome spring and other key seasonal shifts, feasting and the concern for animals and their butchery, not because they were immoral or unchristian but because they represented an alternative ideology and lifestyle for subjugated groups. The key thing here is that the thesis maintains that 'witchcraft' is a label given to a potent subordinate ideology and its rural underpinnings, in order to suppress it.

Cohn argues that such practices never existed and that they were invented by the metropolitan powerful in order to suppress the Other. There never was a subordinate anti-hierarchy within the rural communities which practised magical rites and worshipped mystical beings. His argument is that these were inventions without substance. Where this leaves the underclasses of the period is not in doubt. They were not capable of developing alternative lifestyles and world views. These had to be invented for them. Yet this seems to be a denial of a long line of human thought and is very metropolocentric and Whiggish in its conclusions.

All the evidence for the 'true' Dionysian strand of thinking existing in Europe at that time is seen by Cohn as false and misleading.

Attempts at terrorism by Clan-na-Gael were not successful in terms of the physical and structural damage caused in Great Britain but reforms in Ireland did take place in the late nineteenth century. It is perhaps important to note that the Irish nationalist societies had middle-class, educated leaders but relied on a tradition of Irish peasant lawlessness. But unlike the pattern of agrarian revolt on the continent, no support of any significance came from urban groups. Indeed, the failure of the Easter Rebellion in 1916 was largely due to the hostility of the Dubliners to the peasantry.

CHAPTER 10 *Retro-Organization Theory*

And here, in yet another twist of which this Pandemonium will be full, we come across Dionysus again. But not the god; this time it is a *pseudo* Dionysus – Dionysus the Areopagite – who wrote about the organization structure of Heaven. Gunnar Hedlund (1993: 222) has analysed the organizational image of Paradise which is found in the writings of Dionysus the Areopagite who invented the word 'hierarchy' in the fifth century AD. Of course, its literal but oft-forgotten meaning is that of rule by the sacred. How it came to mean rule by the secular is not at all clear but the Enlightenment did much to destroy the hold of religion on the minds of its congregations – but not as much as is often thought. The hierarchy in this sense, for Dionysus, is eternal and never changing. It is perfect and harmonious. It has enemies outside and only by making it obscure and hidden to the casual gaze of outsiders will it be protected.

The organization structure of the sacred rule is nine levels deep and is unambiguous. There has to be universal subordination within the hierarchy for all issues and all purposes. For those lower down this hierarchy the aim must be to be as much like those above as is humanly possible. As angels proceed upwards, they receive more knowledge and perfection which justifies the one-way flow of communication from the top downwards.

68

The Fenians emerged some fifty years later with the declared aim of complete independence from Britain. Three of its members set up the Fenian Brotherhood in the USA and developed a mode of organization based on the continental revolutionary model of cells of ten, whose members theoretically were unknown to other members of the Brotherhood. But the Irish Republican Brotherhood (IRB), as it was sometimes called, was heavily involved in recruitment in Ireland and indiscriminate in whom it accepted. Because of this, it was riddled with informers. Moreover, it did not train as a military force and each attempt at insurrection was unsuccessful when faced with numerically superior armed militia.

There is, above all, a vertical sealing off of units so that a fallen angel will not and cannot compromise the whole divine system. As Dionysus says, then, in his pseudo-voice: 'our hierarchy is a sacred science, activity and perfection' (Hedlund 1993: 222).

Therefore, Heaven for this pseudo-Dionysus is likely to be a city of numbered streets, a grid structure and wide boulevards (*à la* Haussman) to facilitate the better control of crowds, the prevention of the building of barricades, and the quicker movement of forces around the city. In short, it is a modern city. We should remember, however, that the mining villages of the North-East of England such as Ashington, despite the gridiron design and modernist construction, never fully subdued the life of the people (McCullough Thew 1985). Police patrolled the streets on their bicycles and the overman patrolled the highways and byways of the underground roadways. But always in the dark, the life of the population continued, tempted often 'by bed and the ale-house' (Bennett 1995: 20). Pandemonium, on the other hand, is decidedly pre-modern with numberless houses in close-packed, winding streets. According to Mumford (1960) these are for people to live in and are not for moving through.

secretary. Five such secretaries formed a lower baronial committee and delegates from ten such committees formed the upper baronial committee. Above these were regional and provincial committees. Five members from the provincial committees were selected for the National Directorate which had supreme control over the complete organization. The election was so arranged that only secretaries of the provincial committees knew who had been chosen. Orders and instructions were transmitted downwards in the utmost mystery and secrecy. The leadership itself, then, lay shrouded in mystery and gained thereby some protection from the British. This notwithstanding, many of the United Irishmen were jailed in 1793 for their support of the French and took to swearing oaths of loyalty to their own clandestine organization. At initiation, the new member would say 'I know U' to which the reply was, 'I know N' and so on until the name of the United Irishmen had been completely spelt out. Their badge was the Irish harp combined with the French cap of liberty. The Rebellion of 1798 which ensued was suppressed with great ferocity by the British. Travelling gallows strangled captured rebels to death and many peasants had their heads covered in pitch which was then set alight. Because of this repression the organization that had been the United Irishmen disappeared.

CHAPTER 10   *Retro-Organization Theory*

Whilst Heaven for the pseudo-Dionysus is the celestial hierarchy in which the labyrinthine, the complex, the questioning, the temporary are not welcome, Pandemonium has to be seen in the mirror as reflected, reverse light. Hierarchy in this nether world is no longer sacred. It is profane. It is not obscure from without but clear from within. Rather than being opaque to casual observation it is all too transparent from a position outside the gatehouse. But once you are inside the doors and the tour has commenced the nature of the organizational structure of Pandemonium is profoundly opaque to analysis. There is nothing heavenly about the organization of Pandemonium. It is chaotic, empty of meaning, vacuous.

Just as Lash and Urry (1994: 12) provide 'a dystopic scenario, the dark side of postmodern political economies', [which] 'focuses upon the increasingly rapid circulation of subjects and objects, of multiple space odysseys, and how as a consequence they are emptied of meaning and significance', so, too, will our trip through Pandemonium.

70

Irish agrarian resistance

According to MacKenzie (1967: 178):

> Irish Nationalist societies emerged in the eighteenth century, when an Anglo-Irish Protestant minority consolidated its rule over the Catholic majority. . . . Opposition to such rule usually begins in the form of an open cultural society, set up as a club for the leaders of the oppressed minority. The club progresses from considerations of culture to demands for reform from the occupying power. When these are resisted, the club either splits into moderates and extremists, or goes underground. At this point a Nationalist secret society is formed. Its aim is insurrection, its organization, military.

In the 1780s, the Whiteboys, known as such because of the colour of their frocks and shirts, attacked landlords in the south of Ireland with scythes, clubs and swords. They were a group of agrarian insurgents who fought against 'wealthy monopolists who turned the wretched peasantry adrift' (quoted in Lepper undated: 216). Once suppressed by very strong military action, the name of Whiteboy was used to describe any agrarian bandit but its organizational place was eventually taken by the United Irishmen. The form this organization took was 'comparable to that of a triangle' (ibid.: 230). At the base were small local societies, consisting of twelve members, one of whom was an elected

The circulation of subjects and objects
The increasing domination of the world economy by a small number of
multinational companies is evidenced in the fact that TNCs (transnational corporations) now account for one-third of global output
(Hirst and Thompson 1996). The *World Investment Report* from
UNCTAD found that sales from TNCs were worth $4,800 billion –
bigger than total international trade – and formed the productive core
of 'the globalising world economy'. The global network of TNCs com-
prises 37,000 parent firms which control 200,000 foreign affiliates and
this excludes other numerous non-equity links. Two-thirds of the
parent firms hail from fourteen of the wealthiest nations. Today there
are 26,000 firms involved in this system whereas in 1969 there were
only 7,000 organizations, who were players in a much more restricted
system. But even within this grouping there is an élite.

→

←

DO NOT CROSS THE
CENTRAL RESERVATION

'Yonder peasant who is he
Where and what his dwelling?'
'Sire, he lives a good league hence
underneath the mountain
hard against the forest fence
by St Agnes Fountain.'

And was it ever thus?
  The peasantry always seems to live by the edge of forests, underneath mountains – for here is the least fertile land. It is only on the
Feast of Stephen that any attention is paid to them at all. For 364 days
of the year, they are virtually invisible. Yet when their dissatisfaction
grows with their rulers and lords they adopt equally invisible forms of
organization. Not for them the visible and suppressible. In this discussion, our concern must be to comprehend rurally based
organizations in the contemporary epoch. Two examples will suffice –
both from 'bandit country' – in the UK and Italy. These are the IRA in
County Fermanagh, Ireland and the Mafia in Sicily.

The debate between Thompson and Hirst (1994) and Hedlund (1994) on the meaning of these types of figures is instructive, for what impact shifts of this kind are actually having is an area fraught with contestation. However, the UNCTAD figures suggest that the largest 100 MNCs have $3,400 billion in assets (at 1992 prices) of which about 40 per cent were held outside their own countries. The top 100 include eleven UK firms and together they control about one-third of the world stock of foreign direct investment. TNCs will expand, it is presumed, because of the Uruguay round of GATT talks, NAFTA and bilateral trade arrangements. This will increase the level of *intra*-firm trade from its present proportion of one-third of all trade. Foreign direct investment (FDI) was at $232 billion in 1990 but fell to $195 billion in 1993 as a result of the global recession. US firms invested $50 billion in 1993 and the US was the biggest source and recipient of FDI. The poorest countries of the world have been shunned. For they are peasantries.

Look at the books on globalization (e.g. Waters 1995; Sklair 1991; Robertson 1992) and one can search in vain in what are otherwise admirable texts for any mention of the peasantry. The peasant is seen as lying outside of the global world, having been bypassed in the move to industrialization, post-industrialism and postmodernity. When we speak of the planet upon which we live, and research and write about humanity, it appears that there is no theoretical space for the peasantry (Ghoshal and Westney 1993).

72

which a wildman produced by the newly burgeoning 'science' is created in a Gothic castle, in the east of middle Europe – beyond the mountains – and in a magic kingdom. Romanticism and the monster myth go together. Transylvania was the repository of all that was rural for an urbanizing society in the West of Europa (equivalent perhaps to the boondocks in the USA?). And its social and economic distance from industrial capitalism allowed it to be the repository of 'evil'. If Vlad the Impaler and Ceaucescu had not existed it would have been necessary to invent them.

What has been invented is the benign antidote. The rarity of those of royal blood caring for their peasantry is reported in the Christmas carol about 'Good' King Wenceslas.

In the same way as hunter-gatherers had declined from being 100 per cent of the world's 10 million population in 10,000 BC to 1.0 per cent of 350 million in 1500 AD, by 1960, of the globe's 3 billion people only 0.001 per cent were hunters and gatherers (Giddens 1993: 45), so it was believed that the *peasantry* were a declining segment of society. Yet if there were a third of a billion peasants worldwide in 1500 it is significant perhaps that in 1992 India's population of 861 million contained about one-third of its populace still in the social form of the peasantry. Of China's 1,180 million today, at least a quarter are 'still' classifiable as peasants. In addition to these two countries, 30 per cent of the remaining world population are peasantry (Hobsbawm 1994: 291). With gross guesstimates of this kind, however, all that one is saying is that whilst the *proportion* of the world population who are peasantry has clearly declined, there are many more peasants on the planet today than there were in 1500 when the period of our interest was about to begin. Compared to a third of a billion in 1500, by the year 2000 there will be still 2 billion people who are peasants.

Has organization theory given this statistic anything like a sideways glance, never mind some thought? Giddens says: 'In some of the industrialized societies, such as France and Japan, a fourth class – peasants . . . has also until recently been important. In Third World

73

The interpretations of these myths is not without difficulty but in the latter case, the adult heterosexual male breaks with his mother who is the water monster that has swallowed him – before birth of course. This is a myth of creation, of men, by men, for men. It is about engulfing, archaic 'femaleness'. Similarly the wildman stories, Dracula, and Frankenstein's monster are about unbaptized, crude, highly objectionable violent 'masculinity'. What is important here is that these images all come from the countryside. Think of the origin of the story of Frankenstein. A group of Romantics gathers at night on the side of a Swiss lake and as they talk a woman creates the seeds of a story in

countries, peasants are usually still by far the largest class'(1993: 215).

How can we ignore this? Is it because the peasantry has nothing of note to offer in the way of organizational exemplars? Marx argued, on occasion, that the peasantry interfered with the organization of a social movement for class conflict and rather than offering anything itself, it was a largely retrogressive grouping. It was 'a transitional class', 'left over' from feudalism which is 'an earlier type' of production system. Notice, of course, the linearity and narrative in this developmental approach. Yet today, 100 years since Marx's death, even in the EC one can find significant numbers of peasants, in France, Italy, Spain and Ireland. Add these relevant groups to what we believe are the figures for the LDCs and we begin to recognize just what a significant group, numerically, the peasantry is.

They are significant numerically, but they are also significant proportionately, and they are significant for their ideas about organization. Historically, the peasantry have been a central locale for the development of organizational thought which includes *inter alia* millenarianism and revolt. Millenarianism was very strong in medieval Europe because the movements were frequently the last desperate resort of those who often, quite suddenly, found themselves impoverished. 'The world turned upside down' in which the poor inherited the earth was a favourite response to famine, taxation and disease.

As for revolt, Charles Tilly in *From Mobilisation to Revolution* (1978) looks at four components of collective action designed to overthrow an existing social order. These are, in very brief form:

74

And if the wildman inhabits the high forests, it is archaic female monsters who live in deep water who act as a necessary counterpoint. Way out from civilization, Tlamat the Babylonian monster of the deep is slain by Marduk. Rahab, the Old Testament sea monster is killed by Jahweh when the world is created (Isaiah 51.9) and Grendel is confronted by Beowulf. A very good example is Caoranachk, the female serpent who lived in Lough Derg in County Donegal, Ireland. When she had swallowed St Patrick, the saint hacked his way out of her body with his symbol of Christianity – the crozier, signifying Christianity's victory over the 'female' principle (Cupitt 1994).

(1) *Organization*: this can vary from spontaneous crowd formation to tightly disciplined revolutionary groups.
(2) *Mobilization*: Mao mobilized support from a sympathetic peasantry during the Long March and afterwards.
(3) *Common interests*: these usually are seen to revolve around removing the existing government.
(4) *Opportunity*: chance, random events are either seized or not, at the right time and in the right way – or not.

Where the powerful cannot maintain single sovereignty then the peasantry may well be able to become a truly revolutionary force (e.g. Russia 1917, China 1949). This is despite Marx's own over-determined position on the peasant's capabilities within industrializing societies. Giddens goes so far as to say that 'in the majority of twentieth century revolutions, in fact, peasants have been directly involved' (1993: 623).

There was far-reaching rural reconstruction in China, which Jung Chang's *Wild Swans* (1991) certainly reflects, so that by 1952, 45 per cent of the cultivated land had been removed from the lands of traditional landlords and distributed between over 300 million peasants.

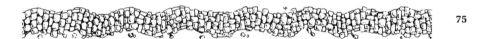

75

less developed in the literature of today. We are imprisoned by our language and its history – and it remains predominantly a neolithic not industrial language. Just as the hearts, clubs, diamonds and spades in (English) cards are agricultural terms, so too, our nursery rhymes are of rural disease (e.g. Ring a ring o' roses; Hey diddle diddle) and our monsters inhabit and come from the countryside. Transylvania is the land beyond the woods – as far into the countryside as is possible. The hirsute wildman, something half-human, half-beast lives a solitary existence deep in rural areas. The Californian Big Foot, the Himalayan Yeti – all the redheaded, violent, big-feeted beasts which are related to the orang-utan are all dwellers of the *campagne*.

CHAPTER 10 *Retro-Organization Theory*

Why then has organization theory missed the pain and fear of the peasantry which lay behind 1917, 1949 and 1975 (in Kampuchea)? When we see that the peasantry still exist within the EC in quite significant numbers why do we not ask more about them? Are we so productivist, so proletarian, so workerist that we cannot see the production of organization going on today within the peasantry and indeed the 'recent' peasantry? Is our interest in the organization of *industrial* production a form of self-enforced blindness? Cannot we abandon fixed linearities and drop the assumption that the peasantry are irrelevant? They are relevant to organization theory in ways of which we have not dreamt. Their pain is a mark of the changing – but not progressing – world. Like the stations of the cross, the pain often felt by the contemporary peasantry should enable us to see how their role has been denigrated, reviled and hurried into an oblivion which it has steadfastly refused to embrace.

As part of this blindness to the peasantry, it is the countryside which is always associated with paganism and misrule. 'Camp' meaning effeminate, challenging transsexual behaviour and cross-dressing comes from the French word *campagne* which means the 'countryside'. For sixteenth-century Parisians, like Euripides before them, saw 'camp' behaviour as *rural* behaviour.

The peasantry and humour often go hand in hand. When I was young I used to laugh like a drain at one joke in particular. But the philosophy of humour was beyond me in those days. Nowadays it is decidedly less amusing because I think its inner meaning is clearer. The joke was told as follows:

'The King of all the manors looks out from the castle battlements at the noise below. His Chancellor fearfully reveals that the peasants are revolting. The cry, 100 feet beneath, is clearly "We want more land. We want more land." The King summons the leaders of the revolt into his presence and bids Tom O'Sheepwash, their spokesperson, to come close. Closer still. Their noses almost touch. "What is it you want?", demands the King, maintaining constant eye contact.

hope. We grow plants and tend gardens. We keep animals. We use the metaphors, myths and tales of agricultural life. Bitches and studs, cows and stallions, goats and kids, toms and vixens, shrews and rats, crows and wasps. We are reminded of a level of knowledge of the country life which is there for all to see in Shakespeare but which is

'"We want more land, Sire," yells the peasant leader directly in his monarch's face. At this, the King suddenly knees the vassal in the testicles and as a spluttering Tom crumples, His Majesty triumphantly proclaims: "Well, there's a couple of achers for a start".'

Marvellous, isn't it? It symbolizes not only the triumph of (male) monarchy over (male) peasantry but also the temporary neutering of this group's leadership and indeed the literal collapse of peasantry in the face of any opposition. Deep down it was obvious to those who listened to the joke that *industrial* workers would not allow this to happen. We knew that in the Russian Revolution, the Bolsheviks – proletarians through and through – actually killed the Tsar. Workers wouldn't stand for the sort of treatment meted out to Tom by the landed aristocracy. It served the buggers (a not totally unreflective label) right anyway.

We in the audience for this joke were swept along by a linearity as powerful as Fukuyama's claim that the end point of 'Mankind's' ideological evolution has been reached in the universalization of Western democracy (Fukuyama 1989: 4). The peasantry, as far as the industrial villagers who heard the story were concerned, were 'intellectually challenged' and were, moreover, a conservative force. On the world-historical stage their time was up. Someone off-stage but in a directorial role and armed with a big crook, needed to pull them off by the neck to allow other groups of actors their rightful place in the limelight.

Suddenly the wall begins to shimmer so that by moving your head you can perceive two separate entries each entitled 'Peasant'.

from West German radio, Warsaw Pact heavy metal, American imports from the black market. (1993: 102)

Cosmonauts have access, as we do in the 1990s, to wine from Chile, fruit from South Africa, woollens from Italy, electronic equipment from Taiwan, automobiles from Japan, movies from the US, fish from Iceland and music from the Andes. Korolev smoked Marlboros laced with powdered Afghani hash. Compare this to the God-forgive-me, two-handled tall mug from which home-made cider was drunk to wash down home-cured bacon and home-made bread as described by Hardy (1979: 60).

Thus, the views of the peasantry exist within the counter-cultures of industrial life, they exist within massive segments of the present world population, they exist within our own psyches. We still look to the sky and ask what the weather will bring. We still consider nature to be something which behaves in mysterious ways its wonders to perform. The night brings fear and trepidation. The spring brings optimism and

Two Contradictory Images of the Peasant

TOWN VIEWS	COUNTRY VIEWS
passé	pained
clodhopper	anti-metropolitan
loutish	rural
villain	victim
superstitious	retains the magical
low intellectual ability	has alternative conceptualizations
lacking discipline	resistant to control
conservative	radical
low sense of morality	no urban pretentiousness
should be 'without' future history	should be within future history
non-Apollonian (i.e. irrational)	Dionysian

78

depends upon the 'attachment to the soil of one particular spot by generation after generation' (1979: vii). Compare this to William Gibson's attempt to develop science fiction writing. *Neuromancer* (1993) is his best-known novel but in the short stories we see 'a future that is recognizably and painstakingly drawn from the modern condition. It is multi-faceted, sophisticated, global in its view' (Sterling in Gibson 1993: 10–11). If Hardy is all about attachment to the soil, William Gibson's 'Red Star, Winter Orbit' is about globalist multiculturalism. It is set in space in the future, not on Earth in the past. Yet, like all science fiction, it is resonant with the present: Korslev is a 'channel surfer':

> Drifting back to his console, he accessed a section of memory where the collected speeches of Alexei Kosygin had been covertly erased and replaced with his personal collection of *samisdata*, digitized pop music, his boyhood favourites from the eighties. He had British groups taped

CHAPTER 10 *Retro-Organization Theory*

In Peking in the late 1940s, the Communist Party established a grading system for all public employees. Twenty-three levels were identified which governed housing, transport, food, medicine and almost all aspects of life. The movement from pre-modern to modern is very evident in this period in post-revolutionary China as the rural comes to be seen as problematic by the urbanites. Recent broadcast material on China shows how rapid industrialization is accompanied by the militarization of learning of factory requirements by peasant women. The killing of a goat in the streets of London by Muslim groups in the mid-1980s created a tremendous furore by invoking the same metropolitan prejudices about a rural lifestyle being brought back on to the streets.

79

In 1896, Thomas Hardy looked back upon the 'Wessex' he had created in a series of articles for the *Cornhill Magazine* beginning in January 1874. The articles became the novel *Far from the Madding Crowd* in which the rural values of Wessex still held sway. He could look back after only twenty-two years and say:

> The practice of divination by Bible and key, the regarding of Valentines as things of serious import, the shearing-supper, the long smock-frocks, and the harvest home, have, too, nearly disappeared in the wake of the old houses; and with them has gone, it is said, much of that love of fuddling to which the village at one time was notoriously prone. (1979: vi–vii)

This was part of his view that rural values had been replaced by urban values in 'the Prostitution of Industrialization and the Rape of the Countryside' (ibid.). Now he faced 'a modern Wessex of railways, the penny post, mowing and reaping machines, union workhouses, lucifer matches, labourers who could read and write and national school children' (1979: v).

Many accused Hardy of portraying a rustic life which was unreal but its beautiful harshness was based upon all but five years of his own life lived in Dorchester. His pessimism and 'immorality' were also attacked but he was convinced that the preservation of legend, folklore, close inter-social relations and eccentric individualities fundamentally

Similarly, in Kampuchea, in the mid-1970s, the de-urbanization of Phnom Penh, as well as the ending of the money economy and the declaration of Year 0, all created revulsion in the West, which came to see it, not as a strategic plan of a group of revolutionaries, but as the work of one madman named Pol Pot. The countryside is seen in modern thought as a dangerous, unpredictable, natural thing which needs taming along with everything which lives within it. In 1979 a student of mine named Derek told me the following story which also demonstrates the tension between the old ways and the new.

In 1953, while performing his National Service in the RAF, he was part of a team which was involved in the radar-mapping of parts of East Africa. At this time, these territories were governed directly or indirectly from London as colonies of the metropolis. Aircraft were to take several overlapping photographs of a given area and, given the technology, required precise positioning in order to do this. The radar beacons, ideally placed on prominent high ground, were essential to the success of the operation. Derek and a team led by his officer entered a small village above which towered a large hill. It had been identified as an ideal locale for a radar beacon by those back in London. The officer asked permission from a village elder to place the radar equipment at the top of this hill, explaining the need for it. The elder refused, explaining in turn that this was holy ground and was indeed the burial site for the village. In true colonial style the young officer indicated that the team needed the site and, despite any and all opposition, would carry out their orders.

80

older, locale-based sense of identity rather than an industrial one. I gave up the identity of 'son of a coal miner' and adopted instead 'son of a line of agricultural labourers'. The pits were closed and so was that part of my sense of self. Hence the present interest in the life of ag. labs then, now and tomorrow. I feel, as almost everyone has the right to feel, part of some industrial heritage but also part of a much longer agricultural heritage. As pits turn into museums, we are fed 'a mythic story' where 'the North-East's unique history [is] conceived as the product of a region blessed with plentiful mineral resources and with a people sufficiently tenacious, inventive and above all, canny enough to exploit its natural advantages' (Bennett 1995: 110).

So rather than live in an industrial museum, one is tempted to seek 'the authenticity of the real past', if one can ever trust oneself not to invent it too much. Is this one any more accurate than any other?

CHAPTER 10 *Retro-Organization Theory*

At this point, the community witch doctor appeared, smeared in human excrement and dressed in various animal skins. His chants and actions were taken to be hostile but once they had stopped the RAF team withdrew and began to set up equipment at the top of the hill. Around the summit and very close to the exact apex was a track which came to play a key role in the affair. Equipment set up below the track worked perfectly but once it was assembled above the track, it inexplicably failed to operate. Generators could produce electricity below the track but once the cable passed over the demarcation line it ceased to deliver voltage. One night a sentry reported seeing 'strange animal shapes moving the equipment around' and was given sick leave as a result. Successively higher levels of the technical command structure of the RAF became involved until the day arrived when, all else having failed, the Air Commodore from the UK was to arrive in his capacity as the national expert on such technical problems. He arrived on site with all the paraphernalia which 1953 technology could command. On the downhill side of the track he was shown that the equipment worked perfectly and as dusk had descended, the movement of the relevant material to the other, uphill side of the track was delayed until morning. On the downhill side that night were assembled scores of white European males, 10-ton trucks, heavy generators, cook-houses, tents, and armed guards – a veritable camp of advanced Western technology.

kept, Freemasonry was indulged in. Whilst trade unions were joined, 'the family' was the defining characteristic. Given that the Northumbrian mines are now all closed, this industrial interregnum has passed. This does not mean the family 'reverts' to an 'ag. lab. mentality'. But nor does it mean that some complete conversion to solidaristic labourism has been successful either. As Ellington Colliery closed in early 1994 and the last pit pony came to the surface, my sister showed me the family 'lineage' back to around the mid-1600s. It's not really a lineage because family historians begin with themselves in a central circle and work their way outwards into the unknown past. But as Sally showed me the huge network of names and lives and deaths, I felt the mantle of identity from mining being replaced by an

In the morning, as dawn broke, something unusual had obviously taken place. *Every* single member of the British military woke up to find his equipment, his accommodation and most importantly himself on the *uphill* side of the track. In the night, everything had been magically moved from where Western technology worked to a place where it did not. Unsurprisingly, the team rapidly withdrew in total confusion to a smaller, local promontory where the equipment began to work perfectly. And, as Derek told me, the whole incident was later euphemistically explained in a *Flight International* issue as due to some local 'magnetic' interference.

The conflict between the two *Weltanschauungen* that Derek witnessed on an East African hillside should not leave us without some understanding. One reading of the tale is that it represents a rural understanding clashing with one derived from urban myths. And in this case the urban mythology insists on ignoring its defeat.

82

of an agricultural labour force cannot be totally successful in just one or two generations. Let me personalize this for a moment. The branch of the Burrell family to which I belong has lived in Northumberland since the English Civil War. This is of interest presumably only to the family in question but what it shows is a family who were agricultural labourers until the middle of the nineteenth century when coal mining developed in the locale. There were two generations of miners spanning births from around 1850 to deaths around 1960 but the children did not lose touch with the rural area or its belief systems. My grandmother, later to become the layer-out, was born to Norfolk agricultural labourers who left the north of that county around 1880. She used to relate the tale of Arthur Henderson addressing the striking miners of Ashington in 1926 – in the middle of this period of King Coal. Henderson spoke on a cloudless July day on the recreation ground. Her story was of a great orator standing on a hay wagon on top of bales of hay. The significance of on what he stood nearly escaped me. She always made this a key part of the story. What does it mean? A victim to be burnt? A man of the people? It signifies (to me anyway) that these miners had easy access to the trappings of rural life and enjoyed it. The annual miners' picnic at Bedlington for example is best understood for what is was: something of the carnivalesque. Not in the full sense, of course, such as the carnival at Romans (Ladurie 1984) but a fair effort anyway. In the community, allotments were cultivated, animals were

A RURAL MYTHOLOGY

THE BURRELLS' MALE LINE

JOHN
b. *c.* 1610–20   Alnwick   ?
|

JOHN   Skinner
b. *c.* 1640–4
d. 2.9.1704   Alnwick
|

JOHN   Glover
chr. 7.5.1667   Alnwick
d. 26.4.1704   Alnwick
|

JOHN   Tanner
chr. 4.7.1703   Alnwick
d. 22.9.1776   Alnwick
|

THOMAS   Ag. Lab.
chr. 1744   Shilbottle
|

THOMAS   Miner
chr. 15.3.1784 Shilbottle
d. 1865   Morpeth area
|

JAMES   Miner
b. 8.12.1819   Shilbottle
d. 11.5.1864   Guidepost
|

JOHN   Miner
b. 17.6.1848   Longhorsley
|

JAMES   Miner
b. 6.9.1879   Shilbottle
d. 9.10.1939   Lynemouth
|

WILLIAM GIBSON   Miner
b. 1.11.1906   Ashington
d. 14.10.1959 Ashington
|

CHARLES MAYES   1) Builder
b. 6.1.1938   Ashington   2) Manager

In Pandemonium, however, such practices of magic certainly do exist. It is the pre-modern city in which the old practices of rural life still dominate. The gridiron streets are not yet built but nor are the systems of thought, which mean the slaughter of goats in the street is seen as unacceptable. It is a rural community in its orientation and animals play a key part alongside humans in its everyday life. Looked at in another way, it is a city in which the hierarchy of the pseudo-Dionysus has not yet triumphed, although it does look upon the target crowds down below in the square as ripe for panopticism and classification into grades. Its only a matter of time before Pandemonium gets itself discipline. But not yet. Not this epoch.

Whilst 'going up-country' (with its masculinist and vaguely sexual metaphor) was what those from cities on the coast did in Kenya or the Gold Coast, it was often the same middle classes who fled their own metropolitan cities for the small and medium sized towns outside the major centres of population. They went up-country to colonize and metropolize and monopolize, hoping, of course, to wipe out those strange and hostile local customs which did not appeal. Yet, even so, the suburbs and new towns which were developed in the 1950s are now reviled by the fully blown urbanities. Once it was Welwyn Garden City and tennis clubs which were seen as *infra dig*. Now it is Tracey and the shopping malls of Essex. Whatever these features are it is from a world not of the countryside nor of the peasant.

So why bother about it? and them? Peasants exist across the planet. Thirty per cent of the world's population exist in this form in an 'untouched' way. Include China and India and the category is enormous (Hobsbawm 1994: 291). Peasant beliefs, understandings and world views have not disappeared from modern societies. These constellations of ideas exist within and lie parallel to industrial ideas. In a structuralist sense they *underlie* industrial viewpoints about factories, the division of labour, the tyranny of the clock. They remain submerged in 'counter' cultures which reject the Protestant work ethic, which mingle work and leisure, which emphasize work 'at home' and not in some *Gesellschaft* or large impersonal association (Weber 1947) which controls how, where and when work gets done. The socialization

Within Pandemonium, the inhabitants think that unilinearity is a
problem, kitsch is a problem, cosmeticization of organizational reality
is a problem. We must come to celebrate and highlight the dirty, the
profane, the obscene. Not so as to encourage their pursuit but more to
throw into relief the huge intellectual cost of ignoring them and pre-
tending to ourselves that if we continue to turn our backs on lust,
pain, disease, death and loathing they may well disappear back into
the streets and remain hidden behind the mist veils. And hiding from
shit does not mean that it will go away. Coming clean is impossible.
Handy Wipes work on nothing but our anxieties.

Luckily, within the Magic Kingdom we shall find exhibits that will
remind us graphically of what it is like on Earth. Only the worst has
been selected for our pleasure. Shall we go in? Come, dear reader,
come. Come and see the miseries which mortals have to undergo somewhere, up there, above us.

→

←

This group works in a closed factory or shop, which has been especially
in the past, often unhygienic, ugly, unaesthetical and unattractive to eyes,
or ears or to the organs of smell or other perceptions. They are surrounded
by the kingdom of dead machinery, steel, iron, coal and oil. Enormous
noises, clangs, grinds, knocks, raps, clatters and taps of machinery and
tools fill their ears. (Sorokin and Zimmerman 1929: 466)

On the other hand – or at the other end of the continuum –

The farmer-peasant environment . . . has been much more 'natural' and
much more identical with that to which man has been trained by thousands of years of preceding history. . . . His standard of living may be as
low as that of the proletarian; his house or lodging may be as bad; and yet
the whole character of his structure of living is quite different and health-
ier and more natural. (Sorokin and Zimmerman 1929: 467)

Such a judgement is easily ignored because of the romantic culture
clearly evident in the perspective adopted and the obvious anti-urban-
ism. It is also dismissable because of its dated nature, perhaps, when
seen from almost seventy years later. In the post-war period cities
became cosmopolitan centres of excitement, fun and energy. But by the
1970s there were clear signs that a flight from the urban environment
was taking place in many societies.

CHAPTER 3

The Magic Kingdom

Hell their fit habitation fraught with fire
Unquenchable, the house of woe . . .

(Milton, *Paradise Lost*, Bk VI, ll.875–6)

'camp' from *campagne* (meaning the countryside) creates the notion
that inhabitants of the rural areas have a tendency to be sexually
'deviant'. Urban cultures see the countryside dwellers as 'provincials',
less intelligent, less fashionable and less socially aware than they are.
They are country bumpkins. If you live in the countryside and are
male, in many Anglophone societies you are likely to be described as
a 'sheep-shagger'. The equation of sexual proclivities which are seen as
questionable with having chosen to live outside the city is a very old
one. Thomas Dekker writing in 1608 referred simply to prostitutes as
'suburb sinners'. If the dwellers of the suburbs are given such treatment, how much more are non-urbanites reviled. But in the UK, whilst
the peasantry may *appear* to have gone, the metropolitans still retain
vocabularies lavish enough to put them down. Yet the metropolitans
are deserting the cities in droves (Lash and Urry 1987). Of course they
do not accept, necessarily, the judgement of Sorokin and Zimmerman
who developed the notion of a rural–urban continuum in their (1929)
book on Chicago. They say that, at that time, the urban proletariat did
not live in a natural or healthy environment:

←

This is a description of West Edmonton shopping mall:

> Imagine visiting Disneyland, Malibu Beach, Bourbon Street, the San Diego Zoo, Rodeo Drive in Beverly Hills and Australia's Great Barrier Reef – . . . in one weekend and under one roof . . . the Mall covers 110 acres and features 628 storeys, 110 restaurants, 19 theatres . . . a five acre water park with a glass dome that is over 19 storeys high. . . . Contemplate the Mall's indoor lake complete with four submarines . . . Fantasyland Hotel has . . . Classical Roman rooms . . . Arabian rooms . . . a Polynesian room. ('Travel Alberta', quoted in Lash and Urry 1994: 271–2)

This is one of the largest examples of an architectural organization of human life where shopping, eating and drinking, leisure, sport, education, sexual encounters and exposure to culture congregate under one roof (Marsden and Townley 1996). It must be noted then that Pandemonium is by no means unique. Indeed it is not even unusual. Architectural fantasy is as old as humanity itself.

Shelley's 'Ozymandias' for example is merely a later variant of a fantastic line of monumental wonders which stretches back, in no particular chronological order, to the baths of Caraculla in Rome (AD 206–17), Hadrian's villa at Tivoli and the Great Pyramid of Cheops at

Surely, the reader says, by now quite clearly stir crazy, the author can't mean that all this trip has been to revisit 'Anti-Organization Theory' (Burrell and Morgan 1979) and its essential romanticism? G.K. Chesterton called this sort of thing 'the Middle Ages by moonlight' and accused several authors of a misty-eyed nostalgia for some supposed golden age. As Eco (1995) has said, when Europeans face a crisis of identity they go back to their roots which were 'born in the Middle Ages'. Our interest then may simply spring from a rootlessness which we are keen to circumvent by a return to some pre-modern idyll. All this stuff on the peasantry sounds very like a naive romanticism. What is its relevance for today?

Relevance lost?

Urban sophisticates hate the notion that the (indeed, their) city is not where the action is. The countryside, by definition almost, is to be avoided at all costs. Henry Ford hated horses, for example, and saw the countryside as something to be controlled, quickly travelled through and tamed by the 'horseless buggy' (Corbett 1994: 123). The label of

El Giza. Architects have found mythology very attractive in design terms and the search for mystical proportions and sacred geometry has exercised the minds of many of them. Sometimes this attraction and allegiance to the ethics of geometry even overshadows that evinced by the Freemasons. The Temple in Jerusalem, taking a highly charged example, has been recreated in the minds of many architects despite the fact that the original was razed to the ground in AD 70. Of course, the past is plundered very often for ideas and its apparent relevance to the present, but the Temple clearly has had huge symbolic value within a number of religious and magical contexts. At the time of the Renaissance, in particular, there were many efforts to fully describe the Temple, with some drawings even claiming to be 'an exact representation' of the edifice built by Solomon.

Later the Romantics, with their concern to rescue for themselves a better world almost lost for all time, drew up plans for buildings even grander than the Temple. Unsurprisingly, imperial designs were held in especially high esteem. Albert Speer, appointed as General Building Inspector for Berlin in 1937, created plans for a Wagnerian fantasy for Hitler's Third Reich in which the 1,000-foot domed hall he designed for rallies would have been so big that it would have had its own microclimate with internal clouds and rain falling on the assembled crowds below. The Art and Power Exhibition at London's Hayward Gallery (1996) showed the importance of monumentalism in architecture to dictators of the period 1930–45. Not only did the Greater Germania warrant such designs. So too did Madrid and Paris, but especially Moscow, where architects were to be 'engineers of the human soul' (Andrei Zhdanov 1934, quoted in Hayward Gallery 1996). The symbolic value of the buildings around us is crucial and this is well recognized in the full masonic, as well as more narrowly defined Masonic, tradition.

Similarly, the concept of the 'pleasure dome' in Coleridge's time finds a tangential expression in the Brighton Pavilion, and in one of the largest tourist attraction in the world, Blackpool, the tower was one of the first industrial attempts to include many aspects of empleasuring oneself under one roof.

88

village had a wise woman or cunning man who were roughly comparable to large numbers of parochial clergy (Thomas 1978: 292). And this was in the face of grave punishments. In Elizabethan Essex, no one lived more than ten miles from a known cunning man or wise woman. These were 'of common or inferior rank' but gained much prestige – and some income – deep in the countryside.

CHAPTER 10 *Retro-Organization Theory*

In the mid-1990s, the Lost City of Boputhatswana, overseen by 'the Sausage king' was opened for business. It contains a 'designer jungle' of 1.6 million trees from around the world including baobab trees that weigh 75 tons and are several hundred years old and 'a simulated night sky', consisting of a fibre-optic representation of the Milky Way, all projected to be at a total cost on completion of £176 million. However, magnificent as The Lost City or West Edmonton mall is today, the Magic Kingdom of Disney has played a key role in bringing the deliberate architectural creation of fantasy from the drawing board into consumptive reality itself (Bryman 1996).

The 'Magic Kingdom' is also known as 'the smile factory', for the Disney Corporation markets its Anaheim theme park in Orange County, California, as 'the happiest place on earth'. During the peak season there are 75,000 people, or 'guests' as they are known, flowing through the park each day. Staff, internally labelled 'the cast', must show a constant smile even to those who are difficult, offensive and threatening. Analyses of the experience of labouring for Disney are now developing and the literature on Disney as an organization has grown apace in the last few years. For example, we know from the work of Van Maanen (1991), who worked at Anaheim until his dismissal for failing to get his hair cut, that the system of staff surveillance is well established and knowing this, the cast seek those blind spots in the panoptical observational array open to their supervisory staff. A large rock or a concrete pillar affords a place of rest, conversation and a well-earned smoke.

$\longrightarrow$

$\longleftarrow$

letters, was animistic. The mechanistic version did not appear to be successful until the 1650s and later. Undergraduates sought to conjure up spirits through seances, to design love philtres and to cast horoscopes. Without these skills they were not deemed to be scholars (Thomas 1978: 269). Thus was knowledge partly democratized and ruralized – although the leading writer on magic in England, it has to be said, was Robert Fludd and he had his work published in Latin and abroad. Village wizards did not often possess books nor depend on theorization. They learned 'the knowledge' from friends or relatives. Intellectuals of the time had little impact upon village magic but the reverse was not true (Thomas 1978: 272). *Plus ça change* – again.

Finally, of course, magic allowed the future to be foretold. Physiognomy was an infallible guide to character and phrenology allowed assessments to be made. So too did palmistry. The Arcandum allowed calculations to be made using the letters of one's name and thus to find out one's fate. At the turn of the sixteenth century, each

CHAPTER 10   *Retro-Organization Theory*

When we are confronted with the cast's attempts to resist the enforced necessity to smile whatever one's mood on the day and with the examples of their attempts to maintain self-respect by disciplining guests who step out of line, through such creative devices as slapping visitors hard across their chests with the seat belt of the ride vehicle if they misbehave, then we must conclude that the 'happiest place on earth' is not entirely a place of mirth and frivolity. It is after all about making profit through the control of large numbers of people who wish to enjoy themselves. And so it is with this thought, dear reader, that we survey the delights to be found in Pandemonium. But here there is little pretence of profit making or enjoyment or of large crowds processing through. Look below in the space for traffic contraflow. Can you see much sign of activity there? So let us consider this part of our textual edifice in the light of places that make no claim whatsoever to be happy. We begin to enter the section of *Pandemonium* which deals with melancholia.

Melancholia: a humour without humour

It is of interest to note that for the Greeks, Melancholia was the daughter of Saturn and this explains her gloomy, saturnine disposition. It was she who caught the imagination of the Renaissance humanists, particularly those who sought to express this view of the human condition in pictorial fashion. She is often depicted with head in hands and surrounded by books – for intellectuals were seen to be prone to melancholia – and often with a skull close at hand. Most importantly, we should recognize that a key part of the image was her depiction as fully involved and associated with the tools of the architect. Compasses, set-squares, rulers, saws, planes and so on were seen as the natural accompaniment to melancholia.

Thus, the architectural fantasies we discussed earlier have to be seen juxtaposed with the post-Renaissance view that architects and their products were a direct reflection of their melancholia and basic unhappiness with the world.

in magic. And with placebo effects, close observation of human beings and knowledge of the countryside, the therapeutic power of magic is surely not in doubt. Richard Burton and Francis Bacon, both early children of the Age of Reason, believed in magical healing and Thomas (1978: 230–1) is at least open minded. Popular magic found lost objects, divined water and identified thieves. It relied upon an understanding of the stars and of magnetism. Elias Ashmole, he of the Museum and Library, was a well-known follower and in 1652 was attracted to the study of magnetism. The universe, for most people of

Architects were dissatisfied with the world as it is and, through their grand designs, sought to make it better. But it has to be said they were not in much hope that this would be an effective or lasting solution.

Medieval philosophy believed that the body contained four types of fluid or humours which determined the temperament of humanity according to their relative preponderance within individual human beings, and furthermore that the organs which secreted them were subject to very strong planetary influence. Such views dominated the world perspectives held by many thinkers for centuries. The following typologies dominated the pre-Enlightenment period.

Phlegm	Phlegmatic	Lamb	Water
Blood	Sanguine	Ape	Air
Yellow bile	Choleric	Lion	Fire
Black bile	Melancholic	Pig	Earth

What is represented here, horizontally, is the humours, their associated temperament, the animals whose nature they were supposed to share and the four elements to which they happened to be linked. This can be expressed diagramically as shown on the next page:

urine. Treatment often involved 'poisons' being recommended and administered in the form of ointments and herbs. *Plus ça change.*

The King or Queen's touch was also assumed to be magical and to invest the receiver with potency. So too was a gold talisman received from the monarch on Good Friday. The soldiers who guarded Charles I in prison irreverently called him 'Stroker' because of his habit of offering to touch them. Seventh sons were also deemed to be very good 'strokers'. They were not without their successes. Many theologicians, keen to see 'wise women' banished from the land, stressed the *potency* of magical cures as well as their wickedness. The Age of Faith, it should be noted well, means faith not only in religion but also

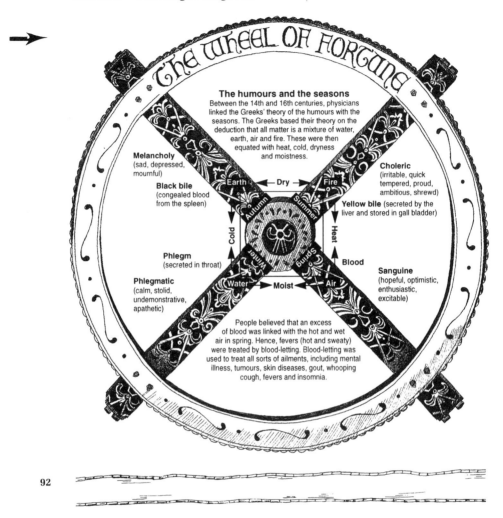

The Wheel of Fortune

The humours and the seasons
Between the 14th and 16th centuries, physicians linked the Greeks' theory of the humours with the seasons. The Greeks based their theory on the deduction that all matter is a mixture of water, earth, air and fire. These were then equated with heat, cold, dryness and moistness.

Melancholy
(sad, depressed, mournful)

Black bile
(congealed blood from the spleen)

Choleric
(irritable, quick tempered, proud, ambitious, shrewd)

Yellow bile (secreted by the liver and stored in gall bladder)

Phlegm
(secreted in throat)

Blood

Phlegmatic
(calm, stolid, undemonstrative, apathetic)

Sanguine
(hopeful, optimistic, enthusiastic, excitable)

Earth ← Dry → Fire

Cold ← Autumn Summer → Heat

Winter Spring

Water → Moist ← Air

People believed that an excess of blood was linked with the hot and wet air in spring. Hence, fevers (hot and sweaty) were treated by blood-letting. Blood-letting was used to treat all sorts of ailments, including mental illness, tumours, skin diseases, gout, whooping cough, fevers and insomnia.

Even if this was labelled the 'Age of Faith' we nevertheless need to recognize that the Elizabethan period was 'the age of greatest religious indifference before the twentieth century' (Stone 1972: 328). Cold indifference and frank hostility of the rural populace to the Church marked the period around 1600 in England. However, support existed for 'cunning men', 'wise women', 'charmers', 'witches' and 'conjurers' (Thomas 1978: 210). Incantations in Latin or Hebrew were used to protect their knowledge and charms which were written on paper were not unusual. Sexing a child before birth was a common request to the midwife and the Rosicrucian desire to have children without 'this trivial and vulgar way of coition' caused some interest. Abortions and their achievement were the focus of much country wisdom. Prognosis and diagnosis were often made on the basis of boiling the patient's

The fact that we are within the labyrinth – a well-known dark, moody and very particular architectural reflection of melancholia – and that the labyrinth is within Pandemonium means that melancholia is the particular humour upon which we must focus.

Queen Elizabeth II, in her 1992 Christmas speech to the Commonwealth, claimed to have had an 'annus horribilis'. Across the globe, however, millions of people do not have horrible years; they have lifetimes of horror. Of course, horror is a relative term and what is horrible to one individual may be commonplace to another. Human beings as a species appear to be able to withstand a tremendous range of life-threatening and sanity-threatening experiences and still survive. But individual members of the species often 'give up' and 'retreat' into madness or suicide. The problem remains though: why should we treat madness or suicide as a sign of failure? Albert Camus wrote, 'Why not commit suicide?'

So according to ancient but well-established theory, there are four principal humours in the human body: phlegm, blood, yellow bile (choler) and black bile. A preponderance of any one of these creates the temper and spirit of mind and body, which by being out of balance, makes for an ill or evil humour. The phlegmatic person is slow, sluggish and not easily agitated. Those who are sanguine are bright of complexion, and optimistic in their orientation. To be choleric is to be easily agitated and irascible.

→

←

WARNING: LINEARITY KILLS

Physicians, surgeons and apothecaries were unable to do very much in the face of this and so there is little mystery about why the population turned to drink. Beer was a basic ingredient of everyone's diet, including children, and estimates suggest everyone drank at least one pint a day. Alcohol flowed most freely at the time of the plague. Malt, it was said, did more to justify God's ways to humanity than the whole of the Bible. So religion, particularly where it reinforced hierarchy and failed to mitigate misfortune, was rejected in favour of magic. Rather, religion was not embraced where magic offered more (Thomas 1978: 3–24).

CHAPTER 10   *Retro-Organization Theory*

Those who are prone to melancholia exhibit pensive sadness and are likely to be depressed. It is interesting to note that particular periods of history may also be assigned the descriptive categories of phlegmatic, sanguine, choleric and melancholic.

In Camus's (1960) provocative question 'why not commit suicide?', the emphasis is very much on the *not*. That period, or more accurately the *Zeitgeist* was much more sanguine than it is today. In the 1990s, the *Zeitgeist* has turned apparently much more towards melancholia. It may well be then, in some cabbalistic kind of way, that at the completion of each century, as the certainty of two zeros on the end of the number for the year approaches, there is a tendency to look back at the lack of achievement and the failures of the preceding century. When there are going to be three zeros in the number the drift to melancholia is likely to be even greater. In fact, the cabbalists of the Middle Ages were chiefly occupied in deciphering charms, mystical anagrams and combinations of letters, numbers and words. As part of this they engaged in intercourse with the dead. At the close of each century and with the mystical evidence in front of them, they too appear to have seen the *fin de siècle* as a period of melancholia and pessimism. This trip through Pandemonium does not come up with an answer to the question posed by Camus. It does not set itself that task. Rather it is predicated on the belief that it is a rather good question to ask (Boothby 1991).

sheep. There were enclosure riots, therefore, particularly in 1607, and bands of peasants pulled down hedges all over the countryside. Even as late as 1688 80 per cent of the British population lived in the countryside with only six 'cities' boasting more than 10,000 inhabitants. Forty per cent of the population were categorized as cottagers, paupers, labouring people and outservants who were used to underemployment deep within the countryside. Every six years or so the harvest would be a disaster and the diet created 'the green sickness' in young women, with its sexual overtones. Large-scale epidemics, including the plague, meant that for 150 years *before* 1665 there were only ten or so years when massive outbreaks of disease did not affect London.

In death or in its contemplation, *Pandemonium* seeks out the occult and an esoteric understanding of necromancy. According to the *Oxford English Dictionary* the term 'occult' dates from 1645. It means 'not understood or able to be understood by the mind, beyond the range of ordinary knowledge'. By 1653, the accepted meaning had extended to cover magic, alchemy, astrology and theosophy which were supposed to contain knowledge that could activate the mysterious and secret powers of nature (Nataf 1991: 1). However, these techniques and beliefs had been invented and systematized in India, China, Mesopotomia and Egypt some 2,000 years earlier. Why they remain hidden today – why they only haunt the collective unconscious (Jung 1945) – why they are still 'esoteric' is because in the West they have been suppressed systematically over the last 300 years. Esoteric knowledge is totally at odds with scientific thought based on logic, for the former relies upon intuition or reasoning by analogy. Analogy brings 'cause' and 'effect' together and looks for what they share in common, using concepts of sympathy and love and association. The aim behind such thinking is the grasp of 'truth' by beginning with fragments and seeking out their holistic interrelationship.

In cabbalism, there is an approach which seeks out the hidden meanings of texts, often using a form of numerology. Since God based the creation of the world on the letters of the Hebrew alphabet, it was believed, and since a numerical value can be assigned to such letters, words have a 'numerical' equivalence and thus have hidden meanings which lie inside the text. Thus, in Hebrew, when 'one' is *ehad* and love is *ahaba* the two words refer to the same transcendental reality because they have the same value (in one case $1 + 8 + 4 = 13$; in the other $1 + 5 + 2 + 5 = 13$). This is known as *gematria* in Hebrew magic. The *notarikon* is another cabbalistic method in which by using the first, middle and last letters of a word it is possible to form another. Some apparently straightforward texts thus have very deep but hidden cabbalistic meanings which are revealed through esoteric techniques. Such techniques often involve secret codes and messages. Watermarks in particular were popular with the likes of Francis Bacon, Ben Jonson

sessed of an entry in the manorial roll. As feudal relations declined, landowners commercialized their links with 'copyholders'. As rents were increased or forced auctions took place, many copyholders were driven off the land and sank to the level of landless labourers. Once they were off the land, it was often enclosed, meaning it was no longer available for anyone to live from and may well have been given over to

CHAPTER 10 *Retro-Organization Theory*

and Nicolas Poussin (Fanthorpe and Fanthorpe 1982). They tended to use the symbol of the grape, or 'blue apples' in much of their work – but hidden on the page from the eye of the casual observer. Bacon went to Cambridge in April 1573 at the age of 12. He became a penetrating critic of the university system and in *The Advancement of Learning* he talks of the 'excellent Liquor' of knowledge. Insight for him came from the produce of the grape. Unfortunately, Bacon was very prone to gout in his later years.

Dr John Dee (1527–1608), a contemporary of Bacon, wrote a 'Treatise on the Rosie Crucian Secrets'. Dee was famous for his skill in mathematics, astrology, crystallomancy and magic in general. He, too, like many Elizabethan intellectuals, saw codes, ciphers and secret societies as important for political survival in a period of intense religious and military upheaval – yet these were also the founts of true knowledge. In attempts to escape from the narrow Aristotelian framework which dominated thinking in the major universities of the time, Dee, Bacon and their colleagues looked to the south and the east for new ideas. These ideas, however, were so challenging that they needed to be 'esoteric' (Ackroyd 1994).

Esoteric knowledge of this kind, in the tradition of Pythagoras, was and is open only to those judged worthy by their way of life, their civility and their commitment to a five-year silence. Esotericism can only be communicated to a few disciples and cannot be – should not be – vulgarized. Only they can see both the literal meaning as well as the mystical meaning of the cabbalistic text before them. Esoterics attempt to recover the 'lost speech', the telepathic interconnections which exist between living things. For example, within the 'language of the birds' – which disappeared with the Fall into our own inner darkness, there are secrets open to humans endowed with the requisite form of understanding. The key to accessing the lost speech is freeing ourselves from the shackles of collective beliefs and embracing Magic. Whilst science deals only with externals, such as symptoms and appearances and their causes, magic is an analogical system in which plants, metals, planets and perfumes all communicate with one

The great mass of the population got its living from the land and there were fundamental changes affecting 'the copyholder'. Copyholders were descendants of former 'villeins' and held strips of land in open fields from the lord of the manor. Their entitlement to live off this land came from a 'copy' they may or may not have pos-

another. Symbols are used to condense these physical and cosmic energies and the manipulator of these – the magician – is conceptualized as barefoot, the better to be in contact with the Earth and its forces. The magician begins to draw a circle which stands for unity and the highly important cabbalistic number, 10. Squaring the circle is the emblem of the quest for spiritual freedom – the philosopher's stone. For Freud and Jung, the circle stood as the whole self, linking psychoanalysis to the Jewish cabbala and the search for esoteric knowledge of the kind mentioned above. The circle is linked to the oroboros – 'the serpent biting its tail' which is the symbol used to depict the achievement of the philosopher's stone by the adept. However, esoteric teaching is to be conceptualized as the handing down from generation to generation of 'an inheritance without instructions' – not a sacred trust fixed for all time. It is mysterious because it cannot be summed up in techniques. It is banal because it goes on day by day, everyday but concerned not with clock time, not 'lived' time but with hermetic time which is 'not of this world'.

In the context of mystery, the commitment of ideas to paper and the extent of the publication of these papers raises the whole issue of secrecy. Now the notions of 'secrecy' which esoteric knowledge rely upon are themselves open to debate. Evelyn Fox Keller (1992) talks of the images of secrets which were held in pre-modern England in the sixteenth and seventeenth century and shows how there was a shift in the locus of 'secrets' from God to nature. For centuries, Arcana Dei guarded arcane knowledge to which only a few could be admitted on condition that they too shrouded this knowledge in secret. Indeed,

by retro-organization theory. It is keen to understand the concerns, beliefs and lives of the peasantry and those who live upon the land. Rather than focus on the Levellers, for example, with their roots located firmly within the cities, particularly London, and their attempt largely to ignore the peasantry in their actions we must recognize that they fall into the category of urban crafts people and minor trades people so our interest does not alight upon them. The anti-hierarchicalism of the Anabaptists (Shaw 1968: 6) reflected the changes going on within English (and British) society much more as food prices increased, wages declined and the population increased (almost 100 per cent) by some 5 million inhabitants (Stone 1966) between 1500 and 1620.

CHAPTER 10   *Retro-Organization Theory*

knowledge and secrets were interchangeable terms. However, with Bacon and others, secrets became seen differently: not as exclusionary but as enticing courtship and demanding penetration. Knowledge became seen as involving the duty of disclosure and not enclosure. Knowledge now became the task of ripping open the veil of secrecy from nature and not one of protecting God. Nature was to become devoid of intelligence and life – in short an object rather than a creative subject. Nature was to be feminized (Jordanova 1989; Easlea 1983).

There is, in this period, a metaphorical linkage made between women, life and nature as the place where secrets lay which did not belong to God. Respect was lost for the way that things are, replaced by a moral imperative for things to change. The secret knowledges possessed by women became seen as a threat to the new reformation of religious thought and to the pressing drive to understand and subjugate nature.

Bonnie Smith (1995) reports on Power's work which has shown how in those most secret of places – nunneries – women acted in a way resistant to the subjugating controls placed upon them by the Church. Nuns behaved in a thoroughly worldly manner. They went reluctantly and sleepily to early service, dropped whole verses out of the litany so as to get back to bed, and acted out the motions of the animals which had provided particular forms of food in order to dishonestly transgress the strictures of silence. These women refused to be subjugated by religious forms of control yet retained their sense of nature and esoteric knowledges which were not religious in origin.

But they have been marginalized from organizational behaviour for too long. We need to consider the international division of labour and ask not about the industrial proletariat and their location. After all, these people are first generation peasants. We should ask about the peasantry today, yesterday and tomorrow for this category has been hidden from organizational behaviour for far too long. Scratch a factory worker and you will find a peasant; scratch an industrial capitalist and you will find a landowner; scratch a manager and you will find someone who is much more of a *Bauer* than they think.

Life in organizations is much more of an everyday story of country-folk than we imagine. And the organization of that everyday life is much more relevant than we might at first think. To understand today we must engage in retro-organization theorizing. Retro-organization theory turns itself at a tangent to the concerns and beliefs of the industrial and clerical worker of the last years of the twentieth century. The interest that organizational behaviour and industrial sociology traditionally have shown in the 'blue-collar proletarian' is put on one side

Yet our views of nuns as unnatural angels and princesses and of nature as the fecund woman ripe for exploitation and possession have their origin in the ways in which the universities developed as off-shoots of medieval monasteries. Bacon said of Nature that it was 'enough if, on our approaching her with due respect, she condescends to show herself'. And this view of science and the development of the university concept were to play a key role in our approach to esoteric knowledge. Secret knowledge was to be legitimized for selected indi-viduals who would be born male and who would inhabit and labour within the laboratories. But knowledge for their purposes had to be torn from Nature, who was to be allowed no independent existence of her own. This is the world of scientific knowledge where nature is seen in t(his) Enlightenment way by the phallocentric scientist. Listen to Sigmund Freud on femininity:

> Throughout history people have knocked their heads against the riddle of the nature of femininity – Heads in hieroglyphic bonnets, Heads in tur-bans and black birettas, Heads in wigs and a thousand other Wretched, sweating Heads of humans. Nor will you have escaped worrying over this problem – those of you who are men: to those of you who are women this will not apply – you are yourselves the problem. (quoted in Oliver 1995: 10)

Hence Freud, whilst attempting to utilize the cabbalistic tradition, makes women into hysterics rather than thinkers. It may be that he did not expect his audience to consist of women, for he was addressing a specialist grouping for whom femininity was an issue considered to be a problem in need of a solution but his stance is nevertheless obvious. This tradition in the sciences and articulated so well by Freud con-tinues on to the present day. Nature is feminized, problematized and

99

There is nothing to say that rural populations are not pornographic. Indeed what we mean by 'pornographic' is often rural in origin any-way. We must beware of romanticizing the Dionysian strand. It may well be too crude for our tastes. In some ways it is always *rude* because this is a word which is associated with the rural. Indeed it comes from the same Latin root. Rude countryfolk are 'rude' by definition. They are villains, they are loafers. They are *Landläufer* or vagabonds.

CHAPTER 10 *Retro-Organization Theory*

seen as in need of solutions. But so it is too in the social sciences for in philosophy, as Kelly Oliver has shown so well in *Womanizing Nietzsche* (1995), there is containment and exclusion of women, femininity and maternity from that discipline. Indeed one might wish to argue that the modern university itself is built around the exploitation of nature and the denial of the MATER-ial world.

At the centre of this misogyny is a rejection of any questioning of the holy of holies – that scientific forms of knowledge are superior to those to which they stand opposed. For if one comes to believe that science is just one form of knowledge amongst many then science's right to legitimize and de-legitimize what is ignorance from what is logic is lost. And this doubt – the fear of the unfoundedness of many of science's claims – has been a key part of the weakness of modernism (Bauman 1995: 294). So science has been forced to attack any and all of those who seek to question its foundations and stave off its opponents with charges of unreason, madness, obscurity and undecidability. In order to do this: 'it strained human imaginative power to the utmost, giving birth to contraptions so varied as, for instance, Descartes's *cogito*, Husserl's *transcendental reduction*, Popper's principle of *refutation*, Weber's *rational constructs*' (ibid.).

Each of these devices was meant to save science from the charge that it was merely one form of knowledge amongst equivalent others and could make no claim to possess 'unequal cognitive power'. The model for science to pursue, which it has done with a will, was to argue for survival of the fittest – which of course means extinction of the less fit – rather than tolerate the knowledge of the cabbalists and other wise folk. Science has sought the eradication of its rivals and has largely achieved this. But not yet in Pandemonium.

100

overtakes in some ways the realities of the present. 'Leapfrogging' creates empirical problems (even if it is conceptually acceptable because of its reliance upon linear thinking). William Gibson observed after visiting Singapore, which has embraced economic modernity with some very old principles of social and political organization, 'How will a society founded on paternal guidance cope with the wilds of 'X'-rated cyberspace?'

But the peasantry in Singapore has been virtually eradicated by social engineering of the city state and the mechanical engineering necessary to cover the countryside with the city. The ex-peasantry may well embrace X-rated CD ROMs and the hard porn they contain.

CHAPTER 10   *Retro-Organization Theory*

If one *were* to embrace cabbalistic notions in writing a contemporary book what would be the implications for style and content? First, perhaps, the ordering of the words would be different from the rationalistic assumptions of the post-Enlightenment period. The concept of linearity within thought, mirroring the concept of progress in human society, is very much associated with the long period of sanguine superiority. The book written in an attempt to mimic the style of the cabbalist of the medieval period would eschew forward-looking linearity and seek to express itself in terms of reversals and circularities and question the structures of that everyday world which is supposed to be straightforwardly understood. Such a text would present the reader with a puzzle and a conundrum. The reader must be willing to pay the price of entering the cabbalist's world and not be seduced by the obvious, the taken for granted and the happily simplistic. Those who would seek to write a cabbalistic text would use intercourse with the dead to articulate the problems and answers upon which they sought to focus. They would concentrate in some cases upon the reviled and the besmirched of previous generations and ask why this vilification had happened. The thinkers who had been hidden from view, rather than the men and women of action, would be those who were interrogated and disinterred and the contemporary value in what they had said, sought. The cabbalistic text would concentrate upon patterns rather than a narrative.

Piore and Sabel (1984), talk of the *Second Industrial Divide* where in the Emilia-Romagna area of the 'Third Italy' old rural practices are fused with new modes of organization and the latest information technology. Rural production of woollen goods is carried out without large-scale production and without being under one roof. It is successful without relying upon single-enterprise organization. For some it offers the hope of 'leapfrogging' established capitalist practice by returning to 'old' social practices yet utilizing modern IT and marketing devices. Whilst the producers are by no means 'peasantry' as we understand it, they are pre-industrial in some senses, agricultural workers in some ways, home-workers in some senses, self-employed in other ways. The concept of 'leapfrogging' allows 'stages' of necessary development to be avoided and the fusion of the old and new

CHAPTER 10   *Retro-Organization Theory*

Narratives are linear in construction whereas the type of book of which we speak might have a pattern in its shape which would be repetitive, mosaic-like, be reminiscent perhaps of the shape of a spiral where entry into it could be at any 'point' and at any 'when' which the reader wished. More than that, a book of the cabbalistic tradition would find patterns in the past which would seem simple and demeaning to our rationalist colleagues. It would look for literary figures at the end of each century who had died in shame and internal exile, who had names that had become synonymous with evil and human misery and whose writings were not commonly available to the desired audience. It would link these names because of their representation of *fin-de-siècle* feelings, despite the fact that a century or more separated their lives.

A book such as that would contain aphorisms and one-liners which reflected the black depths of the human soul. Where one line would do, then that is what the reader would find. Where nothing needs to be said then the reader would find silence. The cabbalistic book would revolve around death and disease and pain and lust. It would concentrate on all the sins that flesh is heir to. In an attempt to escape from the baleful influence of the Enlightenment it would enjoin the reader to embrace those European ages set darkly in the era before the predominance of the printing press. So, let her put her prejudices to one side and enter the world of the cabbalist. To do this all we need to do is to consider Shakespeare.

dragged screaming into 'seminaries of vice', 'dark satanic mills', 'prison factories' and so on. In Japan, the Samurai warriors produced by the feudal-ish system were encouraged to become part of the managerial cadre after the Meiji Restoration. Many committed suicide rather than leave their previous existence, which was to act as a warrior class charged ultimately with the control and subjugation of the peasantry on behalf of their war-lords. Many transferred, however, to managerial activity, so it is little wonder that, even in 1900, legalized murder of those peasantry forced into work in textile mills was allowed and even encouraged by owners and the state.

CHAPTER 10   *Retro-Organization Theory*

Shakespeare and 'The Tempest'

The Tempest was Shakespeare's last play, written in or around 1613. It was intended to be his farewell production on the stage, for we know that he had made arrangements at this date for taking over his house in Stratford-upon-Avon from his cousin Thomas Greene, the town clerk. Faced by the straitened circumstances of his old colleagues, he was persuaded by them to produce *Henry VIII* but during its first performance at the Globe theatre on 29 June 1613, the building burnt to the ground. Nevertheless, it is the Epilogue, spoken by Prospero in *The Tempest*, which Shakespeare intended to mark his 'swan-song'. It is these words by which he wished his audience to remember him.

Shakespeare did not have his plays printed when he produced them because the actors did not favour such a procedure. They feared that publication would have an adverse effect on their theatre's takings for there was a reading public who would devour them very willingly. But since there were no copyright laws, nineteen of his plays were printed in some form or another during his lifetime. Thus, we must always bear in mind that much (or at least some) of what we take to be Shakespeare was not corrected by his own hands but by Heminges and Condell, who claimed to be his literary executors.

The Tempest is Shakespeare's most 'magical' play, in which it is well accepted that the Bard articulates a setting in which the premeditated control of nature is undertaken by the exiled Prospero. He has at his disposal a book of spells and a magic wand, and these give him a 'so potent art' which *usually* works.

→

103

←

But surely, you may say, the vast majority of world trade, world production and world communication *is* between highly organized industrial corporations. Dual economies which contain both industrial and peasant sectors are disappearing along with the peasantry. If organizational behaviour is about anything it is about these types of organization, not a declining sector of agriculturalists.

But as I have attempted to show, the history of corporate growth has been marked by successful assaults upon the peasantry. Industrialization requires that workers are made of peasants; that peasants are

> Now does my project gather to a head;
> my charms crack not, my spirits obey, and time goes
> upright with his carriage
>
> > Prospero, *The Tempest* V.i.1–3

Clearly, this suggests he is not omnipotent, for charms can crack and the spirits might not obey, but generally speaking, his book and staff can command the elves of rural hills *and* those who stand on the sands with printless foot, *and* those demi-puppets who make midnight mushrooms and it is true that graves at his command have opened and let their sleepers go forth. The weather, too, is at his disposal.

Shakespeare here is presenting us with a magician possessed of 'rough magic' in which his wand and book of spells are crucial. In other words, Prospero is more than aware of the cabbala. He is a master craftsman of its art. When he decides to forgo this power and return to Italy all he has to do is the following:

> I'll break my staff,
> Bury it certain fathoms in the earth,
> And, deeper than did ever plummet sound,
> I'll drown my book.

The necessary knowledge is within the mysterious book and its

104

Thus, it becomes much easier to understand Lenin's enthusiasm for Taylorism. 'Do anything to industrialize' is obviously an objective for revolutionary leaders located within non-industrialized societies who see the importance of becoming modern societies. But the first thing that must happen to achieve this objective is the assault upon the peasantry.

The Krodstadt Rebellion was against 'bureaucracy plus the firing squad' but it was also in favour of land for all. As anarchistic principles go, this is quite typical but it explains, perhaps, why an élite concerned to industrialize was much happier dealing with those committed to socialism than with those of an anarchistic-communist bent. The suppression of all those hostile to the *concept* of factory, mill and city comes before hostility aimed at the owners of factory, mill and city. Ultra-Leftism is often very hostile to Leftism for this precise reason. It is against the principles lying behind industrialism and stands not only against the controllers of industrialism.

CHAPTER 10   *Retro-Organization Theory*

associated staff so that these implements have captured the language of magic itself. Hence Caliban, Prospero's victim and powerless opposite, says of his capacity to name and call things.

> You taught me language, and my profit on't
> Is, I know how to curse
>
> (I.ii.363)

Shakespeare's interest in numerology, common at the time, is also expressed in the *Sonnets*. John Padel in 1981 attempted to find a way of making the poems appear to be unified. There were (unsurprisingly, since one always find patterns when one looks for them) subtle unities of resonance and common metaphors but, more importantly, a numerical pattern. It seemed that the sonnets had been written in groups of either three or four; that they made up single poems to be read in their entirety; that they cohere in larger patterns of 17 or 21. The 154 poems thus seem to be explicable as one dramatic text telling of William Herbert and his mother's involvement with Shakespeare in the role of commissioning patron to an artist. Simon Callow, the actor, claims that within the *Sonnets* the poet comes across as someone who feels himself to be 'old, ugly, unloved, unworthy of love, tormented by base desires and crucified by ecstatic aspiration' (Callow 1994: 6).

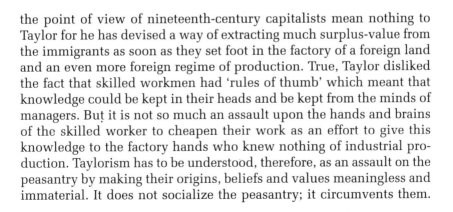

105

the point of view of nineteenth-century capitalists mean nothing to Taylor for he has devised a way of extracting much surplus-value from the immigrants as soon as they set foot in the factory of a foreign land and an even more foreign regime of production. True, Taylor disliked the fact that skilled workmen had 'rules of thumb' which meant that knowledge could be kept in their heads and be kept from the minds of managers. But it is not so much an assault upon the hands and brains of the skilled worker to cheapen their work as an effort to give this knowledge to the factory hands who knew nothing of industrial production. Taylorism has to be understood, therefore, as an assault on the peasantry by making their origins, beliefs and values meaningless and immaterial. It does not socialize the peasantry; it circumvents them.

CHAPTER 10   *Retro-Organization Theory*

Yet, for Padel (1981), the key insight is the numerological patterning of the story, which uses well-established techniques available, indeed commonplace to certain of the educated Elizabethans of the time. These ideas and approaches are drawn, he says, predominantly from cabbalism. One final word of warning, however. Walter Bagehot, the Victorian constitutionalist said something (admittedly about the monarchy) which we need to bear in mind about cabbalism:

> Its mystery is its life. We must not let in daylight upon magic. (1966: 32)

If we are too rationalistic about our analyses of magical phenomena it may well be that understanding at the intuitive level slips through our fingers. To subject any phenomenon to scientific investigation is often, as in the biological sciences, to kill it, to make it lie still, to understand not *why* but *how* it works (Frayling 1995).

Much of the journey through Pandemonium is about 'estoric' thought, where 'estoric' means knowledge intended to be for a restricted or initiated minority because of its abstruse or obscure nature. Essentially, this knowledge came from the southern and eastern edges of the Europe, right into its geographical heartland. The massive influx of refugees and their literary treasures of texts on hermeticism, Gnosticism, Neoplatonism, cabbalism, astrology, alchemy and sacred geometry was triggered off by the exclusion of Jews and Muslims from

from the south of Italy, from Eastern Europe, from Scandinavia and from almost everywhere in Europe where agriculture predominates. It is no accident that Taylor alights upon the 'Dutchman Schmidt' for he is typical, not for his ox-like characteristics but for the fact that he probably knew how to identify an ox and use it in the fields. Taylor's gift to industrialism is not a set of management principles (and there is evidence that he did not write his books at all; that they were ghosted for him). What he provided was a system which put agricultural immigrants into the service of industrialism immediately.

They need not learn English to do the job. They need not have been in a factory in their lives. They may have seen nothing but fields and the Atlantic before their arrival at Ellis Island. These limitations from

Spain in 1492 and the fall of the old Byzantine Empire to the Turks in 1453. Iberian esotericism and the treasures of Byzantine libraries placed at the opposite and far ends of the continent thus met in Western Europe. It was this intellectual confluence, particularly in Italy and Flanders, which contributed so much to the Renaissance (Baigent and Leigh 1990). Estoric thought was taken up in the British Isles with great enthusiasm. Sidney, Spenser, Marlowe and Bacon all embraced it but because it was associated with Catholic houses in continental Europe it could not be dealt with in public fora. Discussion of these ideas by men and women of letters was carried out in secret societies and esotericism was mentioned obliquely through allegory. These shadowy organizations were militantly anti-papist.

The 'arch-magus' of the age was John Dee (born 13 July 1527) who manoeuvred his way through the religious politics of the time but was never untrue to his Protestant beliefs. He was the epitome of 'Renaissance Man': physician, philosopher, scientist, astrologer, cabbalist, mathematician, spy and alchemist. His influence was enormous and he provided the model for Prospero in *The Tempest*. He is written about interestingly and accurately by Peter Ackroyd in *The House of Doctor Dee*. Dee succeeded in fashioning the various strands of esoterica into something relatively coherent and self-contained. He travelled widely and lectured on these filaments of esoteric approaches in Louvain, Paris and Prague. He brought back from his visit to the last city in 1585–6 material of an esoteric kind which later allowed Inigo Jones and Robert Fludd to develop their ideas.

107

Do not cross the North Atlantic

Craig Littler (1982) began this investigation in *The Development of the Labour Process* where he compares UK, US and Japanese developments. Key to the whole issue of the growth of Taylorism in the USA is that it is essentially an assault upon the peasantry. If this point is missed then the discussion of Taylorism is lost from the beginning. Of course, the indigenous peasantry of the USA hardly existed, for the hunters and gatherers had been assaulted by influenza and smallpox and the Deep South had a slave system – even after formal manumission. The USA was a society at the turn of the twentieth century where the 'rural peasantry' did not exist in anything like the numbers that they did in Europe. Taylorism is and was a system to deal with European peasantry, entering the Eastern Seaboard of the USA without any knowledge of anything but the land and its cultivation. Not only is their language not English, as this century dawns, but they are drawn

Prague was important because although it was a Protestant centre debate could take place publicly about those esoteric ideas associated with Spain and Italy which were Catholic to their core. Esoterica became de-coupled from Catholicism in what formed, by common decree, the magic kingdom. It surfaced in the Netherlands, the Palatinate of the Rhine, Württemberg and Bohemia, allowing England to embrace such ideas in the very early years of the seventeenth century. The label 'Rosicrucianism' became attached to these Bohemian ideas and these were of such force they have been spoken of as 'The Rosicrucian Enlightenment' (Yates 1972). As we shall see, they extolled the need for 'An invisible college', a new 'golden age' of utopian harmony and the extension of the spectrum of esoteric teaching.

As Prague and the Protestant Palatinates were overrun by Catholic Counter-Reformation forces in the early years of the Thirty Years War, thousands of refugees fled to Flanders and the Netherlands. In the early seventeenth century Andreas and his German colleagues created a network of so-called 'Christian Unions' which used a 'cell' system for maintaining the corpus of Rosicrucian thinking within a decentralized organizational system. These cells also allowed and facilitated cell members and their friends to be smuggled abroad. In England, an Invisible College was indeed set up, consisting of scholars, philosophers and esotericists which, until 1688, brought together Rosicrucianism, the Royal Society and Freemasonry within one closely circumscribed network of activists.

What is important for our purposes is that the form and mode of leadership and organization adopted by this secret society was cellular

108

with the full embracing of industrialism's large-scale consequences. But this reorientating programme was by no means untypical.

So much has been written about Taylorism it is difficult to draw out anything of great significance that is not a totally well-trodden path. Leaving aside the role of Bedaux in transferring Taylorism back into Europe, what still remains underexplored is the relationship between immigration and Taylorism in the USA, and the relationship between the industrialization of a peasant society and Taylorism.

and not bureaucratic, it was hidden, not transparently 'above board', it was utopian not political in an everyday sense, was collegial and was clearly interested in esoterica. Within the full glare of the Enlightenment it became transmogrified variously into a search for the sacred geometry of control, the Royal Society's push for the expansion of scientific knowledge and experimentation as a method of discovery and the Freemasons' self-serving secrecy to influence personal career. The seeds of the decay in the 'United Kingdom' of this overarching framework were that it was not true to utopianism, nor Rosicrucianism, nor the Invisible College, nor the cell form of organization. Whilst the latter part of the seventeenth century saw the possibility of a Rosicrucianism-led Enlightenment, Rosicrucianism was hijacked by scientists and Freemasons for their own purposes.

So Pandemonium seeks to set some elements in this conjunction of forces free from these historical channellings through which we have come to know about it. What we see around us is esoteric in the full, pre-scientific sense of the word (Easlea 1980).

The Enlightenment, Rosicrucianism and nihilism

The Enlightenment represented the ascendancy of a movement which encouraged the critical reappraisal of existing social institutions and ideas. It did so by an emphasis on Reason. Nihilism, on the other hand, relies upon a complete denial of existing institutions and authority, and a full and firm rejection of any belief in values, the possibility of

The assault on the peasant

Leaving aside the GATT agreement of 1994, China's claim to be modernizing is based on the notion that the benefits of modernization move from the coast to the interior and from the city to the countryside. It is the peasantry of North China who are now being assaulted, as they have in successive generations to become consumers of metropolocentric culture rather than everyday countryfolk. In *Wild Swans* it is shown that Mao encouraged all members of Chinese society to produce steel in the 1949–54 period. Huge efforts were required and expended on tiny-scale production of steel, at great economic cost in terms of fuel wastage, the quality of material finished and so on. Of course, the function of the programme was more to do with forcing the recognition of industrialism's existence amongst the peasantry than

human communication and indeed in existence itself. Both of these stances to knowledge, nevertheless, depend upon a questioning of existing social arrangements and are therefore related. Moreover, they are in some senses modernist or at least derived from modernist notions. Whilst they clearly differ about Reason they are less than conservative in their world views. Rosicrucian thought, however, is essentially premodernist in the sense that it originated and was intellectually important before the Enlightenment blossomed and had a very different view of Reason from the observationally based science of the eighteenth century. In seeking to find a defensible approach which stands outside the modernism of today it may well be worth exploring the pre-modern world of the cabbalists and Rosicrucians to see if their approach to science and knowledge provides us with an alternative world view to that found within the natural sciences of the late twentieth century. What kinds of science, what kinds of ideas about knowledge are to be found in the period after the Renaissance and before the Enlightenment? What is the nature of the horse we could put before Descartes?

Between the Renaissance and the Enlightenment, that is towards the end of the fifteenth century, the Jewish cabbala was centred in Spain. The expulsion of the Jews in 1492 after the defeat of the Arabs led to the setting up of a Jewish centre in Palestine where a new type of cabbala developed. This spread by degrees back to Europe in the late

110

THE BURRELLS' FEMALE LINE

ELIZABETH NORMAN   m. JOHN TAYLOR
        Norfolk   Ag Lab

ANN TAYLOR   m. JOHN HARRISON
b. 13.9.1847   Burgh, Aylsham, Norfolk   b. 10.12.1864 Ag Lab
d.   Bedlington   Blacksmith
                                              Miner

FRANCES TAYLOR HARRISON m. CHARLES ROBERT MAYES
b. 19.2.1891   Bedlington   20.7.1912   Miner
d. 9.9.1980   Ashington

RUBY MAYES   m. WILLIAM GIBSON BURRELL
b. 10.1.1913   N. Seaton   5.6.1933   Miner

SALLY GIBSON BURRELL   m. DEREK STEELE
b. 2.2.1935   Ashington   30.3.1959

CHAPTER 10   *Retro-Organization Theory*

sixteenth century bringing with it a concentration on magical techniques for meditation, ecstatic prayer and an apocalyptic outlook. This set of views and techniques emphasized the beginning as well as the end and as such it eschewed a linear view of human life. There needed, it was maintained, to be a return to a paradisical beginning in order to bring about the end. It was this kind of view which came to rest in Prague in the late sixteenth century under the protection of the court of Rudolph II. Prague soon became the centre not only for Rosicrucianism but for Jewish cabbalism and within the city both lived in relative harmony. Under Rudolph II, Prague came to represent what we now associate with a bohemian approach. It was the focus within all of Europe for alchemy and astrological and magico-scientific studies. Its university acted as a huge and powerful magnet for all those interested in such things. A strongly Protestant city, it enjoyed a period of cultural hegemony in northern Europe. It was linked to Heidelberg and the Palatinate as well as to a newly united England and Scotland. Within this milieu, Rosicrucianism developed as a whole culture, a civilization which is now hidden from view, but which before the Thirty Years War in some senses dominated European thought. Although it only lasted from 1590 to 1620, its brief flowering can be shown to have undoubtedly influenced the likes of Isaac Newton in the middle of the seventeenth century. It relished the written word.

111

notion of using humuments was her idea. I also half inched material from Tom Cooper, Michele Zanini and Kevin Taft. Karen Bull, Hansa Mehta and Rhona Bryan did their bit. Harry Scarbrough told me about Amis and Martin Corbett paid the book the one-word complimentary assessment of saying 'weird'. My siblings were great to me. Supportive and kind through it all like you expect from older brothers and sisters. Sally produced the family trees, one of which ends these acknowledgements and never ever fails to capture my interest in the past. Charles organized the Tasmanian picture which affects me greatly so I owe him $80 and fraternal thanks for the good advice. And I also feel the need to thank our other brother who, in dying on the first day of his life, left me his name. There are times when I feel like a simulacrum of that baby, the original gibson. But life is both verso and recto. So despite her solemn objections to inclusion in *Pandemonium* I must acknowldge K. who, above all, made me think – and write – again.

ACKNOWLEDGEMENTS

𝔓𝔞𝔫𝔡𝔢𝔪𝔬𝔫𝔦𝔲𝔪 𝔐𝔲𝔫𝔦𝔠𝔦𝔭𝔞𝔩 𝔏𝔦𝔟𝔯𝔞𝔯𝔶

Abbott, G. (1993) *Rack, Rope and Red Hot Pincers*, Headline: London.

Ackroyd, P. (1994) *The House of Doctor Dee*, Penguin: Harmondsworth.

Ackroyd, S. and Crowdy, P. (1992) 'Can Culture be Managed?' *Personnel Review* 19, 5: 3–13.

Adams, S. (1993) 'A Gendered History of the Social Management of Death and Dying in Foleshill, Coventry in the InterWar Years', in Clark, D. (ed.) *The Sociology of Death*, Blackwell: Oxford. pp. 149–68.

Adorno T. and Horkheimer M. (1979) *The Dialectic of Enlightenment*, Verso: London.

Alexander, J. (1995) *Fin de Siècle Social Theory*, Verso: London.

Altheide, D. (1977) *Creating Reality: How Television Distorts Events*, Sage: London.

Althusser, L. (1969) *For Marx*, Penguin: Harmondsworth.

Amis, M. (1991) *Time's Arrow*, Cape: London.

Antaki, C. and Lewis, A. (eds) (1988) *Mental Mirrors: Metacognition in Social Knowledge and Communication*, Sage: London.

Anthony, P. (1994) *Managing Culture*, Open University Press: Buckingham.

Arms, S. (1975) *Immaculate Deception*, Houghton Mifflin: Boston.

Aspden, P. (1993) Review of books on Heidegger, *Times Higher Educational Supplement* 10 September: 15.

Atwood, M. (1987) *The Handmaiden's Tale*, Virago: London.

Bagehot, W. (1966) *The English Constitution*, Cornell University Press: Ithaca, NY.

Baigent, M. and Leigh, R. (1990) *The Temple and the Lodge*, Corgi: Ealing.

Baigent, M., Leigh, R. and Lincoln, H. (1982) *The Holy Blood and the Holy Grail*, Corgi: London.

Barnes, J. (1985) *Flaubert's Parrot*, Picador: London.

Barnes, J. (1989) *A History of the World in 10½ Chapters*, London: Picador.

Battersby, C. (1994) *Gender and Genius*, The Women's Press: London.

Baudrillard, J. (1989) *America*, Verso: London.

Bauman, Z. (1989) *Modernity and the Holocaust*, Polity: Cambridge.

Bauman, Z. (1995) *Life in Fragments*, Blackwell: Oxford.

Bede (1907) *Bede's Ecclesiastical History of England*, ed. J. A. Giles, Bell: London.

Bendelow, G. and Williams, S. (1995) 'Pain and the Mind–Body Dualism: A Sociological Approach', *Body and Society*, 1, 2: 83–103.

Bennett, T. (1995) *The Birth of the Museum*, Routledge: London.

Bentham, J. (1838–43) *Collected Works*, ed. John Bowring, Edinburgh.

Bentham, J. (1995) *The Panopticon Writings*, ed. M. Bozovic, Verso: London.

Bentley, E. (1966) *The Life of the Drama*, New York: Atheneum.

Berger, J. (1969) *Ways of Seeing*, BBC and Penguin: Harmondsworth.

Berman, M. (1982) *All That Is Solid Melts Into Air*, Simon and Schuster: New York.

Bernstein, H. (1977) 'Notes on Capital and Peasantry', *Review of African Political Economy*, 10, Sept/Dec: 60–73.

Best, S. and Kellner, D. (1991) *Postmodern Theory*, Macmillan: Basingstoke.

Billington, M. (1994) 'To Play the King', *Guardian* Drama Section 8 April: 4–5.

Blincoe, R. (1992) Interview on Hunter Thompson, *Sunday Times*, 14 October: 10–11.

Blundy, A. (1994) 'Who's a Pretty Boy Then?' *The Guardian*, 21 January: 2/3.

Bly, R. (1990) *Iron John*, Element Books: Sherborne, Dorset.

Bologh, R. (1990) *Love or Greatness*, Unwin Hyman: London.

Boothby, R. (1991) *Death and Desire*, Routledge: London.

Boyne, R. (1990) *Foucault and Derrida*, Unwin Hyman: London.

Bozovic, M. (1995) 'Introduction', in *The Panopticon Writings*, Verso: London.

Brando, M. (1995) *Songs My Mother Taught Me*, Arrow: London.

Braudel, F. (1974) *Capitalism and Material Life 1400–1800*, Fontana: London.

Brewis, J. and Grey, C. (1994) 'Re-eroticizing the Organization: An Exegesis and Critique', *Gender, Work and Society*, 1, 2: 67–82.

Broadhurst, J. (ed.) (1992) *Deleuze and the Transcendental Unconscious*, PLI: University of Warwick.

Bryman, A. (1996) *Disney's World*, Routledge: London.

Buci-Glucksmann, C. (1994) *Baroque Reason*, Sage: London.

Buckley, P., Pass, C.L. and Prescott, K. (1988) 'Measures of International Competitiveness: A Critical Survey'. Paper presented to ESRC 'Internationalization' seminar, University of Bradford, February.

Bull, M. (ed.) (1995) *Apocalypse Theory*, Blackwell: Oxford.

Burchell, S., Clubb, C., Hopwood, A., Hughes, J. and Nahapiet, J. (1980) 'The Role of Accounting in Organizations and Society', *Accounting Organizations and Society*, 1, 1: 5–27.

Burrell, G. (1991) 'The Organization of Pleasure', in Alvesson, M. and Willmott, H. (eds) *Critical Management Studies*, Sage: London.

Burrell, G. (1992a) 'Back to the Future', in Reed, M. and Hughes, M. (eds) *Rethinking Organization*, Sage: London.

Burrell, G. (1992b) 'Sex and Organizational Analysis', in *Gendering Organizational Analysis*, ed. A. Mills and P. Tancred, Sage: London and Newbury Park.

Burrell, G. (1994) 'Modernism, Postmodernism and Organizational Analysis 4: The Contribution of Jürgen Habermas', *Organization Studies*, 15, 1: 1–45.

Burrell, G. and Morgan, G. (1979) *Sociological Paradigms and Organizational Analysis*, Heinemann: London.

Byatt, A.S. (1990) *Possession*, Chatto and Windus: London.

Calas, M. and Smircich, L. (1991) 'Voicing Seduction to Silence Leadership', *Organization Studies*, 12, 4: 567–602.

Calas, M. and Smircich, L. (1993) 'Dangerous Liaisons: The Feminine in Management Meets Globalization', *Business Horizons*, April: 73–83.

Callow, S. (1994) 'Directors', *The Guardian*, 8 April: 6.

Camp, J. (1982) *One Hundred Years of Medical Murder*, Bodley Head: London.

Camus, A. (1960) *The Plague*, Penguin: Harmondsworth.

Carnegie, D. (1973) *How to Win Friends and Influence People*, HarperCollins: New York.

Case, S-E., Brett, P. and Foster, S.L. (1995) *Cruising the Performative*, Indiana University Press: Bloomington.

Chang, Jung (1991) *Wild Swans*, HarperCollins: London.

Chatfield, M. (1977) *History of Accounting Thought*, Krieger: New York.

Checkland, P. (1981) *Systems Thinking, Systems Practice*, Wiley: Chichester.

Child, J. (1964) *British Management Thought*, Unwin: London.

Chodorow, N. (1978) *The Reproduction of Mothering*, University of California Press: Berkeley.

Cixous, H. and Clement, C. (1986) *The Newly Born Woman*, Manchester University Press: Manchester.

Clarke, A.C. (1983) *Childhood's End*, Pan: London.

Cleugh, L. (1963) *Love Locked Out*, Hamlyn: London.

Cockburn, C. (1991) *In the Way of Women*, Macmillan: Basingstoke.

Cohen, R. (1991) *Contested Domains: Debates in International Labour Studies*, Zed Books: London.

Cohen, S. and Taylor, L. (1993) *Escape Attempts*, Penguin/Routledge: London; first published 1975.

Cohn, N. (1976) *Europe's Inner Demons*, Paladin: St Albans.

Cohn, N. (1994) *Cosmos, Chaos and the World to Come*, Yale University Press: New Haven, CT.

Connell, R.W. (1995) *Masculinities*, Polity: Cambridge.

Cooper, R. (1989) 'Modernism, Postmodernism and Organisational Analysis. The Contribution of Jacques Derrida', *Organization Studies*, 10, 4: 479–502.

Cooper, R. and Burrell, G. (1988) 'Modernism, Postmodernism and Organisational Analysis: An Introduction', *Organisation Studies*, 9, 2: 221–35.

Cooper, R. and Law, J. (1995) 'Organization: Distal and Proximal Views', *Research in the Sociology of Organization*, 13: 237–74.

Corbett, J.M. (1994) *Critical Cases in Organizational Behaviour*, Macmillan: Basingstoke.

Crichton, M. (1990) *Jurassic Park*, Arrow: London.

Crichton, M. (1994) *Disclosure*, Arrow: London.

Cupitt, D. (1994) 'Monsters, Myths and Make Believe', *The Guardian*, 14 October: 25.

Czarniawska-Joerges, B. and De Monthoux, P.Q. (1996) *Good Novels, Better Management*, Harwood: Chur, Switzerland.

Dale, K. and Burrell, G. (1995) *Under the Knife: Labours of Division in*

Organization Theory (Warwick Business School Research Papers 198) November.

Dandeker, C. (1990) *Surveillance, Power and Modernity*, Polity: Cambridge .

Davies, J. (1993) 'War Memorials', in Clark, D. (ed.) *The Sociology of Death*, Blackwell: Oxford.

Deal, T. and Kennedy, A. (1982) *The Corporate Culture Debate*, Addison-Wesley: Reading, MA.

De Grazia, A., Juergens, R. and Stecchini, L. (eds) (1978) *The Velikovsky Affair*, Sphere: London.

Deleuze, G. (1983) *Nietzsche and Philosophy*, Columbia University Press: New York.

Deleuze, G. (1989) *Coldness and Cruelty*, Zone Books: New York.

Denzin, N. (1991) *Images of Postmodern Society*, Sage: London.

Derrida, J. (1982) *Margins of Philosophy*, University of Chicago Press: Chicago.

De Sade, Marquis (1966) *The Complete Works of Sade*, Grove Press: New York.

Donaldson, L. (1985) *In Defence of Organization Theory*, Cambridge University Press: Cambridge.

Dopson, S. and Stewart, R. (1990) 'What's Really Happening to Middle Management?' *British Journal of Management*, 1: 3–16.

Douglas, M. (1987) *How Institutions Think*, Routledge and Kegan Paul: London.

Dreyfus, H. and Rabinow, P. (1982) *Michel Foucault*, Harvester: Brighton.

Dworkin, A. (1981) *Pornography*, The Women's Press: London.

Dyer, R. (1985) 'Male Sexuality in the Media', in Metcalf, A. and Humphries, M. (eds) *The Sexuality of Men*, Pluto: London. pp. 28–43.

Easlea, B. (1980) *Witch-hunting, Magic and New Philosophy*, Harvester: Brighton.

Easlea, B. (1983) *Fathering the Unthinkable*, Pluto: London.

Eco, U. (1987) *The Name of the Rose*, Picador: St Albans.

Eco, U. (1995) 'Interview' by C. Farling reported in *The Sunday Times*, 21 May: 21.

Elias, N. (1978) *The Civilising Process*, Polity: Cambridge.

Emery, F. and Trist, E. (1965) 'The Casual Texture of Organisational Environments', *Human Relations*, 18: 21–32.

Enzensberger, C. (1973) *Smut: An Anatomy of Dirt*, Boyars: London.

Euripides (1973) *The Bacchae and Other Plays*, ed. and trans. Philip Vellacott, Penguin: Harmondsworth.

Factory Commission (1833) Royal Commission on Employment of Children in Factories, Report Parliamentary Papers XX.

Fanthorpe, P. and Fanthorpe, L. (1982) *The Holy Grail Revealed*, North Hollywood.

Featherstone, M. (1987) 'Leisure, Symbolic Power and the Life Course', in Horne, J., Jary, D. and Tomlinson, A. (eds) *Leisure, Sport and Social Relations* (Sociological Review Monograph 33).

Featherstone, M. (1991) *Consumer Culture and Postmodernism*, Sage: London.

Featherstone, M., Hepworth, M. and Turner, B. (eds) (1991) *The Body*, Sage: London.

Feingold (1983) 'How Unique is the Holocaust?' in Grobman, A. and Landes, D. (eds) *Genocide*, Simon and Schuster: Los Angeles.

116

Feldman, D. and Klitch, N. (1991) 'Impression Management and Career Strategies', in Giacalone, K. and Rosenfeld, P. (eds) *Applied Impression Management: How Image Making Affects Managerial Decisions*, Sage: London.

Filicove, J. and Filipec, B. (1986) 'Society and Concepts of Time', *International Social Studies Journal*, 107: 19–32.

Ford, S. (1990) *The Casting Couch*, Grafton: London.

Forester, C.S. (1952) *Lieutenant Hornblower*, Little, Brown: New York.

Fortunati, V. (1993) 'The Metamorphosis of the Apocalyptic Myth', in Kumar, K. and Bann, S. (eds) *Utopias and the Millennium*. Reaktion: London. pp. 81–9.

Foucault, M. (1977a) *Archaeology of Knowledge*, Tavistock: London.

Foucault, M. (1977b) *Discipline and Punish*, Allen Lane: London.

Foucault, M. (1979) *The History of Sexuality Vol. 1*, Vintage: New York.

Fox Keller, E. (1992) *Secrets of Life, Secrets of Death*, Routledge: New York.

Frayling, C. (1995) 'New Light on a Time of Darkness', *Sunday Times*, 21 May: 10–8, 9.

Frazer, J. (1993) *The Golden Bough*, Wordsworth Press: Ware.

Freud, S. (1958) *The Standard Edition of the Complete Psychological Works of Sigmund Freud*, ed. J. Strachey, Hogarth: London.

Fuchs, C. (1995) 'Michael Jackson's Penis', in Case, S., Brett, P. and Leigh Foster, S. (eds) *Cruising the Performative*, Indiana University Press: Bloomington.

Fukuyama, F. (1989) *The End of History*, Free Press: Glencoe, IL.

Gambretta, D. (1993) *The Sicilian Mafia*, Harvard University Press: Cambridge, MA.

Gaskell, P. (1836) *Artisans and Machinery*, Parker: London.

Ghoshal, S. and Westney, E. (eds) (1993) *Organization Theory and the Multinational Corporation*, Macmillan: Basingstoke.

Gibson, W. (1993) *Neuromancer*, HarperCollins: London.

Giddens, A. (1993) *The Transformation of Intimacy*, Polity: Cambridge.

Gilman, S. (1985) *Difference and Pathology*, Cornell University Press: Ithaca, NY.

Ginzburg, J. (1983) *The Night Battles: Witchcraft and Agrarian Cults in the 16th and 17th Centuries*, Routledge and Kegan Paul: London.

Goffman, E. (1959) *Asylums*, Penguin: Harmondsworth.

Goffman, E. (1967) *The Presentation of Self*, Penguin: Harmondsworth.

Gonzalez-Crussi, F. (1988) *On the Nature of Things Erotic*, Picador: London.

Gouldner, A. (1970) *The Coming Crisis in Western Sociology*, Cambridge University Press: Cambridge.

Greenwood, R. (1888) *Museums and Art Galleries*, Simpkin, Marshall and Co.: London.

Grosz, E. (1994) *Volatile Bodies*, Indiana University Press: Bloomington.

Habermas, J. (1989) *The Structural Transformation of the Public Sphere*, Polity: Cambridge.

Hall, J. (1974) *Hall's Dictionary of Subjects and Symbols in Art*, John Murray: London.

Handy, C. (1994) *The Empty Raincoat*, Penguin: Harmondsworth.

Hardy, T. (1979) *Far from the Madding Crowd*, Penguin: Harmondsworth.

117

Harvey, D. (1990) *The Condition of Postmodernity*, Blackwell: Oxford.

Hayward Gallery (1996) *Exhibition Notes to 'Art and Power: The Art of the Dictators 1930–1945'*, London.

Hearn, J. and Parkin, W. (1985) *'Sex' at 'Work'*, Wheatsheaf: Brighton.

Hedlund, G. (1993) 'Assumptions of Hierarchy and Hetarchy', in Ghoshal, S. and Westney, E. (eds) *Organization Theory and the Multinational Corporation*, Macmillan: Basingstoke. pp. 211–36.

Hedlund, G. (1994) 'International Economic Governance and the Multinational Corporation', *Organization*, 1, 2: 345–52.

Heidegger, M. (1978) *Being and Time*, Blackwell: Oxford.

Heller E. (1974) *Kafka*, Fontana: London.

Henrion, F. and Parkin, A. (1967) *Design Co-ordination and Corporate Image*, Studio Vista: London.

Hirst, P. and Thompson, G. (1996) *Globalization in Question*, Polity: Cambridge.

Hobsbawm, E. (1975) *The Age of Capital*, Weidenfeld and Nicolson: London.

Hobsbawm, E. (1994) *The Age of Extremes*, Abacus: London.

Hofstede, G. (1992) *Cultures and Organizations*, McGraw-Hill: London.

Hollway, W. (1991) *Work Psychology and Organizational Behaviour*, Sage: London.

Höpfl, H. (1990) 'The Semiotics of British Airways', unpublished, Bolton Institute.

Hopwood, A. (1987) 'The Archeology of Accounting Systems', *Accounting, Organisations and Society*, 1, 1: 207–34.

Hoskin, K. and MacVe, R. (1986) 'Accounting and the Examination', *Accounting, Organisations and Society*, 105–36.

Hoskin, K. and MacVe, R. (1988) 'The Genesis of Accountability', *Accounting, Organisations and Society*, 13, 1: 37–73.

Hoy, D. (ed.) (1987) *Foucault: A Critical Reader*, Blackwell: Oxford.

Hughes, H.S. (1959) *Consciousness and Society*, Paladin: St Albans.

Huxley, A. (1932) *Brave New World*, Penguin: Harmondsworth.

Ignatieff, M. (1978) *A Just Measure of Pain*, Heinemann: London.

Innis, H. (1951) *The Bias of Communication*, University of Toronto Press: Toronto.

Irigaray, L. (1985) *Speculum of the Other Woman*, Cornell University Press: Ithaca, NY.

Jackall, R. (1988) *Moral Mazes*, Oxford University Press: Oxford.

Jackson, M. (1987) 'Present Positions and Future Prospects in Management Science', *Omega*, 15, 6: 455–66.

Jacob, M. (1991) *Living the Enlightenment: Freemasonry and Politics in Eighteenth Century Europe*, Oxford University Press: New York.

Jay, M. (1985) *In the Empire of the Gaze*, London: ICA Papers.

Jennings, H. (1985) *Pandemonium*, Papermac: London.

Jordanova, L. (1989) *Sexual Visions*, Harvester Wheatsheaf: Hemel Hempstead.

Jung, K. (1945) *Nietzsche's Zarathustra*, Routledge: London.

Kafka, F. (1948) *Diaries 1910–13*, trans. M. Brod, Secker and Warburg: London.

Kafka, F. (1953) *The Trial*, Penguin: Harmondsworth.

Kafka, F. (1961) *Metamorphosis and Other Stories*, Penguin: Harmondsworth.

Keegan, J. (1989) *The Second World War*, Arrow Books: London.

118

Keegan, V. (1993) 'Has Work Reached the End of the Line?', *Guardian*, 28 September: 2–3.

Keneally, T. (1982) *Schindler's Ark*, Hodder Headline: London.

Kumar, K. (1995) 'Apocalypse, Millennium and Utopia Today', in K. Bull (ed.) *Apocalypse Theory*, Blackwell: Oxford. pp. 200–24.

Kumar, K. and Bann, S. (eds) (1993) *Utopias and the Millennium*, Reaktion: London.

Kundera, M. (1985) *The Unbearable Lightness of Being*, Faber & Faber: London.

Ladurie, E. (1984) *Carnival in Romans*, Penguin: Harmondsworth.

Lasch, C. (1979) *The Culture of Narcissism*, Norton: New York.

Lash, S. and Urry, J. (1987) *The End of Organized Capitalism*, Polity: Cambridge.

Lash, S. and Urry, J. (1994) *Economies of Signs and Space*, Sage: London.

Latour, B. (1988) *The Pasteurisation of France*, Harvard University Press: Cambridge, MA and London.

Law, J. (ed.) (1991) *A Sociology of Monsters*, Routledge: London.

Leder, D. (1984) *The Absent Body*, University of Chicago Press: Chicago.

Leigh Starr, S. (1991) 'Power, Technologies and the Phenomenology of Conventions', in Law (1991) pp. 26–56.

Lely, G. (1962) *The Marquis de Sade: A Definitive Biography*, Grove Press: New York.

Lepper, J. (undated) *Famous Secret Societies*, Sampson Low, Marston: London.

Lingis, A. (1989) *Deathbound Subjectivity*, Indiana University Press: Bloomington.

Littler, C. (1982) *The Development of the Labour Process*, Routledge: London.

Luhmann, N. (1986) *Love as Reason: The Codification of Intimacy*, Cambridge University Press: Cambridge.

Lyon, D. (1994) *The Electronic Eye*, Polity: Cambridge.

Lyotard, J-F. (1983) *The Condition of Postmodernity*, Manchester University Press: Manchester.

McCullough Thew, L. (1985) *The Pit Village and the Store*, Pluto Press with the Co-operative Union: London.

McDonald, L. (1988) *1914–1918: Voices and Images of the Great War*, Michael Joseph: London.

McKendrick, N. (1973) 'Josiah Wedgwood and Cost Accounting in the Industrial Revolution', *Journal of Economic History*, 45–67.

MacKenzie, N. (ed.) (1967) *Secret Societies*, Aldus Books: London.

Marsden, R. and Townley, B. (1996) 'The Owl of Minerva', in Clegg, S., Nord, W.E. and Hardy, C. (eds) *Handbook of Organizational Studies*, Sage: London.

Martin, R. (1977) *The Sociology of Power*, Routledge and Kegan Paul: London.

Marx, G. (1988) *Undercover: Police Surveillance in America*, University of California Press: Berkeley.

Massey, D. (1993) *Scientists, Transcendence, and the Work/Home Boundary* (Warwick Papers in Industrial Relations No. 48) 17–25.

Meštrović, S. (1991) *Fin de Siècle Sociology*, Routledge: London.

Miller, P. and O'Leary, T. (1987) 'Accounting and the Construction of the Governable Person', *Accounting, Organisations and Society*, 12: 235–65.

Mills, A. (1995) 'Man/Aging Subjectivity, Silencing Diversity: Organizational Imagery in the Airline Industry', *Organization*, 2, 2: 243–70.

Mills, A. and Tancred, P. (eds) (1992) *Gendering Organizational Analysis*, Sage: London.

Milton, J. (1980) *Complete Poems*, Dent and Sons: London.

Morgan, G. (1986) *Images of Organization*, Sage: London.

Morgan, G. (1989) *Imaginization*, Sage: London.

Moss Kanter, R. (1990) *When Elephants Learn to Dance*, Harvard University Press: Cambridge, MA.

Mousnier, R. (1965) 'Trevor-Roper's General Crisis', in Aston, T. (ed.) *Crisis in Europe: 1560–1660*, Routledge and Kegan Paul: London. pp. 97–104.

Mouzelis, N. (1975) *Organization and Bureaucracy*, 2nd edition, Routledge: London.

Mumford, L. (1960) *Art and Technics*, Columbia University Press: New York.

Nakanishi, A. (1979) 'On the Life of Luca Pacioli', *The Accounting Historians' Journal*, 53–60.

Nataf, A. (1991) *The Occult*, Chambers: Edinburgh.

Nietzsche, F. (1968) *The Will to Power*, Viking Books: New York.

Noble, D. (1994) *World without Women*, Oxford University Press: Oxford.

Oakely, A. (1981) *Subject Women*, Pantheon: New York.

Okely, J. (1975) 'Gypsy Women: Models in Conflict', in Ardener, S. (ed.) *Perceiving Women*, Malaby Press: London.

Okely, J. (1979) 'Trading Stereotypes' in Wallman, S. (ed.) *Ethnicity at Work*, Macmillan: London.

Okely, J. (1983) *The Traveller-Gypsies*, Cambridge University Press: Cambridge.

Okely, J. (1994) 'Thinking through Fieldwork', in Bryman, A. and Burgess, R. (eds) *Analyzing Qualitative Data*, Routledge: London.

Olins, W. (1978) *The Corporate Personality*, Design Council: London.

Oliver, K. (1995) *Womanizing Nietzsche*, Routledge: New York.

Orbach, S. (1979) *Fat is a Feminist Issue*, Hamlyn: London.

Orwell, G. (1954) *Nineteen Eighty-four*, Penguin: Harmondsworth.

Owen, W. (1983) *Complete Poems and Fragments*, Chatto and Windus: London.

Padel, J. (1981) *New Poems by Shakespeare*, Herbert Press: London.

Paglia, C. (1990) *Sexual Personae: Art and Decadence from Nefertiti to Emily Dickinson*, Yale University Press: New Haven, CT.

Parker, M. and Jary, D. (1995) 'The McUniversity: Organization, Management and Academic Subjectivity', *Organization*, 2, 2: 319–38.

Pascal, B. (1995) *Pensées*, trans. H. Levi, Oxford University Press: Oxford.

Perkin, H. (1979) *The Origins of Modern English Society*, Routledge and Kegan Paul: London.

Peters, T. (1987) *Thriving on Chaos*, Macmillan: New York.

Peters, T. (1990) 'Towards the Entrepreneurial and Empowering Organization'. Presentation at Royal Lancaster Hotel, London, 13 February.

Peterson, I. (1988) *The Mathematical Tourist*, W.H. Freeman: New York.

Peterson, I. (1990) *Islands of Truth*, W.H. Freeman: New York.

Pfeffer, J. (1982) *Organisations and Organisation Theory*, Pitman: Marshfield, MA.

Pfeffer, J. (1994) *Organizational Science*, Pitman: Marshfield, MA.

Phillips, T. (1987) *A Humument*, revised edition, Thames and Hudson: London; first published 1980.

Pick, D. (1993) *The War Machine*, Yale University Press: London and New Haven, CT.

Piore, M. and Sabel, C. (1984) *The Second Industrial Divide*, Basic Books: New York.

Poster, M. (1990) *The Mode of Information*, Polity with Basil Blackwell: Cambridge.

Pratchett, T. (1983) *The Colour of Magic*, Corgi: London.

Pratchett, T. (1991) *Moving Pictures*, Corgi: London.

Pratchett, T. (1994) *Men at Arms*, Corgi: London.

Radhakrishnan, R. (1994) 'Postmodernism and the Rest of the World', *Organization*, 1, 2: 305–40.

Ramazanoglu, C. (ed.) (1993) *Up Against Foucault*, Routledge: London.

Ravetz, J. (1972) *Scientific Knowledge and its Social Problems*, Penguin: Harmondsworth.

Rees-Mogg, W. (1992) 'Is This the End of Life as I Know It?', *The Independent*, 21 December: 17.

Reiser, P. (1994) *Couplehood*, Bantam: New York.

Rich, A. (1977) *Of Woman Born*, Virago: London.

Ripa (1970) *Iconologia*, Lubrecht and Cramer; first published 1593.

Ritzer, G. (1993) *The McDonaldization of Society*, Sage: Newbury Park, CA.

Robertson, R. (1992) *Globalization*, Sage: London.

Robins, K. and Webster, F. (1988) 'Cybernetic Capitalism', in Mosko, V. and Wasko, J. (eds) *The Political Economy of Information*, University of Wisconsin: Madison, WI.

Rocks, D. (1994) 'Golden City', *High Life*, British Airways: London. pp. 76–80.

Rose, N. (1989) *Governing the Soul*, Routledge: London.

Rosenau, P. (1992) *Postmodernism and the Social Sciences*, Princeton University Press: Princeton, NJ.

Rothschild, R. (1987) Letter to Editor, *Fulcrum*, University of Lancaster, 30 April.

Routledge (1994) *Atlas of the World's Languages*.

Russell, B. (1961) *The History of Western Philosophy*, Allen and Unwin: London.

Sacher Masoch, L. von (1990) *Venus in Furs and Selected Letters*, Blast Books: New York.

Sawday, J. (1995) *The Emblazoned Body*, Routledge: London.

Scarbrough, H. and Burrell, G. (1996) 'The Politics of Management', in Clegg, S. and Hardy, C. (eds) *The Handbook of Management*, Sage: Newbury Park, CA.

Scarre, G. (1987) *Witchcraft and Magic in Sixteenth and Seventeenth Century Europe*, Macmillan: Basingstoke.

Scarry, E. (1985) *The Body in Pain: the Making and Unmaking of the World*, Oxford University Press: Oxford.

Scase, R. and Goffee, R. (1989) *Reluctant Managers*, Routledge: London.

Segal, L. (1994) *Straight Sex*, Virago: London.

Seidler, V. (1994) *Unreasonable Men: Masculinity and Social Theory*, Routledge: London.

Semler, R. (1993) *Maverick*, Warner Books: New York.

Sennett, R. (1996) *Flesh and Stone*, Faber and Faber: London.

Shanin, T. (ed.) (1971) *Peasants and Peasant Societies: Selected Readings*, Penguin: Harmondsworth.

Shaw, H. (1968) *The Levellers*, Longman: London.

Shearing, C. and Stenning, P. (1985) 'From Panopticon to Disneyworld', in Doob, E. and Greenspan, E. (eds) *Perspectives in Criminal Law*, Canada Law Books: Aurora.

Shearman, C. and Burrell, G. (1987) 'The Structures of Industrial Development', *Journal of Management Studies*, July: 325–45.

Shearman, C. and Burrell, G. (1988) 'New Technology Based Firms and the Emergence of New Industries', *New Technology, Work and Employment*, 3, 2 (Autumn).

Shelley, M. (1994) *Frankenstein*, Penguin: Harmondsworth.

Shilling, C. (1993) *The Body and Social Theory*, Sage: London.

Shilts, R. (1988) *And the Band Played On: Politics, People and the AIDS Epidemic*, Penguin: Harmondsworth.

Sinclair, U. (1985) *The Jungle*, Penguin: Harmondsworth; first published 1906.

Sklair, L. (1991) *The Sociology of the Global System*, Harvester: Hemel Hempstead.

Smith, B. (1995) 'Gender, Objectivity and the Rise of Scientific History', in Natter, W., Schatzki, T.R. and Jones III, J.P. (eds) *Objectivity and its Other*, Guilford Press: New York.

Sohn-Rethel, A. (1977) *Intellectual and Manual Labour*, Humanities Press: Atlantic Highlands, NJ.

Solzhenitsyn, A. (1971) *Cancer Ward*, Penguin: Harmondsworth.

Sorokin, P. and Zimmerman, B. (1929) *The Life of the Peasant*, University of Chicago Press: Chicago.

Spender, D. (1982) *Women of Ideas*, Ark: London.

Stallybrass, P. and White, A. (1986) *The Politics and Poetics of Transgression*, London: Methuen.

Steiner, G. (1975) *After Babel: Aspects of Language and Translation*, Oxford University Press: Oxford.

Stone, L. (1966) *Crisis of the Aristocracy, 1558–1641*, Oxford University Press: Oxford.

Stone, L. (1972) *The Causes of the English Revolution, 1529–1642*, Routledge and Kegan Paul: London.

Stone, L. (1979) *The Family, Sex and Marriage in England 1500–1800*, Penguin: Harmondsworth.

Sudjic, D. (1994) 'Set Pieces', *Guardian*, 8 April: 12–13.

Susskind, P. (1989) *Perfume*, Penguin: Harmondsworth.

Swift, J. (1994) *Gulliver's Travels*, Penguin: Harmondsworth.

Sylvester, D. (1988) *Interviews with Francis Bacon*, Thames and Hudson: New York.

Taft, K. (1995) 'Consumption Patterns in Edmonton'. Unpublished paper. Warwick Business School.

Taylor, A.J.P. (1979) *How Wars Begin*, Hamish Hamilton: London.

Thomas, K. (1978) *Religion and the Decline of Magic*, Peregrine: London.

Thompson, E.P. (1968) *The Making of the English Working Class*, Penguin: Harmondsworth.
Thompson, G. and Hirst, P. (1994) 'Globalization, Foreign Direct Investment and International Economic Governance', *Organization*, 1, 2: 277–304.
Thompson, H. (1972) *Fear and Loathing in Las Vegas*, Paladin: New York.
Tilly, C. (1978) *From Mobilisation to Revolution*, McGraw-Hill: New York.
Townley, B. (1994) *Reframing Human Resource Management*, Sage: London.
Turner, B. (1991) 'Recent Developments in the Theory of the Body', in Featherstone, M., Hepworth, M. and Turner, B. (eds) *The Body*, Sage: London.
Turner, B. (1992) *Regulating Bodies: Essays in Medical Sociology*, Routledge: London.
Umiker-Sebeok, J. (1987) (ed.) *Marketing and Semiotics*, Mouton de Gruyter: New York.
Urry, J. (1990) *The Tourist Gaze*, Sage: London.
Van Maanan, J. (1991) 'The Smile Factory', in Frost, P., Moore, L.F., Louis, M.R., Lundberg, C.C. and Martin, J. (eds) *Reframing Organizational Culture*, Sage: Newbury Park.
Veblen, T. (1995) *The Theory of the Leisure Class*, Penguin: Harmondsworth; first published 1907.
Vidal, G. (1981) *Creation*, Abacus: London; repr. 1988, with introduction.
Vonnegut, K. (1971) *Slaughterhouse V*, Paladin: London.
Waters, M. (1995) *Globalization*, Routledge: London.
Watzlawick, P., Bavelas, J. and Jackson, D. (1968) *Pragmatics of Human Communication*, Norton: New York.
Weber, M. (1947) *Theory of Economic and Social Organization*, Routledge and Kegan Paul: London.
Webster, F. and Robins, K. (1989) 'Towards a Cultural History of the Information Society', *Theory and Society*, 18: 323–51.
Weeks, J. (1981) *Sex, Politics and Society*, Longman: London.
Weeks, J. (1986) *Sexuality*, Ellis Horwood: Cirencester.
Williamson, J. (1978) *Decoding Advertisements*, Marion Boyars: London.
Willmott, H. (1992) *The Great Crusade*, Pimlico: London.
Winterton, N. (1992) *Maternity Services Report*, HMSO: London.
Wittgenstein, L. (1973) *Philosophical Investigations*, Macmillan: Basingstoke.
Yates, F. (1972) *The Rosicrucian Enlightenment*, Routledge and Kegan Paul: London.
Zanini, M. (1994) 'Pharmaceutical companies and the Mafia'. BSc Management Sciences Project, University of Warwick.
Zwicky, J. (1992) *Lyric Philosophy*, University of Toronto Press: Toronto.

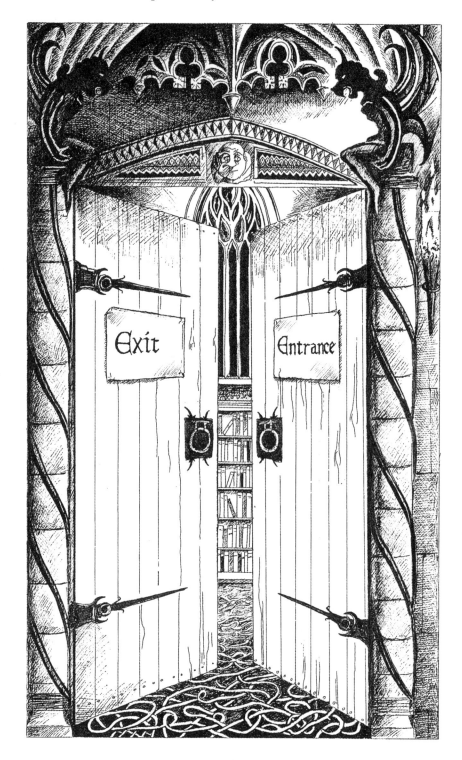

124

In the same way as Hughes (1959) points out the crucial importance to us of the period 1890–1920 to our own century, the period of 1590–1620 marked the seventeenth century in an indelible way. A number of Rosicrucian publications were of major importance in this all too brief time span. While still in his teens, Johann Andreas wrote *A chemical wedding* (1607) which deals with alchemy, death and change. He was later to describe it as a 'ludibrium', which means a fiction, a jest, or as of little worth. In 1604 Studion wrote a book at the same time called *Naometria* which evidences a great concern for prophecy through the use of numbers and chronology. John Dee also contributed to this Rosicrucian movement with his text *Monas Hieraglyphia* where magic, alchemy and the cabbala were unified. He made the plea that 'magicians, cabbalists, physicians and philosophers ought to collaborate with each other' but he was speaking not of the activities of his native Britons but of life in the streets of Prague and in the rooms of its university. All of these three texts paid lip-service to the red cross whence Rosicrucianism gets its name and to the fabled German, Christian Rosenkreuz in whose name the movement developed. All three used political imagery from animals in the same way as English pubs did at this time. When much of the population cannot read one finds that politics is carried out through the use of pictures of elephants and donkeys.

125

𝒜 𝑐 𝑘 𝑛 𝑜 𝑤 𝑙 𝑒 𝑑 𝑔 𝑒 𝑚 𝑒 𝑛 𝑡 𝑠

Many people have helped bring this book into being. The Board of Sage Ltd voted on whether to accept the manuscript and the text won its existence by the odd one. The people who regrettably I no longer see but who read the manuscript in a very early version were Julia and Andrew McConaghy, Gill and Roger Shaw, Sue and Alan Searle. Sue Jones then at Sage was crucial in forcing progress to be made and made creative interventions which were really helpful. I owe her a lot. Luckily, very luckily, I still see, meet, talk to and revel in the existence of Clare (BA Dunelm!), Anna and Katy whose vitality holds magical powers for their father. Christine helped in her own way. Bob Cooper, *to page 111* Keith Hoskin and Mike Reed were supportive and constructive at the right times. In Warwick, Francesca Coles was inspirational and the

They all expressed, too, a belief in millenarianism, in a harmony of theory which would unite macrocosm and microcosm and a belief in prophecy through tentative enquiry.

They all saw music, and the theory of number behind it, as an occult source of explanation. They were not Enlightenment philosophers. They were bohemians in the full sense of that word. The crucial elements of Rosicrucianism then were as follows: its adherents expressed a belief in a utopia, a concern for doing good and brotherly love, a concern for healing the sick free of charge, disseminating knowledge through a reformed system of education, bringing humanity back to its Paradisical state; the view that one's published work should be a ludibrium, one should undertake to wear no distinguishing dress; to be members of an invisible college and to seek secrecy. To stress the difficulty of ideas they mystified knowledge and encouraged closure of discourse. They sought a magical, revelatory science, seeing themselves as conjurors and magicians; wall art, magico-science and artisanal craft were all used to educate, and musical instruments, the alchemist's forge and architectural mathematics were the key devices to be used in their activities.

126

They have a way with nature that is the essence of the magical tradition. The urban sophisticates say of Ankh-Morpork that: 'maybe it is a bit like hell would be if they shut the fires off and stabled a herd of incontinent cows there for a year but you must admit that it is full of sheer, vibrant dynamic *life*' (Pratchett 1991: 14).

What we are interested in here, however, is not the story of the urban sophisticates who think that life begins and ends at the gates of the big city but 'an everyday story of countryfolk' (*The Archers* BBC Radio 4 serial).

Our focus, as we exit the city, is not so much upon the industrial proletariat or the labouring aristocracy; nor is it primarily upon the managerial and white-collar groups of large organizations. It is the peasantry. The signing of the GATT accord in Marrakesh after seven and a half years of negotiations is meant to increase world trade by about $2.50 billion. Most of the LDCs (less developed countries) have welcomed the treaty for this reason. But for 30 per cent of the world's population who have to live on the 3 per cent of the world's output, the agreement may well be a disaster. For they are low-income, commodity producers and much of their population remains peasantry. They receive little or no thanks for their effort.

Although Rosicrucian thought is primarily associated with Heidelberg and other parts of Protestant Germany, Bohemia and to a lesser extent the new United Kingdom, were also centres of activity. Francis Bacon (whose namesake appears later in *Pandemonium*) in *The Advancement of Learning*, first published in 1605, placed music in the role of the chief of the sciences since it is based on number. Bacon did not believe that science or knowledge progressed forward in a straight line. The prevalence of that sort of view is still fifty years into the future. He saw, along with the cabbalists and Rosicrucians, that such a view went against the idea that a *return* to the Garden of Eden was the primary mechanism by which humans might be saved. On the other hand, he was much more in favour of openness and of speaking to the masses than were many in Prague at the time.

127

In the pre-modern world of which retro-organization theory speaks, Pandemonium is the city which is contained, hidden away, inside the university. Thus, as you leave Pandemonium you may well be reminded of Ankh-Morpork (Pratchett 1983). The walls of the city are marked with slogans drawn from this inspiration. To the left, high on the uppermost courses, is one about university vice-chancellors – a timely reminder before we re-enter the campus world.

> The senior wizard in a world of magic had the same prospects of long term employment as a pogo stick tester in a minefield. (Pratchett 1991: 18)

To the right, low down and almost obscured by dustbins, is the selection procedure followed by the senior wizards in electing a new unseen University Archchancellor.

> 'Just the chap,' they all said. 'Clean sweep, New Broom, A country wizard. Back to the thingumajigs, the *roots* of wizardry. Jolly old boy with a pipe and twinkly eyes. Sort of chap who can tell one herb from another, roams-the-high-forest-with-every-beast his brother kind of thing. Sleeps under the stars, like as not, knows what the wind is saying, we shouldn't wonder. Got a name for all the trees, you can bank on it. Speaks to the birds, too.' (Pratchett 1991: 19)

Thus, Pratchett recognizes that within the magic kingdom that is Ankh-Morpork countryfolk are best placed to bring that magic about.

On 9 November 1620, after the Battle of the White Mountain which took place just outside Prague, René Descartes entered Prague as one of the Catholic forces. It was a year to the day since he had claimed to have had a life-changing dream in which he came to believe that mathematics was the sole key to understanding. A Jesuit by origin, the Frenchman had entered a city in which Protestantism was about to be suppressed and Rosicrucian thought with it. In 1623, Descartes's friend, Mersenne, launched a massive attack on the Renaissance, and Rosicrucian ideas with it. He saw these as the product of evil doctrines, promulgated by subversive agents. He was one of the first to show followers of cabbalism as diabolical members of a secret society and, in an effort to rid Europe of this evil, he sought to exorcise all Renaissance philosophy from the territories France now controlled. In its place, Mersenne was to advocate Cartesianism and ideas of a 'mechanical' kind. Not magics but 'mechanisms', not the conjuror but the mechanical philosopher were to be Mersenne's gift in his support, encouragement and proselytization of Descartes's ideas.

Interestingly, when Descartes returned to Paris in 1623, the propaganda against Rosicrucianism was turned against him. He was thought likely to be a member of the invisible college and his name was widely associated with witchcraft scares. His interest in solitude (and hence, it was thought, secrecy) was a decided disadvantage in facing these charges.

128

For Shakespeare, it is important to note, indulgence has a double meaning. It means tolerant treatment offered as a gift. It also means a remission of a sin which can be *bought* after the guilt has been forgiven. It can be both a gift and a commercial transaction. Well, you *have* indulged the author, probably in both senses, if you have managed to get thus far by carefully following the traffic laws in operation in Pandemonium. But one presumes it is the reader who wishes to be 'set free' much more than the author. It has been an effort to reach this point for us both and much has been expected of the university-based tourist within the city (Urry 1990). Your gaze has been required and the eyes are now sleepy. All that remains is the final haul out of the pit for feet weary with travel and minds weary with universities.

CHAPTER 10   *Retro-Organization Theory*

To overcome this problem, Descartes often showed himself in Paris to demonstrate to all who were interested that he was visible, and as a 'seen' person he was not and could not be a Rosicrucian (Yates 1972: 116). Most of the *positive* interest in Rosicrucianism had ended across Europe by around 1620 when it appeared that the Counter-Reformation was to triumph everywhere. Witch-hunts, led by these forces, had sent the ideas of the pre-Enlightenment period into retreat. John Amos Comenius (also known as Jan Komenský) was in a deep depression caused by the propaganda against Rosicrucian ideas. He had attempted to build a form of universal knowledge or Pansophia, himself, in Bohemia which he called a 'theatre of all knowledge'. But libraries and seats of learning were deliberately destroyed in Prague, and Comenius lost his wife and child between 1620 and 1622. This terrible time led him to write *The Labyrinth of the World,* which although written as a ludibrium, envisages a dystopia where all sciences lead to nothing and all knowledge is unsound. The damage to libraries and the threat to Protestantism had created for him a personal and political labyrinth from which escape was perceived to be very difficult. Nevertheless, in 1640, the English Parliament asked Comenius to come to the country to build a *utopian* society like Bacon's 'New Atlantis'. For him, using theatrical imagery, 'the play was still on'.

In reflecting upon Pandemonium and its six exhibits, I do feel as if my 'strength', such as it was, has been severely depleted. It would be very nice to think that it will 'come back again, soon' but it may well be some way into the next century and the welcome onset of retirement before the muse visits again. If so, then to use a phrase often thought to hold back Pandemonium itself, 'all well and good', and I will await the visitation of one of the nine of Calliope, Clio, Erato, Euterpe, Melpomene, Polyhymnia, Terpsichore, Thalia and Urania. Somehow, I know that I won't be on the calling list for many of the nine sisters, however long I wait.

CHAPTER 10 *Retro-Organization Theory*

By 1641, all this had disappeared. The impact of Rosicrucianism lingered on in the work and ideas of Elias Ashmole but his particular interest in Freemasonry (he joined a lodge in 1646) has influenced how we see the former phenomenon today. He was in favour of true magicians but against necromancers, conjurors and witches. Similarly, Newton saw that ancient myths foreshadowed science, and in the myth of the seven strings of Apollo's lyre he saw deep secrets of alchemy. But Yates (1972: 206) is keen to maintain that Rosicrucian ideas are separate from Freemasonry and that the supposed unities are vague and inaccurate; indeed they are 'below the notice of the serious historian'. Nevertheless, Newton, it might be maintained, was the last and perhaps greatest of the Rosicrucians.

That being said, the Jewish cabbalist and Protestant Rosicrucians who flowered in 1590–1630 produced a set of ideas which are pre-Enlightenment in time and spirit.

cross the central reservation

CHAPTER 10

Retro-Organization Theory

Now my charms are all o'erthrown
And what strength I have's mine own,
. . .
As you from crimes would pardon'd be
Let your indulgence set me free.

(Prospero, speaking for Shakespeare in his exit
from playwriting. Epilogue, *The Tempest*,
lines 1–2, 19–20)

Cabbalism would tell us to reject any need to find diachronicity, linearity and progress in human life. Reject any need to find linearity in writing and communication. Search pre-Enlightenment thought for ideas to plunder and violate. Reject concerns about chronology, anachronisms, narrative and antecedent causality.

Assume synchronicity and juxtaposition, for time and space compression allow much to happen directly in front of us. A 'three minute' culture encourages the quick movement through time and space so we can and will channel-hop. Be conscious of being diabolical (cf. Nietzsche and Sade). Be self-congratulatory about being consumed by 'barbaric madness'. Reject formal Apollonian representation in favour of formless Dionysiac delirium. Believe in utopia as well as dystopia 'against this time, in favour I hope, of a time to come' (Deleuze 1989: 3). Believe in disseminating knowledge through a reformed system of education. One's work should be a ludibrium. Knowledge should be mystified, be kept secret amongst a secretive inner group and its diffi-culty of understanding expressed. It is not open to all. Seek a magical, humanist knowledge for non-industrial (i.e. peasant) subordinates wherever they may be. Be revelatory.

131

But there are other types of necropoli we need to consider alongside the death camps and the monuments to the powerful. What about Stratford-upon-Avon as a necropolis? The home of Will the Quill has become the centre of a very successful tourist industry. It is 'bardola-try' – an organized evangelical religion. With the Puritanism of the mid-seventeenth century, Shakespeare's plays fell into disuse and it was only when David Garrick organized the first Shakespeare Jubilee in 1769 that his reputation gathered apace. It was a battle in which competing cultural and commercial interests were played out. Forgery and fabrication were rife within the 'bardolatrous trade'. Today, Stratford has become a necropolis in which the most obvious false-hoods have been removed, but Anne Hathaway's Cottage still remains problematic. She may or may not have lived there – and she may or may not have married Shakespeare. What is crucial here is not the real-ity of the events *au fin du siècle* some 400 years ago but the fact that millions believe the locales and places to be correct. It is a site for the hagiographic display of a playwright – and because of this, an eco-nomic resource of considerable worth. Lash and Urry (1994: 266) call phenomena like Stratford, 'place-myths'. For us, on our way out of Pandemonium, they are, very usually, necropoli. The vast majority of organizations, in this sense are also necropoli – machines for the sup-pression of death – and they do this through a form of mirrors.

CHAPTER 9 *Sixth Exhibit: The Hall of Mirrors*

Horse Guards Parade

The revelation which comes to mind immediately we enter the confines of Horse Guards Parade is that there are clichés everywhere. The temperature suggests a climate which is splendidly temperate. The air is full of the scent of roses and night stocks. The sky is an azure blue and the sun shines as if it was a May morning. The atmosphere is one of happiness, contentment and satisfaction.

We are in a square which is a great public space standing in front of a castellated edifice of monumental proportions. It is an enclosed area where earlier arrivals are mingling with us on their way out. They don't appear to be unhappy. In fact when they see us they begin to smile and wave. We wonder what they are thinking and why they smile so much. What lies ahead cannot be that bad. Now we have left Prague Castle behind and its medieval fustiness no longer depresses the spirits we are entering a less melancholic part of the city . . . Aren't we?

We smile as we leave because we have just *left* scenes of indescribable futility. We know, now, that perfumes are used both to mask the smells of whatever we have confronted but also in an attempt to change our moods. In the same way as Susskind's *Perfume* (1989) shows how this might be done and the Mule in Asimov's the *Foundation* trilogy shows how it can be achieved with music, we are fully aware that supermarkets blow the smells of baking bread back into the store rather than expelling them. We are all consumers of these technological breakthroughs as we mingle in Horse Guards Parade. Yet we smile; we feel better. Horse Guards Parade smells and looks wonderful. What is to come next? Our guide appears, wearing the mask of Janus.

'My friends,' says the author bringing the magic to an end, 'is Pandemonium a utopian or dystopian city?' As guests, we are now asked to believe that the exhibits we are about to see on our trip are from *our* mundane organizational world. The inhabitants of Pandemonium see where *we* live to be strange, exotic and terrifying. They have produced six fearful sub-tours for our misery. Each threatens to reveal to us what our world is really like. A smell of sweat and fear blows in our direction. Above the opening door stands a banner upon which the legend of the Bohemian magic kingdom's last stand is imprinted in blood.

The invaders came from the West, bringing with them, for Christ's sake, fucking science.

We must travel under this banner, we are told, and leave the magic kingdom through this single door. Where we are going is shown in the title emblazoned in distant flashing neon. We leave behind lights powered by the ethereal energy of Pegasus' wings and, as we proceed, the noisy clatter of a diesel generator signals our entry into the first exhibit.

133

Many are named after companies but these companies are often named after people – usually men. To write one's name in the sky is possible with dominating buildings. Resistance to these forms of power, therefore, comes in the form of smashing the building to the ground or in overshadowing it, or in declaring it obsolete, expensive and decrepit. We see in urban development the playing out of egos and the attempts to suppress death through monumentalism. We see other attempts to suppress the memories held of the powerful. The smashing of Lenin's statues, the renaming of Stalingrad, the forthcoming Indian sabotage of Mount Rushmore are all examples of resistance to the powerful. They are often marked, of course, by the newly powerful displacing the old, as in Ho Chi Minh City, and John Moores University. But they, in turn, as monumental 'necropoli' may well be renamed in new monumentalism. They are all halls of mirrors.

CHAPTER 9 *Sixth Exhibit: The Hall of Mirrors*

CHAPTER 4

First Exhibit:
Abattoirs and Death

Death Grinnd horrible a ghastly smile, to hear
His famin should be filld, and blest his mawe.

(Milton, *Paradise Lost*, Bk II, ll. 845–7)

The women must wait, in a state of virtue of course, otherwise the men's chivalric sacrifice will have been in vain. Hence the 'joke' said through gritted teeth *vis-à-vis* the Americans in the Second World War: 'overpaid, oversexed and over here'.

War memorials offer a way of re-asserting community. After all: 'In the Great War over 60 million men had been mobilised (from a continent of approximately 120 million households), 22 million had been wounded and 10 million killed' (Davies 1993: 124).

Yet architecture in the form of war memorials is a work of fiction, it is 'parable art', designed to show what lessons should be drawn from conflict. So too is the corporate architecture of the leading world cities. Within New York, Los Angeles, Tokyo, London, Paris, Johannesburg, Sydney and Hong Kong we see not vibrant cities but *necropoli*. Consider the skylines of the major cities and the attempts by the powerful to etch their lives upon the citizens below. This is monumentalism in its high modernist form. It is in the cities of Asia that the largest towers are now being built. The limitation of building materials in the last decades has been in their flexibility. Beyond certain heights and wind speeds, these buildings bend too far for the occupants to be comfortable. New technologies of flexible but counteracting materials, balanced by electronic techniques, allow building heights to soar yet again.

CHAPTER 9   *Sixth Exhibit: The Hall of Mirrors*

Putting Descartes before the horse

It is 1889 and we are in Turin. Friedrich Nietzsche is in the first stages of madness supposedly brought about by tertiary syphilis. In the street he sees a coachman severely beating a horse with a whip. He runs towards the horse and cradling its head in his arms, he begins to cry (Kundera 1985: 290). Does madness this way lie? Nietzsche had rejected Darwinism as a false science of optimism. The society of the modern had not brought about the survival of the fittest but, on the contrary, had brought about the survival of the most degenerate. These soulless pygmies wielded giant power within the burgeoning bureaucracies of the time. As close observation of the cardiac muscle of humans will show to the pathologist who has eagerly crunched her way through the sternum, after death the heart assumes the shape of a pyramid (Barnes 1989: 22). And, of course, the pyramid is the classic bureaucratic shape or structure which reveals to all its heartlessness. For Nietzsche, bureaucrats, theologians and state officials were all 'despisers of the body' expressing their contempt for things visceral and carnal. The coachman whipping the horse in that street in Turin was a despiser of the body in like manner. It did not matter that horse flesh is not human flesh, for the abattoir makes little distinction.

135

laying of the cornerstone of the Capitol on 18 September 1793, Washington descended into the trench in which the stone was placed and laid around it containers of oil, corn and wine – standard symbols of Freemasonry. Both the White House and the Capitol building became focal points in the elaborate geometry of the nation's capital city. Washington and Jefferson both changed the original design to produce specifically octagonal patterns with the particular cross used by Freemasons within them (Baigent and Leigh 1990: 348–50). So we see here the links between architecture and attempts to develop cities in which Freemasonry plays a central town planning role.

Jon Davies (1993) has done some interesting work on war memorials. Despite a consistent misspelling of Bambrough in Northumberland, he illuminates the significance of these very common features of the British landscape. Pressure for memorials in the local villages and hamlets throughout the UK often came from the mothers of the dead.

Other 'boys' who had returned were given village medals, but their sons – until the memorial – had nothing (Davies 1993: 115). Monuments thus carry much working-class weight in iconography as well as aristocratic or naturally based feelings. However, they are about *men*. They mark off the responsibilities of men and of women in which the former claim the 'life of honour' through a sepulchral monument.

CHAPTER 9   *Sixth Exhibit: The Hall of Mirrors*

Note here that the Italian word *manegiare* which means, among other things, horse handling is one of the twin origins of the English word 'management'. Whipping and physical pain were part and parcel of the techniques available to coachmen and thence to the early managers and soulless bureaucrats who adopted a role consonant with a view of a workforce made up of dumb animals. Clearly, managers everywhere are tempted to put the horse before Descartes. From the treatment of the Dutchman Schmidt by F. W. Taylor who saw him as a 'dumb ox' to the use of parts of the body and not the mind to describe contemporary workers, it is clear that the treatment of human beings as if they are animals is very well established.

Daniel Pick, in *The War Machine* (1993: 3), tells of the French regiment in 1917, at a time when the French army was rocked by mutinies, who went to the front baa-ing like lambs on the way to slaughter. From 1860 onwards, Pick argues: 'technology, factory production and calculated death were coming together in many new ways'. Chicago became the greatest cattle market in the world as animals were delivered to the stockyards by railway and the carcasses dispatched all over the United States and sometimes beyond. The search for the perfect abattoir went on in Europe too as the scale of slaughter increased. Sinclair's 1906 novel *The Jungle* describes the stockyards as 'a very river of death'. A. J. P. Taylor argued that the First World War was dragged into being by the inexorable logic of the railway timetable. Whereas it had been cattle that had been ferried around Europe, it became the troops for the front who travelled in the very same trucks over the very same tracks on the very same schedule.

136

member to the Third Degree. Also crucial is the emphasis upon the supposed basic premises for master builders lying in geometry. It was to be in structures based upon geometry and not embellished with representational art that God's presence was best accommodated. The synagogue, the mosque and the temple all share a concern for sacred geometry and abstract mathematical principles rather than pictures. These were not to be merely 'houses of God'. They were musical instruments tuned to resonate with God for all those who entered their portals. The most perfectly pitched building had been Solomon's Temple and the best musician, Hiram.

Cities, too, could be based upon geometric and sacred patterns. At the inauguration of George Washington on 30 April 1789, Freemasonry was much in evidence. On the American dollar bill was placed the 'Great Seal' of the USA. It is undoubtedly Freemasonic, with an all-seeing eye in a triangle above a 13-stepped, four-sided pyramid. At the

The war poet Wilfred Owen said that, once there, the soldiers 'died like cattle'. As we will see, Bauman saw the selfsame processes at work twenty years later in Auschwitz which was 'a mundane extension of the modern factory system'. Martin Heidegger provocatively said in 1949:

> Agriculture today is a motorised food industry, in essence the same as the manufacture of corpses in gas chambers and extermination camps, the same as the blockade and starvation of countries, the same as the manufacture of atomic bombs.

In *The McDonaldization of Society,* Ritzer (1993: 103) discusses the ways in which calculability and predictability have invaded many aspects of our lives – and deaths. Using some Weberian insights he begins to describe factory farming:

> A broiler producer today gets a load of 10,000, 50,000 or even more day old chicks from the hatcheries and puts them straight into a long windowless shed. . . . Inside the shed, every aspect of the birds' environment is controlled to make them grow faster on less feed. Food and water are fed automatically from hoppers suspended from the roof. The lighting is adjusted . . . for instance, there may be bright light 24 hours a day for the first week or two, to encourage the chicks to gain [weight] quickly. . . .

architecture, including number, shape, measure and the practical uses of geometry. Solomon's Temple, strictly speaking, was Hiram's Temple. One day, Hiram was praying near to his almost complete edifice when three villains attacked him, searching for knowledge not appropriate to their inferior rank. They asked for the secret word, sign and grip appropriate for a master craftsmen – an 'arche-tekton'. When he refused to divulge these secrets, he was attacked with three blows: one from a hammer, one from a level and the third from a plumb. He received each blow in a different doorway of the Temple but ultimately died at the east door. The arche-tekton's body was buried under loose earth nearby and a sprig of acacia placed on top. His body was only discovered seven days later by nine of his servants, also masters. As they disinterred the body, one of them says 'Macbenae', which means 'the flesh falls off the body', and this becomes the 'new word' of the Temple. When Hiram's body is reinterred in the Temple, the masters wear aprons and gloves of white to show that not one of them has stained his hands with Hiram's blood.

For some, this story is one of human sacrifice in a new building to propitiate the God(s). The symbol of Hiram was the skull and crossbones and his death is re-enacted in Freemasonry at the elevation of a

→

> Towards the end of the 8 to 9 week life of the chicken, there may be as lit-
> tle as half a square foot of space per chicken – or less than the area of a
> sheet of quarto paper for a 3 and ½ pound bird.

What Ritzer is claiming here is that McDonalds represents the epitome
of late twentieth-century control in the processes of food production.
What he fails to note on both counts is that McDonalds is an organization dependent very much on death and that its organizational
antecedents lie not only in modern factory farming but in the concentration camps of Auschwitz and Buchenwald as well. McDonalds
requires the profitable death of cattle and chickens in profusion.
Without automated death the cost of a Big Mac would be even higher
than it presently is. The Nazi concentration camps relied upon the relative automation of death at a much earlier stage than fast food
companies. The death camps were fast and were specifically designed
to be so. After much trial and error, as soon as the doctrine of the
Final Solution was accepted in late October 1941, experimentation
was undertaken which soon produced mass deaths relatively efficiently and effectively.

However, the links between the automated production of death as
witnessed in the abattoir and the growth of technically efficient production techniques are long ones. Henry Ford developed the notion of
mass assembly production having seen the system of mass *disassem-
bly* in the Chicago meat packing plants before the First World War.

138

Architecture and death

The Enlightenment hope was of a world in which humans came to
rival God. To do so, 'Man invented himself'. As part of this invention
the products of humans would have to rival those of God and so
monumentalism in architecture became very important. As we have
seen, the Freemasons saw themselves as following in the tradition of
the ancient architects and came to terms with death very quickly.

Freemasonry actually contains a major element of Judaic tradition
filtered through Islam. The building of Solomon's Temple is a story
which comes to us from the Old Testament and contains a central element in Freemasonry's development – the murder of Hiram Abiff.
Hiram was a 'Master' of Phoenician Tyre, well versed in the secrets of

←

Whereas cattle started whole and ended up by being cut into pieces in the abattoir, in the Highland Park automobile plant cars began as little pieces and ended up at the bottom of the production line in a complete form. The assembly line could be run in both directions, as Ford's genius recognized. One could construct or destruct, manufacture or murder, assemble or disassemble simply by reversing the flow of the processed item. The selfsame processing techniques used by the Nazis in the later period of the war have become the focus of a tremendous amount of interest recently.

The Holocaust

Put simply and into the English language, the Age of 'Illumination' was brought to a screaming halt by the period of 'burning'. For in English, 'Enlightenment' means to shine light upon something in order to reveal it more clearly. Whilst the origins of the term 'The Age of Enlightenment' are German and come from 'das Zertalter der Aufklärung' with a meaning, essentially, of to throw light on or 'to clear up' or 'to brighten up something or someone', in the Anglophone world it came to be known as the Age of Reason. Everything could be questioned, made rational and become subject to appraisal and improvement; even, as became all too clear, the right to exist of a whole religious belief and its followers.

'Holocaust' means 'the burning of everything' and has come to signify great destruction and loss of life, especially from fire. The sense of being a 'burnt offering' which is there in the Ancient Greek meaning has been lost, more or less, although there is a sense in which Roman

become a 'presence in an absence' – a great unspoken feature of life and living. But has organization theory itself not conspired in the hiding of death behind many masks? Habermas, in addressing Fascism, began to construct a position for organization theory into which it will be forced to retreat as the century ends. There is a view gathering support which claims that the modernist project created Auschwitz (Burrell 1994). Taking a broader perspective, Feingold (1983: 398) has written that:

> The final solution marked the juncture where the European industrial system went away; instead of enhancing life, which was the original hope of the Enlightenment, it began to consume itself.

CHAPTER 9   *Sixth Exhibit: The Hall of Mirrors*

Catholic acquiescence in what was going on in Eastern Europe in 1941–45, particularly in Poland, has to be understood not only in terms of anti-Semitism but also, perhaps, as a sacrificial offering for that organization's continued existence and the retention of some of its influence under Fascism.

Zygmunt Bauman's marvellous book on *Modernity and the Holocaust* (1989) shows the importance of bureaucratic organization to the death camps; and how Reason itself comes to be used for insane purposes. The light is finally extinguished by flames. In the spring of 1933, the newly elected Rector of the University of Freiburg talked of the 'greatness and glory of a new dawn'. Four months earlier, Adolf Hitler had been named Chancellor of Germany and Martin Heidegger had joined the Nazi Party. Whilst he was not a member of the Party for more than nine months and refused to ratify the dismissal of anti-Nazi deans, that quote of his, earlier in this section, seems crassly insensitive. Making little difference between techniques for growing vegetables and those for killing many of a people who would have populated German universities in any other period seems inexcusable. His collectivism and consequent rejection of the bourgeois individualism upon which much of current philosophy rested at that time (and this?) have made it clear that he was prey to National Socialism and its calls for national identity.

140

dieting for the beer belly, colouring dyes for hair, vein-stripping for varicose veins, amyl nitrite or penis extensions for sexual potency, steroids for faster times. If one eschews bio-engineering of this particular kind and embraces old age gracefully, they tell me, then one has escaped body politics in the new age. But one has not. Everywhere in the hall of mirrors that one looks there are injunctions to change one's appearance, to change the contents of one's stomach, of one's arteries, one's image in the mirror. It is not only that fat is a feminist issue (Orbach 1979), or that some worry about hair loss can be avoided. The same techniques used to sell Clinton, or Blair or the Principal of London Business School to their respective constituencies are now used to sell a different 'us' to ourselves. And we watch. For we are *numero uno* to ourselves.

Attempts to suppress death – either one's own or that of one's loved ones – are probably as old as *Homo sapiens*. Organization theory itself needs to escape from euphemisms and stop playing a part in the suppression of the great fear – the fear of our own death. Today death has

But surely he is much more than a Black Forest Neanderthal – 'a Schwarzwald redneck', in Rorty's hostile evaluation (Aspden 1993: 19)? Gadamer gave his views to George Steiner on the man who lamented 'the forgetting of Being':

> 'He grabbed me by the shoulders, lifted me off the floor and said: 'Steiner, Steiner, it is so simple. Martin was the greatest of thinkers, but the smallest of men'. (quoted in Aspden 1993: 19)

What this thinking provided, besides showing the underlying violence of his political beliefs, is a recognition of the bureaucratic and Cartesian nature of mechanized barbarism and the angst that this causes. Bureaucratic systems when fused with rationality, of course, need not produce the death camps. But once put in the context of racial purity and the ideology of extermination, bureaucratic rationality found it relatively easy to produce a system of physical extermination carried out in a dull, routinized way.

Originally, the Nazi plan had been to put Jewish individuals in Madagascar or east of a line drawn between the Asian cities of Archangel and Astrakhan. But extermination was decided upon on

The rise of neo-Fascist art

As John Berger (1969) has shown, the links between artistic representations and the powerful are all too clear throughout history. In management theory, Anthony (1994) has pointed out that corporate culture and the engineering thereof has sought to develop myths, stories and symbolic representations of the organizationally powerful through which to manipulate lower-order members. Unsurprisingly, today's imagineers use Fascist art and its conventions to portray corporate leaders as far-seeing superhuman figures who, through charisma and leadership qualities, can produce results which others would find impossible. There is collectivism here but it is of a corporatist kind. Members of the organization are encouraged to undertake 'followership' and gaze upwards, admiringly, at the Führer figure.

Subtle differences in expression, the line of the audience's vision, the size of the monumental leader and so on are all carefully orchestrated to imagineer a representation of the unchangeable supremo-*numero uno*. At the same time as the corporate *Übermensch* concept is developed a similar rise in neo-Fascist body politics is visible within the wealthy parts of the population. Cosmetic surgery is undertaken to take years off the clientele who suffer from the biological ravages of time. Liposuction for cellulite, exercise for pectorals,

cost grounds from 21 October 1941 and the classic Weberian elements of precision, speed, unambiguity, knowledge of the files, continuity, discretion, unity, strict subordination, reduction of time, reduction in material and in any 'personal' elements were all put in place in order to achieve this goal.

First of all, the system created a climate of moral indifference. Not more than 10 per cent of the SS were 'abnormal' in terms we would understand today were we to use clinical psychological tests. Few gave way to outbursts of sadistic cruelty and many would easily have met the entry criteria for selection by the present US and British army. Feelings of 'animal pity' for a crying child, let us say, were overcome, not by the selection of cruel individuals but by bureaucratic procedures. Indeed, over-zealous and particularly keen SS members were weeded out from the camps to keep the use of specific individual initiative to a minimum. Violence is authorized from above, is routinized by exact specification of the roles, and victims are dehumanized in the classic ways identified by Erving Goffman (1959). This is to say they lose all trappings of individuality by having their identity stripped away from them, are treated as numbers not human beings and undergo degradation ceremonies to reduce their status. Indeed, some 'victims' identify with the oppressor, wear scraps of Nazi uniforms as a sign of their allegiance and are more cruel than the guards themselves. They become almost willing participants within this particular theatre of cruelty.

142

So the interest in the visual is not only about the superficial, the surface, the exterior. It is an interest in the visual because of its symbolic value. The waiting rooms of hospitals, the Dean's Office, the queues at Disneyland and the airliner's décor all have symbolic purpose and sometimes unintentional symbolism within them. It may appear to be cosmetic but actually it is of rather deep significance. So the move in several social sciences towards a more self-conscious awareness of philosophical issues raised by optocentrism has to be welcomed. This is beginning to be noticeable even in marketing, where Jean Umiker-Sebeok's *Marketing and Semiotics* (1987) and Williamson's *Decoding Advertisements* (1978) are both directly based upon thinking in social philosophy. This trend has been noticeable for a while in accounting (Hopwood 1987; Miller and O'Leary 1987), operational research (Checkland 1981; Jackson 1987), but as part of this movement let us suggest that the issue of optocentrism in French philosophical thought with which we began this exhibit is of direct relevance to organizations.

'Killing at a distance' more or less maintains the invisibility of the victims to their executioners. 'Sanitation officers' placed the Zyklon B tablets in the gas chambers from containers labelled 'disinfecting chemicals'. They were specifically not allowed to see the pathetic contents of the gas chambers and the results of their murderous actions. The labels used were sophisticated distancing devices keeping actors discrete from the action in so far as was possible. There was also the dissociation of the ends of the process from any morality by a strict functional division of labour. No sense was allowed to those actively involved of the whole enterprise and its purpose. The task of baby-burning, which for any civilized people we fondly imagine would have been abhorrent, was split into minute, functionally separate tasks. No one person could be identified with responsibility for this set of activities. All were 'cogs in a machine'.

Scientists within Germany – and, let us acknowledge, elsewhere – failed to complain about the use of scientific techniques generally in the Holocaust. When Jewish scientists were taken from their work, often in the universities and sent to the camps, complaints that were made were not about the act itself but about the loss of expertise to the war effort. Moreover, much of Nazi science in companies like I. G. Farben was used specifically to further the achievement of the Holocaust.

The editorial boards of the leading journals remained virtually unchanged in the period of Hitler's regime. Science, both natural and social, abetted the killing techniques used in Auschwitz and elsewhere. And this logic is by no means dead. Since 1945 bureaucratic rationality has been used in the aircraft brake scandal (Corbett 1994), in the Ford Pinto scandal (ibid.), in seeing Vietnam as 'an electronic battlefield' and using 'smart weapons' and 'surgical strikes' in Iran. Research projects concerned with making warfare more cost effective, on getting a 'bigger bang for the buck', are still with us. Organizational behaviour and management in general can be relied upon easily (one might say on almost every occasion) to provide technical services for the armed forces if required. Few of our graduates today, had they been born in Germany fifty years ago, would have not taken part in the Holocaust in one way or another. Indeed, their grandparents in the USA or Britain may well have played tiny parts in 'Slaughterhouse 5' (Vonnegut 1971), in the bombing of Dresden, or of the Los Alamos research leading to Nagasaki and Hiroshima. Had the outcome of the Second World War been different, these scientists, bureaucrats and managers would have been reviled in Northampton perhaps instead of Nuremberg.

If history is the propaganda of the victors then we should not ask too many questions about the sinking of the *Belgrano*, carpet bombing, collateral damage and Agent Orange, and the millions of those employed, still, despite 'the Peace dividend' in the 'Defence' sectors of the First World. In classic Orwellian 'Newspeak', of course, defence means war, the 'Final Solution' meant genocide and '*Lebensraum*' meant the Slavic killing fields. What we really face here in the Square of Pandemonium is 'cidocracy'. Certainly the Enlightenment did not create rule by killers – but it made them much more efficient in waging war. As we have seen, the division of labour within the death camps helps employees remain sane and divorces them, to some extent, from the consequence of their actions. Yet hospitals too rely upon such systems of de-personalization. As Amis (1991) shows us, a simple reversal of time's arrow would produce a world in which the death camps took in the dead and produced relatively healthy individuals before speeding them back in trains with the locomotive at the rear to the urban centres of Europe. Similarly, when time runs backwards, hospitals become places of disease acquisition. You enter a hospital feeling well with an operation 'wound' which would have healed up, only to have surgeons open you up, and after much hard work, place malignant tissue within your body. Hospitals, in reversed time, send you out into the world with disease and cancerous growths and make sure you feel like shit as you exit through their doors.

144

Wally Olins tells the following anecdote:

> my colleague Michael Wolff once interviewed the personnel manger of an advanced engineering company. The rain dripped from a hole in the roof of the unheated, prefabricated structure where they sat together. It slowly trickled onto the head of the personnel manager and ran down his nose. Apparently oblivious of this, he explained . . . that what they wanted in the company were young people really in sympathy with . . . the white-hot technological revolution. (Olins 1978: 176)

In a recent review of measures (both qualitative and quantitative) of competitiveness (Buckley et al. 1988), no mention whatsoever is given to visual criteria, not even to design. Yet, as Watzlawick, Bavalas and Jackson (1967: 38) have written:

> No matter how one may try, one cannot *not* communicate. Activity or inactivity, words or silence, all have message value: they influence others and these others, in turn, cannot *not* respond to these communications and are thus themselves communicating.

CHAPTER 9   *Sixth Exhibit: The Hall of Mirrors*

Ludicrous? Possibly. But note that pregnant women in the UK of the mid-1990s may well see up to forty healthcare professionals on a 'production line' basis (Winterton 1992). Women may not see the same midwife twice. They do not know the names of those who are delivering their babies nor can they establish caring relationships with 'professionals' who see themselves as governed by the exigencies of expediency and efficiency and thus are unable to develop 'long-term' emotional ties. Should the labour go badly wrong, or the perinatal child suffer from some defect, the system permits distancing and blame avoidance. There is strong evidence that where the pregnant woman in labour is known to the healthcare professionals there is less use of analgesia, the forceps delivery rate is lower and the woman's perception of the birth is much more positive. Where the relationship is almost entirely depersonalized, the very circumstances which depersonalized relationships are designed to better manage are more likely to occur.

Jill Tweedie, a writer and journalist, had been feeling weak and ill for some time. After a series of tests she was given the somewhat shocking news by a senior doctor that she had multiple sclerosis. He asked her to speak to someone on the way out, another professional, who would offer her help and advice on how to deal with this tremendous shock.

Olins (1978) advocated the creation of well-articulated corporate identity programmes in which the visual was paramount. But in a sense all organizations emit visual stimuli, consciously or otherwise, The 'given offs', visible to observers, may go unnoticed by the organizations themselves for years. Indeed, there is no guarantee that the signals organizations seek to emit regarding their competitiveness, products, status, quality of service and future success will actually be perceived as reflecting the intended message. For example, it is not obvious that corporate location is necessarily a conscious or deliberate expression of choice or manifestation of corporate imagineering. Often few sites are available, particularly to smaller organizations constrained by limited resources, so that issues of a purely symbolic nature may well give way to those of a more substantive nature. 'Front' may be subservient to labour supply, for example. Cambridge Science Park, for example, contains one company which makes much of its high-tech location, to the extent that even the science park landscaping features in much of their publicity. Instead of electricity pylons of the normal girder construction marching across the former ammunition dump owned by Trinity College, the site possesses two single mast type pylons.

CHAPTER 9   *Sixth Exhibit: The Hall of Mirrors*

She was then ushered into a side room, still shaking, to be confronted not with a counsellor but with a technician – to be measured for her wheelchair. The technician indicated that the sooner she learned to expect what awful consequences the passage of the disease would have on her body, the better it would be for all concerned. This took place without any prior counselling whatsoever. Indeed, the 'measuring' *was* the counselling she received. She was to be processed in a way which would make her less difficult to deal with within the system. The production line mentality for health care as well as for death dealing are both very well established because of the economic cost factors. The human costs, naturally enough, are lost in these systems. That, after all, is *what they are designed to do*.

In *The Dialectic of Enlightenment*, Adorno and Horkheimer (1979: 231) argue that a love–hate relationship with flesh and the human body dominates twentieth-century culture. For:

> Europe has two histories: a well-known, written history and an underground history. The latter consists in the fate of the human instincts and passions which are displaced and distorted by civilisation. . . . The relationship with the human body is maimed from the outset.

This understanding that the history of civilization is one of a progressive maiming of the human body has been well understood by several keen-eyed commentators. Kafka (1961), for example, writing 'In the

146

The pleasant, open-plan character of the lounge will have much to remind him of his own student days or, if he prefers, will provide him with an opportunity to drop in on the conversations of staff as they discuss matters of academic interest. Alternatively, he may wish to seek out a quiet corner where he can peruse the previous day's *FT* or last year's Blackwells Management Books catalogue. Certainly, he will have time to form an impression of what we at (University X) have to offer. (Rothschild 1987)

Since neither a change of location nor building in this case was possible the 'imagineering' (Morgan 1989) conducted to overcome these difficulties was implemented almost exclusively at the level of décor.

The concentration hitherto on the 'givens' – that is, the deliberate and conscious signals emitted by the organization – however, only gives us one side of the picture. Equally important are the 'given offs'.

Penal Settlement' describes a situation of a prisoner who is to be executed by a torture machine designed by the camp's commandant, who is a genius. The commandant is at the same time soldier, mechanic, judge, chemist and draughtsman. The very drawing itself of this torture machine is an object of veneration to those in the penal colony and those who touch it are required to clean their hands first. In the course of the slow death which the torture machine brings about, it engraves itself upon the body of the victim. The executing officer has not told the victim of his fate for 'He'll learn it on his body.' But for Kafka the undoubted pain the victim is to suffer is also going to be a source of ecstasy. The officer in charge of the execution describes the face of the condemned man as the Harrow pierces his flesh.

> But how quiet he grows at just about the sixth hour! Enlightenment comes to the most dull-witted. It begins around the eyes. From there it radiates. A moment that might tempt one to get under the Harrow with him. (1961: 180)

In actual fact, the officer does at a later point take his own life under the Harrow in a passage which is one of Kafka's most terrifying. It ends with the phrase redolent of the slaughterhouse: 'through the forehead went the point of the great iron spike' (ibid.: 197).

147

Do not cross the central reservation

Picture, if you will, the arrival in campus of the Managing Director of a medium-sized company, bent on acquiring top-class advice. Having parked some distance from Gillow House (unless he visits during the vacation) he will have the luxury of a choice: the swamp (scenic but awkward in really wet weather) or the garbage bin route (direct if aesthetically unrewarding).

Once in the rear foyer he may have a little difficulty in locating the toilets, but the prospect of being able to purchase a Twix or some crisps will be more than adequate compensation unless he is absurdly fastidious. A few enquiries will bring him to Enquiries and the coffee lounge, and provided that he has 15p in very small change he will be able to avoid the disappointment of finding the change machine out of order.

Depending upon the time of day, a spell in the queue will enable him to make useful contacts and ultimately take him to an attractive wall-mounted dispenser and a selection of practical cups and cutlery. If he is still early for his appointment, a few minutes spent selecting a chair which will take his weight without collapsing will be well rewarded.

CHAPTER 9 *Sixth Exhibit: The Hall of Mirrors*

It is also reminiscent of Kafka's dreams where he claims to have welcomed images in which he has been stabbed through the heart with a knife. Indeed, Heller (1974) argues that the notion of the 'wound' is a central motif throughout the work of Kafka. It is not totally surprising to learn, therefore, that Kafka was considerably influenced by the work of de Sade, whom he described as ' the true patron of our age'. A similar view of the human body and the pain which it endures and sometimes loves is to be found in the work of Francis Bacon. In 1966, he wrote: 'we are meat, we are potential carcasses. If I go into a butcher's shop I always think it's surprising that I wasn't there instead of the animal' (Sylvester 1988: 46).

This division between animal meat and human flesh, between the crucifixion and the abattoir, may seem disgusting to some but that is precisely why Bacon (an apt name for a commentator on such issues if ever there was one) raises it to our consciousness. The human body is made up of meat and bone and through this recognition comes a new understanding of human misery. Now, millions of people upon the planet may think that this is no revelation, for each day as they wake the harsh realities of life's pain and suffering may be all too obvious.

So too does company interior décor and the buildings themselves. IBM is sometimes known as Big Blue and the role of Eliot Noyes in creating a corporate image – including the architecture and interior décor – is well recognized. Noyes designed the IBM office in Garden City, New York, which just happens to look like a typewriter with adornments reminiscent of typewriter keys. The ANZ Bank building in Sydney, Australia, has the appearance at certain times of the day of a gold brick dominating the city. Buildings can – if the clients can afford it – reflect the corporate image consciously desired.

For those organizations (commercial or otherwise) less well financially endowed, interior décor offers a relatively cheap and quick means of manipulating the visual front. In these days of budget costs and industry ties, even universities are waking up to the importance of visual fronts. Having decided to change its name from the 'School of Management and Organizational Sciences' to the simpler 'School of Management' and having selected a new format for its letterheads and literature, my erstwhile institution refurbished its management building in an attempt to signal to the outside world a change in its attitudes, markets and products. This was, in part, influenced by a letter to the university newspaper from a member of staff which is reproduced here in full:

CHAPTER 9   *Sixth Exhibit: The Hall of Mirrors*

For others, the idea that we are daily 'cut down to size, packaged in plastic and offered for consumption complete with instructions for preparation and a sell-by date' (Boyne 1990: 100) may seem abhorrent, yet, as we are beginning to see in this text, the metaphor of the abattoir is very strong in its suggestiveness for the organizational world. The organizations of and for death – the necrorgs – are all around us, were we only to look.

But looking is dangerous and frightening and what we may find is something which carries the terror of the unknown or – even worse – of the void which has immobilized human self-reflexivity for millennia. The tale from under the rim which is based upon an observer who has looked into the void and reports what might be there is likely to be a very harrowing story indeed.

The mechanization of death, of course, is not entirely new. The system which was utilized by the Blackfoot tribe in Southern Alberta of slaughtering buffalo is suggestive of a highly organized approach to the production of meat. The debate on whether it represents more than this still rages. At a cliff edge named 'Heads smashed in', the Blackfoot would drive a whole herd of buffalo over the precipice until there was enough meat to feed the tribe over the year. This involved neither the spearing of the animals nor the shooting of arrows which figure in movies such as *Dances with Wolves* (1990).

149

and Parkin (1967), for example, are quite clear that the concentration of power in the hands of very large corporations is one reason why *corporate* rather than industrial design has become more important in the post-war period. Part of this interest is manifested in the ways in which very large organizations have focused on corporate location – that is, the choice of geographical positioning. Pfeffer (1982: 263) gives the following examples:

> Safeway, a retail grocery store chain with annual sales of well over $10 billion, has its corporate headquarters in an older, three or four storey building located in the produce market and industrial warehouse section of Oakland, California. There is no other corporate headquarters nearby. By contrast, Fidelity Financial, the parent company of Fidelity Savings and Loan, a $2 billion California savings and loan outfit, built a new headquarters building near Kaiser Center in Oakland, a multistorey building near Lake Merritt and numerous other high rises. This was done even as Fidelity incurred substantial financial difficulties.

Corporate location therefore has tremendous symbolic significance for many large organizations who wish to make signals to their client audiences.

CHAPTER 9   *Sixth Exhibit: The Hall of Mirrors*

On the contrary: this organized herding of the animals to their death used gravity rather than weapons. The debate concerns the issue of whether or not only enough animals to supply the tribe's requirements for meat, glue and hides were killed or whether, in a demonstration of human mastery of nature, as many animals as possible were killed. At the base of the cliff archaeologists have found large numbers of remains which are intact. In other words they have not been stripped of their hides or their flesh. They have been left there as they fell, which suggests that their death meant nothing to the economy or survival of the Blackfoot Indians.

Whatever the reality of the meaning of the 'Heads smashed in' cliff, it demonstrates that what went on at Chicago concerning cattle was by no means totally innovative. Human ingenuity in dealing death to animals had been well developed in that same geographical region long before the white settlers arrived. It is possible to argue that all organizations are involved in death, partly because all organizations are involved in life itself and there is always the presence of death amidst life. But, more importantly, because to organize – to use the organon – is a death-suppressing impulse, we tend to forget that to organize is to kill (Dale and Burrell 1995).

Frances Taylor Mayes (née Harrison) was a caretaker at the local Methodist church and treasurer of 'the sisterhood'. When asked by the neighbours she would also act as 'the layer-out' (Adams 1993). In the absence of trained medical staff to deal with the dead and the high prices charged by undertakers she would step in and 'lay out' dead bodies as soon as summoned. Layers-out tended to be 'very efficient', trustworthy or 'spotlessly clean' (Adams 1993: 158) for their duties were onerous and they expected in return, not money, but considerable respect. They would straighten out the limbs of the dead person, place pennies on the eyelids, tie the chin with a bandage, fold the arms across the chest and tie the legs together. The body was then washed, all orifices plugged (with the penis tied in the man), the hair brushed and the

Pfeffer (1982) has argued, little research has been done on linking the physical attributes of organizations into organization theory itself. Measures of relevance, he suggests, are the number of square feet devoted to an activity (since large size has symbolic and expressive effect) and the amount of money expended on 'finish' per square foot.

Olins is not alone in concentrating upon the very large corporation and neglecting the role of 'front' in their smaller counterparts. Henrion

CHAPTER 9   *Sixth Exhibit: The Hall of Mirrors*

fingernails cleaned. It would be dressed in a clean nightgown and rendered as odourless as possible. Male relatives may well have had to be cajoled into moving the body downstairs to be placed in position for the paying of the last respects. Frances did this sort of task at least once a year throughout the 1930s when she was in her forties. She gave up the 'job' when she contracted eczema in her early fifties and the 'medicalization' of death had made her role increasingly peripheral and controversial. By 1948, 'layers-out' had all but disappeared from many parts of the UK. Their relationship to undertakers, doctors, midwives and community nurses had usually been a tense one and the victory of the centralizing state in the Second World War had created the welfare state and a victory for the medical profession. The privatized services of the 1930s were in retreat and with them the layer-out. Frances Mayes, who happened to be my maternal grandmother, never regretted performing this role. It allowed the old, the young, the male, to escape from death as best they could in a context where death was commonplace.

The dimensionally disadvantaged

Featherstone (1987) has noted that the importance of the ageing process to the social classes differs. Working-class members may well see the body as 'a machine in decline' but for the middle classes who see their bodies as possessing physical capital the deterioration threatens the 'body-as-project'. Acute anxiety thus develops. The notion that the body and death itself are perceived differently in time and space is expressed clearly by Shilling (1993: 177):

It comes as no surprise, for example, that the Windscale nuclear reprocessing plant changed its name to the apparently less emotive Sellafield or that Townsend-Thorensen, in its post-Zeebrugge phase, renamed itself P&O Ferries. Names are important and continue to be a key facet of organization identity. Olins argues that the complexities of contemporary organizations with complicated ownership patterns and brand differentiation impose a tight discipline on visual styles. This is why, he says, corporate identities of major companies have such marked similarities. Labels and images have to be recognizable on a global scale, non-offensive in a variety of languages and equally useful in northern Nigeria and Bond Street. Thus the tendency is almost always towards visual homogenization and diminished originality – a process seen by Olins as likely to affect the following visual elements within corporate identity – corporate paper, signs, vehicle identification, uniforms, advertising, sales promotion material, packaging design, product design, exhibitions and environmental design. As

→ I view death as having become a particular existential problem for people as a result of modern forms of embodiment, rather than being a universal problem for human beings which assumes the same form irrespective of time and place.

So, when we look at the ways in which death has been approached by differing societies, we must avoid the assumption that death has a universal meaning. Yet, it may well be that the 'escape' from death has taken on a widespread architectural significance. On one hand, this concerns the architecture of the body and how it is shaped, maintained, decorated and repaired. On the other it revolves around architectural expressions of the dead – now without bodies.

i.e. One minute walking along, the next minute dead. Why?

THINK OF IT MORE AS BEING . . . DIMENSIONALLY
DISADVANTAGED

(Pratchett 1994: 24)

152

optocentrism and the revelations it engenders in the notion of *organizational front*. In doing so, let us begin with the work of Erving Goffman who was one of the first to develop the idea of 'fronts', although at the level of the individual. Goffman speaks of the 'givens' – the conscious and deliberate symbols expressed by a person in an attempt to be as s/he is seen – and the 'given offs' – the impressions rather than expressions which are picked up by the observer which are not a deliberate and/or conscious part of the presentation of self. In the following mirrors a look will be taken at both the *givens* and the *given offs*. The clearest articulation of the importance of the visual givens is Wally Olins's book, *The Corporate Personality* (1978). In the Preface, Olins states that he is primarily 'concerned with the way the corporation manifests its identity visually, so the book has a bias towards visual matters' (p. 39). Moreover, 'it is about how the appearance of an organization can be controlled and how this can make the company more effective, more profitable and a better place to work in' (p. 9). In Goffman's terminology, the 'corporate personality' is about the 'givens' consciously manipulated to produce a sense in the viewer of a corporate identity. Olins takes his examples from many sectors including food, aircraft, automobiles, banks and the oil industry and is particularly keen to point to what he sees as the crucial importance of the self-labelling process of acquiring a name and its subsequent role in corporate identity. Although his book is now somewhat dated and his examples necessarily almost two decades old, the salience of his points remains.

CHAPTER 9   *Sixth Exhibit: The Hall of Mirrors*

And that is how many of us within the baby-boomer 'generation' see it. Nothingness instead of existence. The body as project gives way to remembrance of the body as project. One way is to say 'This is my body: as you eat, remember me.' Another is to say, 'Look at this. I did that.'

The way in which death has been seen and portrayed over the centuries is very instructive to observe. As the cabbala points out, at the turn of a century – any century – approaches, death plays a more important part in thinking. For the end of the century – like the end of the year – marks closure, finality and endings. Each *fin de siècle* means that death is reconsidered anew by the generation facing the end of a period. For many centuries, death was seen as a tame thing. Most illnesses and diseases claimed their victims by dehydration and so those about to be called by death knew for two days or so that they had time to make peace with their 'Maker', whoever that was, allocate their goods and chattels to relatives and friends and prepare for death's coming. It was 'tame' in the sense that when it was likely to occur would be foreseen. Outside of warfare and sudden fatal accidents of a similar kind, death was predictable. For it took effect over the period

→

153

←

WARNING: LINEARITY KILLS

the optical and power. Here the labels we give to those in authority prove very instructive: overseer, supervisor, colliery 'viewer' and so on are redolent with the power/knowledge dimension. And finally, there is the contemporary concern with corporate *image* and 'imagineering' where images can be created, shaped, transformed and restructured by specialist agencies.

All these processes and conceptualizations should be familiar to the reader who has got this far on the tour. These foci on the visual – be they from psychology, accounting, corporate strategy, marketing, social theory or psychoanalysis – all show an optocentrism in the development of our understanding of the symbolic world which we would do well to reflect in our approaches to and analyses of the processes of organization. Drawing on work done with Claire Shearman (Shearman and Burrell 1987), I wish to encapsulate this

in which dehydration took place. Even in war, the soldier knew when the battle had been organized to take place and could also prepare for death as a possible outcome.

The commissioned pictures of the Renaissance show death riding a nag – a slow mount – which wore a bell around its neck to forewarn that he was coming. Death was ponderous and not unkind. Everyone could see it coming.

But with Brueghel the Younger (1564–1638), death takes on a macabre appearance, reflective perhaps of a moral crisis facing the Church and organized religion. Death becomes seen as rape. Women (and men) run from death. They are seen as supine and being 'taken' forcibly. This is no longer a tame death but a violent, nasty experience, especially for those who have not been moral. Notions of human choice about morality reflect important changes in beliefs, in that it was now becoming possible to consider 'individuals' as meaningful categories. Tombstones and wall plaques grew up in the eighteenth and nineteenth centuries as indicators of individuals who had lived 'significant' lives which needed to be marked or celebrated. Prior to this, the fate of all but the nobility was the charnel house where bodies were left to rot and the bones thrown into unmarked graves. Note the fate of Mozart, for example. Jung Chang describes how in China in the 1940s prisoners of the Japanese who had been garrotted were taken to the outskirts of a town called South Hill where they were tipped into a shallow pit:

> The place was infested with wild dogs, who lived on the corpses. Baby girls who had been killed by their families, which was common in those days, were also dumped in the pit. (Chang 1991: 91)

This would have been typical for millennia in Europe also.

154

This ties in again with Erving Goffman's (1959) seminal work on the *presentation of self* where the centrality of the concept of 'we are as we are seen' is such that the dramaturgical metaphor more frequently alluded to by commentators on his work is in fact secondary to his explicit optocentrism. Much recent work on cognitive maps highlights the visual representation of business activity and relates back to 'ways of seeing'. Further visual dimensions are suggested by the notion of *environmental scan* where, in the area of business strategy for example, the organization uses the 'cognitive map' produced by its 'way of seeing' to 'scan' the environment for resources or noxiants (Emery and Trist 1965). Foucault (1977b) meanwhile has highlighted the notion of *gaze*, pointing to the inter-organizational surveillance and discipline to which we are all subjected and underlining the connections between

By the nineteenth century in Europe however there was a tremendous growth in the fashion for opulent funerals, particularly of the military. Lord Nelson, for example, was not buried at sea, which was the classic fate for navy personnel prior to this occasion. After the Battle of Trafalgar, his body was placed in a barrel of brandy to preserve it on the trip northwards and was duly delivered to Portsmouth for a state funeral back in London. Unfortunately, perhaps, sailors had drilled into the barrel and having 'tapped the monkey' siphoned off the contents, day by day, to keep themselves in alcohol on the way home. The barrel was virtually dry when the cask was opened in London. We do not know what state the body was in when it was finally buried. What we do know is that a huge funeral was organized in which for virtually the first time there was a protocol worked out which was to become standard throughout the nineteenth and twentieth centuries for state funerals of British royalty and military alike.

Today, death has become an important service sector industry and whilst there are seasonal fluctuations in trade, undertakers can rely upon a steady stream of business. Death is no longer tame, nor macabre, nor commemorated. It is scientized into debates on the organism and what might be rescued for foetal research or organ transplants, on whether the brain stem is really dead or not and on when to switch off life support machines.

155

What points of departure then might we seek in our use of visual metaphors in getting to grips with the corporate world? First, there is the notion of *ways of seeing*, developed by Wittgenstein and others, in which it is posited that there are mutually incompatible ways of viewing reality, the field of vision in each of which is characterized by a narrow exclusive myopia. The area of corporate strategy is replete with examples of 'ways of seeing' and their relative merits. Secondly, there is the notion of the *mirror stage* as developed by Jacques Lacan and others in which the human being is seen as becoming truly human when s/he learns to be reflexive and to see themselves as others almost do – as if in a mirror. In their discussion of the genesis of accountability, as we have seen above us, Hoskin and MacVe (1988) argue that double-entry book-keeping only became possible with the use of the metaphor of the mirror or spectrum in medieval accounting theory: that is, one side of the balance sheet reflects the other. Thirdly there is the related notion of *reflexivity* recently utilized by social psychologists in their studies of social knowledge and communication (Antaki and Lewis 1988).

CHAPTER 9 *Sixth Exhibit: The Hall of Mirrors*

The attempts to prevent death's total victory no longer revolve solely about the reproduction of one's DNA in the form of children. Today, it can involve organs surviving death as much as genes surviving the visit of the grim reaper. Yet this does not mean death has lost its sting. In a world of narcissistic individualism, the fear of death cannot fail to be significant. But whereas death, when it was tame, took place with one's family close around, when all important business had been completed and when one, personally, was prepared for it, today it takes place in a hospital. The organization of death is therefore much more obvious. It is possible that a declaration of death will not be made until the body is within the confines of the hospital. It is unlikely that close relatives will be allowed within an intensive care unit so that they may well miss the moment of death. Medical opinion often fights against the idea of telling the dying person of this prognosis because it makes management of the situation more difficult. Death has become highly organized and sanitized. Since it is dirty and profane it is kept separate from life, both geographically and psychologically. Words and phrases developed in the Victorian era as euphemisms for death: 'departed', 'shuffled off this mortal coil', 'gone to meet her Maker', 'gone before' and so on, adorn the gravestones of the nineteenth century. Death is hidden.

156

with advertising, design and corporate image (Williamson 1978; Henrion and Parkin 1967; Olins 1978) where the dictum 'we are as we are seen' has taken hold. As a guiding principle, this is of limited value, for a focus exclusively upon such elements as appearance, gloss, fronts, façade and image may well miss the reality, substance and essence of the phenomenon under observation. Nevertheless, in the analysis of organizations, it would be easy to maintain that the visual aspects have been de-emphasized. Concern has focused upon the 'objective' data of company performance which are taken to represent a real situation within the organization. Originally, reality was approached through *listening* to organizational members account for their activities over a period of time. The 'audit' was essentially something that was aural. Today, the audit is a visual affair manifesting itself in company accounts and reports which are to be read rather than listened to. Thus, accounts have moved from the realm of the aural to the realm of the visible. The study, in a careful and theoretically informed way, of the visual aspects of corporate life in all its manifestations is what this hall of mirrors is all about. By having a counter-moving set of text rush by well above them, readers should already be only too aware of the importance of the visual.

CHAPTER 9   *Sixth Exhibit: The Hall of Mirrors*

The realities of visceral decay, necrotic collapse and flesh removal by a sequence of bacterial and animal actions is very rarely spoken of in polite dinner circles. These processes take place in individualized coffins below ground and not, as before, on the surface in full view of visitors to the charnel house. And this is partly why the battlefields of the First World War were so shocking to those brought up in late Victorian times. For here, the visibility of the trenches as charnel houses was all that was available for a whole generation from a whole continent and several nations from beyond Europe. The realities of death could not be hidden across the front lines of the Somme. There were periods in the First World War when the ordinary infantry came close to calling the war off. Not only did the Russian army mutiny, but as we have seen the French army baa-ed its way to the front. The famous frontline football match at Christmas 1914 between Scottish and Saxon troops in the no man's land between Frelinghein and Houplines is but one example. The truce lasted a week, despite orders for it to be discontinued. When it was finally broken, it was done covertly:

> We sent someone over to tell the Boches, and the next morning at 11 o'clock I put 12 rounds into the farmhouse, and of course, there wasn't anybody there. But that broke the truce – on our front at least.
> (2nd Lt. Cyril Drummond in McDonald 1988: 52)

157

```
DO NOT CROSS THE
CENTRAL RESERVATION
```

It is an idea which has been developed within the realms of French philosophy in general and in the work of Michel Foucault in particular. Indeed, Foucault's emphasis upon the faculty of sight is such that his concern (1977b) for surveillance, the gaze and the panopticon is seen (*sic*) by Jay as a reflection (*sic*) of his essential optocentrism. Put simply then, optocentrism asserts that 'we are as we are seen' or perhaps we are as we pretend to be.

This exhibit demonstrates that the analysis of organizational life might show the contemporary movement towards the visible – that is how organizations have adopted a more optocentric orientation. The importance of the visual has long been recognized by those concerned

CHAPTER 9 *Sixth Exhibit: The Hall of Mirrors*

At Christmas time the year afterwards, in the Ypres area, the same thing happened – despite strong warnings against it. One lieutenant, the only British officer to go into no man's land, was sent home in disgrace (McDonald 1988: 116–17). As the war progressed attacks on officers by their own men using *inter alia* fragmentation grenades i.e. 'fragging' (Corbett 1994) was also in evidence and officers in the British army began to lead from behind and not in front of their men. Yet, the overwhelming experience was not fraternization with the enemy and resistance to superior officers. It was, of course, hatred of the enemy. Captain Agius in 1915 related the following story :

> I was supporting the attack with my 25 pound guns and I'll never forget seeing a Gurkha coming across in front from the German lines, holding something in his hands – and when I looked it was the face of a German! It wasn't his neck or his head, just his face cut vertically down. (quoted in McDonald 1988: 66)

A sanitation officer describes the realities of death thus:

> It's a brutal business is war. To spray dead bodies with disinfectant is no assistance in wartime. After lying in positions where it is not safe to go out and bury them, the best that can be hoped for is that nature should not

158

'Postmodernism' in the 1980s, he says, meant a set design which was hyper-realist, as in the National Theatre's fabrication of a full-size floating canal boat for Ayckbourn's *Way Upstream* (1982) and the unforgettable helicopter landing in *Miss Saigon* (1987). The naturalism of Page's *The Tempest* in a recent London showing was so great that plastic macs were distributed to the first three rows to prevent them from being drenched by Caliban and his fellow swamp creatures. There is, says Sudjic, a return to an architectural 'modernism' in set design in the mid-1990s. Whatever the accuracy of this labelling his conclusion is surely beyond doubt. He argues: 'The audience is the subject of illusion and sleight of hand. Of aesthetic flourishes and tricks of light and perspective.'

And since 'all the world's a stage' these same sleights of hand are to be found in almost all organizations. Organizations are halls of mirrors. In a beautifully crafted piece entitled *In the Empire of the Gaze*, the Berkeley social scientist Martin Jay talks of the rise of *optocentrism*, a concept referring, of course, to the centrality of the visual and optical, both in prioritizing the sense-data which we as individuals seek to understand *and* in developing ways of understanding the societal interactions around us.

CHAPTER 9   *Sixth Exhibit: The Hall of Mirrors*

be retarded in its process of bacterial dissolution and nothing should ever be placed on a dead body to prevent a rat eating it. If it cannot be buried, get it down to the state of bleached bones as soon as possible. (McAveen in McDonald 1988: 204)

Bodies were lost in the quagmire that was the front only to be stood upon, used as sandbagging in preparing trench defences and constantly reappearing within the battlefield in one obscene form or another. Some soldiers resisted death with the most horrific mutilations; others embraced it much more quickly than was the norm for their very minor injuries (McDonald 1988: 252). It was a common phrase in the First World War that someone who had '*gone west*' had died (Owen 1983). It is clearly a euphemism for those processes attendant upon mortality which the previous quotation demonstrates. Interestingly, it comes from the direction in which prisoners coming from either the Tower or Newgate Prison would travel on their way to the 270 acres of rough ground bisected by the Ti bourne (or little stream). About 50,000 people died at Tyburn and the majority of them went west by being dragged the three miles or so on a 'hurdle' or sledge.

159

What we are asked to do in this part of Pandemonium is to look at the 'impression management' undertaken by large bureaucratic organizations and see these attempts at visual communication as reflective of an ecstatic outgrowth of videocy under postmodernism. Moreover, in this part of the tour it will be demonstrated that much of the source for visual imagery in the 1990s appears to be influenced, to a greater or lesser extent, by Social Realism and neo-Fascist art. Photographs and publicity material reveal that these 'New Right' ideas have taken root in the corporate world of the West. If we live 'in the empire of the gaze', the surveillance that we undertake and that is undertaken of us is less free than we might have expected. The hall of mirrors traps us in a particularly unhappy epoch in world history.

The importance of impression management to theatrical performance is well recognized (Sudjic 1994: 12–13), Sudjic argues that the exhibitionistic design of sets can be a key factor in getting audiences to come through the door. Sometimes it can replace content almost entirely (as in, for example, *Starlight Express*). Often this alienates the performers who obviously prefer to see themselves as occupying a greater position of importance than the setting. Yet theatrical design and architecture are ultimately linked. Inigo Jones began his career as a designer of court masques and John Nash was also initially a theatrical designer. The Bauhaus too was active in the theatre. Today, says Sudjic, architecture impacts much more on the theatre than vice versa.

CHAPTER 9   *Sixth Exhibit: The Hall of Mirrors*

A horse and cart were used to ensure the victims arrived at Tyburn alive and thus did not disappoint the awaiting crowds. If one had 'gone west', therefore, it was to a place of execution and inevitable death (Abbott 1993: 196).

The importance of the gibbet is that it is visible from miles around. It is no use having a spectacle that people could ignore or avoid or from which they could avert their eyes. The gibbet, to be successful, had to be placed in a position in which every passer-by, every member of the populace who looked up in their everyday lives would see the inevitable – a victim of the state. In Transylvania, Vlad the Impaler recognized the necessity of the state making an exhibition of the perpetrators of misdemeanours. One day he came across a man whose shirt was unclean and unkempt. The monarch asked of the man if he were married and on learning that he was proceeded to give the order that his wife should be flayed and then impaled upon a pike for failing to look after the appearance of someone who had come into the sight of the great and terrible Vlad. About 10 per cent of the state's population were impaled in this period and each of the victims was left there, usually outside his castle, as a spectacle to encourage the rest. The terrible sight that the populace had to behold and appreciate was intended to frighten and subdue a people who were thought to be recalcitrant.

Not only were the poor and powerless impaled in the land beyond the woods. The wealthy, the educated and the powerful all felt the spear invade their body cavities. And burial was not permitted. For this punishment of the soul was seen as even worse than the physical pain which the body was forced to endure. Display of your body took place until the flesh had fallen from your bones and the carrion had had their fill. And all in sight of your loved ones and your supporters.

Gallows were typical of many European towns in the medieval period and beyond. There is a story of a sailor being shipwrecked around 1600. On being washed up on a strange beach he looked up and saw some gallows and promptly fell on his knees to thank God that he was in a Christian country. Over 72,000 people were hanged in the reign of Henry VIII alone, so gallows were not ornamental devices. As Foucault has shown us, these societies were controlled by 'the spectacle' – the constant, almost random violence directed in a harsh, visually arresting way to encourage others to desist from the activities for which the elements of the spectacle had been invoked.

In the sixteenth century there was a beggar's prayer: 'From Hull, Hell and Halifax, Good Lord deliver us.' The middle location is self-evident. Hull was feared as a place where beggars met with 'punitive charity', whereas Halifax was infamous for its gibbet (Abbott 1993: 216–18). The word 'gibbet' here is a misnomer, for a gibbet is a structure from which the body of a hanged individual was suspended until the flesh rotted from the bones. This was usually sited at a public crossroads. The University of Warwick, a centre in some areas of disciplinary excellence, stands upon Gibbet Hill Road in the medieval city of Coventry and close to such a site (Foucault 1977b). The Halifax gibbet, however, was a beheading machine of a unique kind. But it was deemed better to use a word non-locals would have heard of, rather than to invent another which would not frighten outsiders. The Halifax gibbet claimed many lives but was most active in the period 1589–1623 (Abbott 1993: 218).

161

Central to this agenda is *videocy* or the language of the visual. It displaces older, more established discourses based on orality and the print media. It introduces new media logics and media formats (Altheide 1977) which restructure the relationship between the 'real' and 'the person'. As will be shown, the concept of *virtual reality* is very important here because this is a new technology of representation in which the 'real' disappears, to be replaced by a computer-generated simulation of what the real is supposed to look like. Baudrillard, for example, argues that these new technologies turn human life into a theatrical spectacle where it is not clear who is the observer and who is actor. Noel Edmonds's TV programme contains, as we have seen, a slot in which viewers watching the television in the privacy and comfort of their own home suddenly become viewed by the audience. The videocy here reflects the breakdown of traditional doctrines such as observer/observed, participant/onlooker and sight/reflection. This creates an ecstasy of communication (Baudrillard 1989).

CHAPTER 9   *Sixth Exhibit: The Hall of Mirrors*

→ Almost any discussion of death, discipline and punishment has to include the execution of the regicide Damiens in 1757 so vividly outlined by Michael Foucault in *Discipline and Punish*. What Foucault does is to give the sentence of the court on 26 March which is almost unique in its sheer savagery. What he does not do is to describe the 'real' events of that day. Damiens was subject to 'questions ordinaires et extraordinaires' to make him confess the names of his accomplices. The house in which he was born was to be demolished on that day and no other building or monument ever erected on the spot. His legs were forced into the dreaded boots, in which wedges were driven for three quarters of an hour, splintering leg bones and tearing his flesh. Everything went wrong as one of the torturers, Monsieur Soubise, detailed to obtain the necessary lead, sulphur, wax and resin, became too drunk to buy the commodities and the wood for the fire was too damp to ignite. Responsibility was handed over to Charles-Henri Sanson, at that time 18 years old. He was later to achieve his career-best figures at the height of the Terror in executing 2,831 aristocrats in the 26 months from April 1793 to July 1795. Sanson sent his assistants to the shops, while Damiens sat around on the scaffold waiting for the next part of the ordeal to begin.

162

DO NOT CROSS THE CENTRAL RESERVATION

Hoy 1987; Best and Kellner 1991). He points to a line of thought from Nietzsche through Heidegger to Derrida.

A romantic nostalgia for the past, an authoritarian populism and the rise in popularity of televised religion were all part of the New Right's agenda. It seized control of popular culture by placing *on* the agenda the body, the family and patriotic individuality, and by taking *off* the agenda both civil and human rights (Denzin 1991: 6).

CHAPTER 9   *Sixth Exhibit: The Hall of Mirrors*

Casanova, the Italian of some notoriety, was a witness to the whole scene. He wrote in his memoirs:

> I watched the dreadful scene for four hours but was several times obliged to turn my face away and to close my ears as I heard his piercing shrieks, half his body having been torn away from him. (quoted in Abbott 1993: 187–9)

The links between rationality and death are very strong. As Foucault shows, the rationale of 'the spectacle' and the obvious, cruel and violent end to which many found guilty of anti-statist activities were put was seen as a means–end form of rationality. In the absence of self-discipline and self-control, order imposed from without upon the body of the populace – often in the form of individual bodies within it – was seen as both possible and desirable. 'Pour encourager les autres' is a dictum used when death is deemed necessary because there is little else to be done to discourage the others.

Mousnier (1965: 103–4) has argued that the seventeenth century witnessed a 'great crisis of ideas and feeling, a revolution in the manner of thinking and of understanding the universe, almost an intellectual mutation took place at that time in Europe. It marks the end of Aristotelianism, the triumph of quantitative rationalism, of the notion of mathematical function, of experimental rationalism, with Descartes,

163

'Surely,' you say, 'we've left Pandemonium and are in Manhattan, Docklands, Frankfurt am Main, La Défense . . . somewhere which is not diabolical. We've surfaced.'

Your guide reminds you there is still a long way back to the Exit of Pandemonium. All you see before you is postmodern superficiality. The edifices are insubstantial monuments to a 'culture' of visual immediacy. Postmodernism can be viewed favourably by those on the political Left who see it as a breakout from notions of 'High Culture' and the domination of human creativity by the bourgeoisie and its values. Postmodernism may well be celebrated by the Left for allowing cultural pluralism. On the other hand, postmodernism may be seen as a reflection of bourgeois values and allowing the further development of Far Right political belief and practices. Here postmodernism can be perceived as allowing neo-Fascism in some rather alarming forms to be viewed with sympathy. For if liberal democratic values and rationality are to be questioned and if history can be plundered for images and concepts, then why cannot the Holocaust be rediscovered and revitalized? This is a worry best expressed by Habermas, who sees the rejection of reason as opening up the possibility of seduction by anything that just happens to come along – like neo-Nazism (Habermas in

the Medianistes and Newton; it is present in the "Catholic Renaissance" and the mystical movement . . . in the growth of witchcraft.'

This quotation, despite the obvious point that its author does not have English as his first language, reveals the sympathy – not antipathy – between rationality and witchcraft. And we can witness this conjunction in an exceptionally clear form in the New England town of Salem as the seventeenth century draws to a close. The tension between rationality, witchcraft and death all surface around 1692 in this part of the American colonies.

Instrumental in this colonization of the Eastern Seaboard of the USA was the Royal Navy. The British navy in the seventeenth century had not reached the apogee of its dedication to the experimental rationalism of which Mousnier speaks. Nevertheless, both experimentation and mathematicization were developing apace. British naval ships in the late seventeenth century were comparable to those even of the Netherlands and were, in effect, the spacecraft of the day. They contained the most advanced forms of social and technological organization that their societies could conceptualize. It was possible for ordinary seaman, through the evidence of their exemplary seamanship, to rise to be captains – often by the age of 21. At a time when the average life expectancy of a landlubber in these parts of Europe was 35 and when seaman went to their ships at the age of 11 or 12, this becomes more understandable. Shipbuilding involved

164

You begin to sense a movement in the air which suggests the horrors of the exhibits are now behind you, for up ahead the electric lights are again visible. For hours, it has been murky and dusklike but in the distance it seems much lighter. You enter a bright area which looks like a waiting room for interviewees. Everywhere you look seems to be a mirrored reflection of itself. You are caught in a constant self-referencing of photons.

This part of Pandemonium is just like the central business district of a major Western city. Skyscrapers, brilliantly lit, tower above, representing corporate achievement, bureaucratic hierarchy and the extensive brains of the firm. Most of the buildings are 'postmodern' in design. You recognize this landscape. Architecturally, you may find them interesting. Or not. Before you lies what the 'modern' architect considers to be the high points of culture. Much money has been spent on the façades of the buildings. More dollars, yen and marks have been expended on their interiors. How the buildings are clad, masked and decorated tells you much about how the denizens of within will be clad, masked and decorated.

advanced engineering, the latest in materials technology, the most up-to-date navigational devices, a meritocratic structure (to some extent) within the context of a very dangerous occupation and the backing of merchant adventurers or the state who, because of the doctrine of mercantilism, usually saw economic benefit as the rationale for any activity.

Salem was full of British merchant vessels in the late seventeenth century. Indeed, since the draughts of these vessels were small it was later to become the major American port for trade with the British Isles. Thus within the harbour of Salem were the expressions – the exemplars – of marine rationality in an experimental form. Surely then, the witch trials that were about to take place were antithetical to such examples of applied rationality? Salem was founded in 1626 by Roger Conant, a pacifist who named the village after the Hebrew word for peace – Shalom. In 1692, several young women in the town, including a daughter of the Reverend Parris, had visions and convulsive fits. One view, originating within science, is that the wheat from which the villagers' bread was made was tainted with a fungal growth which produced LSD. Since women often ate together it is possible that one particular batch of bread contained enough acid to produce this collective effect. We must note, however, that LSD conceptualization of the disappearance of the crew of the *Marie Celeste* has also been given credence and it becomes a useful, indeed highly convenient

$\longrightarrow$

$\longleftarrow$

We have left behind us the five exhibits which form the core of Pandemonium and in moving from Panopticon City into the area of the pillory it has been drawn to our attention that 'appearance' and the 'spectacle' are crucial in the empire of the gaze. Our everyday presence is demanded by large organizations – if we are fortunate enough to enjoy employment. We have to be seen to be there, at work and to be giving our hearts and minds in the pursuit of corporate goals. On the other hand, the narcissistic infatuation with self, with what is seen in the mirror, with the image and not the substance, places great emphasis on the visual features of the individual and how these might be controlled.

As we begin to leave this part of Pandemonium a harsh sign says FROM NOW ON EVERYTHING'S AN EXHIBIT.

CHAPTER 9   *Sixth Exhibit: The Hall of Mirrors*

way of explaining unusual human behaviour. But in Salem, the young women did not 'fly' overboard chasing the moon: they accused many middle-aged women in the village of tormenting them. A doctor was summoned and concluded that they were victims of witchcraft.

Governor Sir William Phipps, on arrival in Boston from London, immediately set up a special court to listen to the testimony through-out the spring and summer of 1692. Events moved on at a pace. More than 200 people were accused of witchcraft, 150 were imprisoned in Salem jail and 19 villagers were condemned to death by hanging. One elderly farmer was 'pressed' to death for not recognizing the legitimacy of the court to interrogate him. A wooden door was placed on his chest and stones placed on it in order to crush him. It took him three days to die and towards the end, having protruded from his mouth, his blackened tongue was forced back into place by the sheriff's cane. Most infamously however, Bridget Bishop, a 53-year-old 'hotelier', was executed for having about her body the classic signs of a female witch. She had red hair, she possessed a third nipple with which to feed her familiar but this signal mark disappeared from one medical examination to another; she told lies, her neighbour lost a sixpence having just seen her on the road, neighbours' children developed speech impediments and lameness after her presence near them and so on.

How can this be rational in a port where leading examples of rationality supposedly lay moored in the harbour? Well it *is* rational, of course, when seen within the context of late seventeenth-century thought. It is *wertrational*. Moreover, it is *zweckrational* when one considers that the

166

CHAPTER 9

Sixth   Exhibit:
The   Hall   of   Mirrors

all access was thronged, the Gates
and Porches wide, but chief the spacious Hall

(Milton, *Paradise Lost*, Bk I, ll. 761–2)

jury 'knew' the following to be true. Witches exist and it is not possible to tell a lie if you value your external soul; thus any liar must not value their soul and must be possessed, therefore of a demonic influence. However, most importantly, it is *spectral* evidence which is seen as quite acceptable and rational, that plays the key role here. Spectral evidence is admissible when someone who is God-fearing has seen a spirit or shape undertake some activity. Alibis are therefore useless for even if everyone in the local tavern clearly saw and even talked to someone there at midnight this did not show incontrovertibly that this person's *spectre* was not elsewhere undertaking diabolical tasks. Since 'spirit' and body are separable if the individual *wished* them to be so, the mere physical evidence of an alibi was not enough. Spectres walked around at night within the port of Salem and it was these sightings that formed the bulk of the evidence upon which nineteen people were executed.

This is 'rational' in the same way as physical evidence today within forensic science is seen as 'rational'. Fingerprinting, retinal patterns and genetic 'fingerprinting' are supposed to be 'unique' in a meaningful statistical way but for many generations it was believed that upon the retina of a murdered person would be found a picture of the murderer since this would be the final image seen there. Similarly fingerprinting, genetic comparisons and retinal patterns all require 'expert' interpretations of incomplete data. Forensic evidence in the case of the Guildford Four and the Birmingham Six, for example, turned out to be quite 'spectral', yet were believed in a late twentieth-century court.

167

paramount reality? Clearly the notion that the universities still represent ivory towers is part of the idea that the institution itself is a flight from reality. But those who articulate such a viewpoint have not been near a university in the British Isles for a decade and a half. The alienation of the academic from the institution is gathering apace; staff feel as if they are victims and fear that they too will 'go west'. With these sorts of feelings will come more and more efforts at escape.

In so doing, of course, academics and managers will be severely pilloried by their hierarchical superiors. Escape attempts are not welcomed in the present situation for there are clear signs that socio-economic forces at the organizational level have created a group of employed who are prone to more and more pressure to attend work and increase their hours and a groups of contracted workers who are in work part-time. Outside of this are the 'dispossessed': those marginalized from the labour force and excluded from paid employment. Each of these groups is punished. Each of them has things to confess. Each of them has been subject to a lambasting. Each has suffered violence of the tongue.

CHAPTER 8   *Fifth Exhibit: The Pillory*

The Salem witch episode came to an end when the urban and urbane Sir William Phipps found his own wife had been accused of witchcraft. Very quickly indeed, spectral evidence was said to be inadmissible in any future trials and they were forthwith discontinued. But it would be foolish to think that the sophisticates of Boston saw rustic madness as having overstepped the mark. For the seafarers in Boston and Salem harbours, for all their scientific rationality, saw spectral apparitions all the time. St Elmo's fire, sea monsters, mermaids, sirens, krakens all abounded in the North Atlantic. Tall men in low gangways continually cracked their heads (Forester 1952). And everyone knew from their infancy that the Devil existed, that witches celebrated his earthly existence and that, thankfully, techniques developed during the Inquisition could reveal them in their diabolical awfulness.

And perhaps they were right. To understand how witchcraft survives, perhaps, we might assume that witches need to be executed. To understand terrorism's attraction, perhaps, we should understand that terrorists need to be executed. They exist in and through their death. They do encourage the others.

168

Surrealist violence;
Surrealist disruption;
trips to the edge;
dice throwing;
Eastern mysticism;
madness;
sensory deprivation;
beastliness (e.g. Crowley, Rasputin);
mass murder;
Stirnerism (anarchistic individualism);
sabotage;
the Quest (e.g. Siddhartha and Sir Gawain).

Their descriptions begin with 'distancing' in terms of the role adopted by the individual and goes on to discuss sex, drugs and not quite rock and roll. It is important to note that some of these attempts involve a submergence in paramount reality and as such are highly individualistic and have little capacity for changing the social fabric. But others would necessitate a transformation of the society from the paramount reality into something fundamentally different. Within the ranks of middle management escape attempts may take the form of organized revolt, but this seems unlikely (Scarbrough and Burrell 1996). And what of the universities as representing the high points of modernity and the modern world? Are we replete with escape attempts from

CHAPTER 5

Second Exhibit: Pain and Disease

this dark and dismal house of pain

(Milton, *Paradise Lost*,
Bk II, l. 823)

→

←

'My friends,' says the author bringing an end to the smells, 'Stan Cohen and Laurie Taylor, in their seminal work, *Escape Attempts* (1975) attempt to deal with escape attempts from 'paramount reality'. They describe the following:

distancing – detached, ironical cynicism and self-awareness;
novelty – new experiences (changing towns, partners, jobs);
role reversals – identity transformations;
fantasizing – daydreaming (e.g. Walter Mitty);
hobbies: a special room at the bottom of the garden;
games;
gambling;
sex – masturbation/'straight' sex;
holidays;
movies, TV and art 'escapism';
drugs – including alcohol;
therapy (e.g. psychoanalysis, T. groups, feelie groups, etc.);
communes;
obsessive behaviour;

CHAPTER 5   *Second Exhibit: Pain and Disease*

→ As I write this page, my second bout of gout has me doubled up in pain. The first took place some four years ago and some anti-inflammatory drugs worked the trick. It is a Sunday and my doctor's appointment is for tomorrow. Until 9 a.m. tomorrow all that is available is aspirin. God knows what the experience of gout was in the seventeenth and eighteenth centuries but if it was worse than this then I do not know how they handled it. This chapter was not meant to be written from 'within' pain but it seemed too good an opportunity to miss, to experience the agony – for this it how it feels and there is no attempt being made here at hyperbole – and write at the same time.

It does not work very well because all my efforts are upon keeping my left foot pressed firmly to the floor, for this is when the pain eases off, and are not directed towards the creative task of communicating pain. If writers such as novelists require distress in order to enrich their writing then it can only be from within a modicum of pain. The agonizing stuff doesn't allow you time, nor energy, nor inclination to be creative. You are too busy trying to control 'it' – the messages from nerves, tissues and flesh saying 'something's wrong, something's wrong' – to choose words and phrases as carefully as you might.

170

However, there are other alternative realities which it is possible to escape into, which offer places and times which are free of the everyday constraints of paramount reality. To access these alternative realities one can seek, as a manager or not, access which is merely a momentary slip through the fabric of the space-time continuum or a life within this alternative reality which is permanent. However, these possibilities pale into insignificance when seen against the huge growth in the supply of situations aimed at 'enclaving a free area of activity' where within paramount reality it is believed that a free area or enclave exists where it would be possible for individuals to find some escape from the rigours of the bureaucratic prison in which they find themselves. In other words, escape attempts for managers and the population as a whole become packaged and subject to bureaucratization. They are not real escape attempts, but are ones which are sanctioned, encouraged and even profited from by the owners of large organizations.

And out of the gloom suddenly you are assailed by a heady mixture of aromas. A glimmer of bright sunlight offers a welcome way out from the Pillory.

←

CHAPTER 8   *Fifth Exhibit: The Pillory*

Of course, you bloody well know that 'something's wrong' so the warning function of the central nervous system has been served. Why the hell does it need to keep sending the same signal? I know only too well that crystals of uric acid are embedded in the joint of my left big toe and this represents the classic symptoms of gout. I know that. But that knowledge doesn't control the inflammation. Thus this chapter of *Pandemonium* begins – and no artistic licence is being invoked here – in real agony. I hope, with all my heart, it will be better tomorrow. But the next section was written weeks ago.

'Pain is never the sole creation of our anatomy and physiology' (Bendelow and Williams 1995: 83). Rather, it emerges at the intersection of bodies, minds and cultures. Descartes, however, in 1664, saw pain in a straightforward kind of way as the result of receptors in the skin conveying messages to the brain. Mind is thus dichotomized from body and the treatment of pain is medicalized. As Leder (1984: 262) has said, 'whereas in day to day events we are our body without hesitation, suddenly pain renders the body disharmonious with the self'. This, at least partially, explains the tendency of those who are in pain to write about the body, because for them it is problematized. Indeed the very meaning of pain may be to negate meaning itself. Pain unmakes our world of habit and provides no means for organizing our experience. Scarry (1985) suggests that torture is a mimed attempt to recreate the horror of war and to imitate death for the victim. The individual is depersonalized. But in this context it is important to note that these forms of inflicting pain are supposedly highly gendered (Grosz 1994).

> *After death, the heart assumes
> the shape of a pyramid*

Escape attempts in middle management are probably very little different from those in the rest of the population. If managers come to accept that they live in an alienated world characterized by technocratic distortion then the question becomes one of how authenticity is to be achieved. Thus, within the West at least, there has been the growth in forms of escape from this paramount reality. In the framework provided by Cohen and Taylor (1993), 'paramount reality' is that reality which is governed by pragmatic concerns for organizational functioning, for individual career and for confronting a world in which predictability, economic progress and understandability predominate.

CHAPTER 8   *Fifth Exhibit: The Pillory*

→ Pain is measured in dols and the highest possible rating for some reason is 10.5. How something as subjective as pain can be recorded and measured objectively remains a mystery but it appears that childbirth approaches the highest levels of measurable pain in some cases. Here is Suzanne Arms (1975: 279) describing the feelings that engulf many women when they are about to give birth:

> At this point the woman, nearly sapped of energy, must rally her reserves to begin pushing the baby out, yet she is now confronted with contractions even more violent than before, coming so hard and fast that they seem to meld together in successive waves, culminating in a shattering explosion that overwhelms her entire body. . . . Suddenly nauseous and chilled to the bone, the woman turns to the nearest figure of authority with beseeching eyes and a look on her face that no one who has ever attended a delivery will forget.

But during pregnancy the entire pelvic area increases in vascularity, which greatly increases the capacity and intensity of orgasms because of the increased responsiveness of the clitoris and the strengthening of the relevant muscles (Rich 1977: 183). The links between pain and pleasure through the medium of ecstasy are very unclear but obviously such links are to be found. For at a physiological level the stimulation of nerve endings can lead to sensations of pain and/or pleasure and sometimes they are very difficult to separate out in consciousness.

172

Maybe the best description of where we are heading from a products standpoint came from a speech given by a professor from the University of Miami in 1989 to the International Airline Pilots Association describing the aircraft of the year 2005. He said the crew would consist of one pilot and one dog, the pilot's role being to feed and nurture the dog. The dog's role would be to bite the pilot if he tried to touch anything.

Is this what we have come to, then – the surveillance of intelligent skilled human beings by electronic toilets and vicious dogs? But the information human beings use is much more valuable than many organizational collections of humanity grouped in large firms. The *Official Airline Guide* which contains data on airline schedules is valued more highly than many airlines represented within it. In 1989 the *TV Guide* in the US was worth $3 billion, which made it more valuable than the companies who made the programmes it contained (Peters 1990: 5).

So is delayering and information technology (IT) displacing whole firms, and all middle managers in all firms? Dopson and Stewart (1990) think not but the consultants apparently do. In the face of this sort of pressure (Scase and Goffee 1989) many middle managers begin ← to contemplate escape.

When Kafka did record happiness in his diaries – and these occasions were very rare – he speaks of transforming torture into bliss. The entry for the night of 2 November 1911, for example, is the very famous:

> This morning, for the first time in a long time, the joy again of imagining a knife twisted in my heart. (Kafka 1948)

In Greek mythology such tortures were part of the lexicon of understanding what it was to be a god. Their tortures were on a larger scale than the normal everyday ones faced by mere mortals. Tantalus for example was a king who was punished in Hades by the sight of inaccessible water and fruit. The Procrustean bed was made to fit by the stretching or lopping of its victims. For Kafka, however, even the legend of Prometheus was not enough. He wrote:

> 'everyone grew weary of the meaningless affair. The Gods grew weary, the eagles grew weary, the wound closed wearily.' (Kafka 1948)

There is a sense here, as there is in Nietzsche, that the greatest torture in life is Life itself. The most terrifying idea is meaningless and goalless existence, 'without a finale into nothingness'. But, and this is an important but, for Nietzsche there are Dionysian raptures to be enjoyed from accepting the tragedy of meaninglessness! Out of human pain comes pleasure, and out of pleasure comes pain (Featherstone et al. 1991).

173

you are a middle manager, whether you are chief executive officer, is if you look at that number and think it is amusing, you do not understand what is going on around you.

A great believer in the notion of the age of information technology, Peters also claims that the new advances will bring about shifts in what we regard as expert fields and what we regard expertise as being legitimately about. One example of each is to be found in this extract from his (1990) speech.

> In a catalogue that comes from the Toilet Bowl Division of American Standard there is a picture of American Standard's top of the line, $36,000, 'Smart' bathtub. In Japan, 10 percent of the toilets are now 'Smart' toilets, and they are now heading for 'Smart Smart' toilets.
> The new toilets in Japan take all of a person's vital signs, blood pressure and so on, and electronically transmit them directly to one's doctor. A toilet is not a toilet.

CHAPTER 8   *Fifth Exhibit: The Pillory*

→   In Central London there is a performer who does the following things for a living. He swallows razor blades and regurgitates them. His partner throws darts into his back, he escapes out of strait-jackets by dislocating his arms from their sockets. He allows people to stand on his head while his face is buried in broken beer bottles. Business in the mid-1990s is booming. His 'Jim Rose Circus Sideshow' has appeared on a TV programme called *The Word* in which he is celebrated as an example of 'grunge culture'. His colleagues in this circus eat slugs and worms and crickets. They ingest a mixture of beer, chocolate sauce and ketchup through the nose and regurgitate it. They skewer their nipples with kebab implements and lift breeze blocks with them. The Amazing Mr Lifto swings suitcases with his tongue. The tongue, of course has to be pierced with a lifting hook in order for this to work. Household irons are suspended from his nipples – also tastefully pierced. He swings large household objects from a hook attached to his foreskin, malformed as a result of an unsuccessful circumcision. The lead act is 'The Torture King'. He begins by sticking a long hatpin through both cheeks. His cheeks stick out like elasticated rubber before the skewer appears. He places one hand in the sparks of an electric generator and lights a neon tube on his head. The show lasts for two hours and con- sists solely of this type of performance.

174

The trouble is that the corporate world is run by people not exactly bust- ing keen to lose their parking lots, let alone to subject themselves to monthly scrutiny by people whom, currently, they can hire and fire. Even corporate turkeys don't vote for Christmas.

And this is the issue. Middle management are now perceived to be cor- porate turkeys; anti-democratic, anti-change and ripe for culling.

And speaking of prophets, Tom Peters (1990: 1) has also put a gloss on this issue. He claims that a radical restructuring of corporate staff will be necessary whether the firm is British or German or Swiss or Swedish or American. 'It is that bad.'

When I was here in May, I came across a short newspaper article that reported on a speech by the Chief Executive Officer of Asea Brown Boveri. With no headline on the article, with no major story involved, he commented that during that first year of Asea's owning Brown Boveri they had managed to modestly trim the corporate staff of Brown Boveri back from its prior 4000 people down to 100. Now some of you snicker when I say that, some of you weep. Some of you become ill at your stom- ach. All three responses are appropriate. My simple comment, whether

←

CHAPTER 8   *Fifth Exhibit: The Pillory*

The cast in the 'Show' take the usual fainting in the audience as a sign of a good performance – the equivalent, they say, of a standing ovation. They see that what they are doing is the same as the old circus sideshows in the nineteenth century in that they offer up to the audience the curiosity of the body.

Tony Bennett in *The Birth of the Museum* (1995) maintains that the twin forms of entertainment in the nineteenth century, the museum and the fair, gave way to the exhibition which was a composite form of both. He argues that

> the activities of fairs, museums and exhibitions interacted with one another: the founding collections of many of today's major metropolitan museums were bequeathed by international exhibitions; techniques of crowd control developed in exhibitions influenced the design and layout of amusement parks; and nineteenth-century natural history museums throughout Europe and North America owed many of their specimens to the network of animal collecting agencies through which P.T. Barnum provided live species for his various circuses, menageries and dime museums. (Bennett 1995: 5)

Prior to this, the exhibition complex had often taken the form of 'the cabinet of curiosities' in which the bodies of the deformed, the bearded lady, the giant and the dwarf were presented alongside skeletons of the same, with the intention of presenting 'small and ugly creatures' juxtaposed with 'showy ones'. Thus the sideshow exhibited the bodies of the grotesque in order to make money. Just as today, using normal

Memos are confined to one page. Semler does not have a desk and there is no receptionist. He 'empowers' his employees. Semler argues that modern times are over and the problem of what is happening to the giant corporations of the present century such as IBM has *no* solution. Because, it is said, this is an historical process coming to an end. To democratize the organization Semler has shed seven layers of management. This has created, he says, an end to autocracy, for each manager is assessed by the workforce anonymously on a scale of 0 to 100. Scores around 50 are not good enough. Elections of managers is to come next, as is self-setting of salaries. The pyramidal structure has gone, to be replaced by three concentric circles. And 'the books' are open to everyone. Clearly then, knowledge and skills are seen as residing throughout the 200-person organization and not just in senior management. Managers hired for their abilities to command, organize and lead will find themselves facing a workforce who are now asked to command, organize and lead themselves. As Keegan (1993: 13) says

CHAPTER 8   *Fifth Exhibit: The Pillory*

bodies, but in grotesque ways, the Rose circus fuses fairground with performance with exhibition.

Because everybody (*sic*) has to live in one, the abnormal manipulation of the normal body raises some important issues for us all – even if we were to faint in a Rose circus performance. In his defence, Rose even quotes William Blake, who said 'the road to excess leads to the palace of wisdom'.

But whilst these perpetrators of grunge culture may have some philosophical backing it is difficult to see why *The Word* would advertise for members of the public who were seeking fame for 15 minutes by defiling their bodies in some deliberately nauseous way to appear in front of camera. The programme had one offer from someone who wished to suck out the contents of a tramp's nostrils, but refused to stage it on the grounds that they could not guarantee that the contents of the said nasal cavity would be sterile. Indeed. At least Rose and his troupe are not seeking to disgust but to remind.

In *Wild Swans* (Chang 1991) there is a description of another form of human pain which is also for show and profit.

176

However, the concept of experience has made its appearance here, yet again. Is this feminization of the service class not another reminder of the expertise which senior management define as being necessary to the organization being lost then re-found by hiring it in? Despite Calas and Smircich's justifiedly suspicious approach to this new 'expertise' being sought and encouraged, might we not wish to argue that expertise of unusual kinds will always empower its possessor? If so, the wave of relayering now going on describes *new* expertise being defined as crucial to organization for its survival. Of course, the organizational superordinates are defining, ordering and monitoring this expertise. Nevertheless it demonstrates the point that 'new' expertise will always be identified and sought after. The organization can never control all the forms of expertise it defines as essential. Indeed, there is a sense in which when the organization already possesses knowledge this will *not* be defined as expertise to anything like the same degree as knowledge it does not possess. Prophets are not recognized in their own land. Well, not always. Ricardo Semler, a Brazilian, has attempted to impact upon the Anglophone world through his book *Maverick* (1993). The story supposedly is that 'Mr Semler is turning the world of work upside down' (*Guardian*, 28 September 1993: 2, 3). Expertise is recognized to exist throughout the organization in São Paulo: employees reorganize their factories, central computers have been dispensed with, so too have filing cabinets.

CHAPTER 8   *Fifth Exhibit: The Pillory*

In China, the author's grandmother had her feet bound from the age of two in ways which were designed to give her the gift of 'golden lilies'. These were feet which would be no longer than four inches. Her mother refused to loosen the bound feet for she knew her daughter would never forgive her if she was to relent. Families, in the Mandarin category at least, would inspect new brides who had entered their family and if the feet were longer than four inches the bride would be ostracized and shunned by her new family. The shame was such that mothers knew that no respite could be offered. The description offered by Jung Chang of her grandmother's feet is absolutely horrific:

> she would set about cutting off pieces of dead skin. The pain came not only from the broken bones, but also from her toenails, which grew into the balls of her feet. (Chang 1991: 32).

Yet how is this different from the self-inflicted distortions of the body done for paid entertainment as described above? The not uncommon fetishistic connotations of feet are also relevant here.

The *Annalistes* tradition of social history writing in France has been keen to show how the body – particularly it has to be said of the lower orders – becomes the victim of social forces. The vantage point of this type of history is those who 'struggled in a prison with their brother the rat, their guest the flea and their enemy the plague'.

177

super-information highway the concern is about encouraging the bringing into being of large multinational companies (and networks thereof) rather than how these mega-organizations will be managed on a day to day basis. But once the networks are firmly established the emphasis will not be upon the 'empowered' managers playing a role in a 'decentralized' system. It will be upon a centralized schematization in which one or two global players do as much as possible to circumvent the power of their own lower-order staff. The lessons of May 1968 still live on.

As Calas and Smircich (1991) have shown, the globalization process, in so far as it affects management, has moved the focus of power from the senior management of some newly delayered companies to a very small number of headquarters staff located in some 'transnational' space. At the Seville Expo of 1992, for example, Coca-Cola refused to base themselves in the USA building. They went instead into the 'World Trade Building'. The gap left in these multi-internationals by successive waves of delayering has been filled by a high proportion of women who are stereotypically skilled in 'healing the wound' left by delayering. Thus the decline in the service class is further evidenced, in some eyes, by its feminization (Calas and Smircich 1991).

CHAPTER 8   *Fifth Exhibit: The Pillory*

The Inquisition developed the art of torture of the human body in ways which now seem barbaric, in order to make witches confess. Witches were said to convey their evil intention with a potent but invisible emanation from their eyes. The victim, almost always male, was said to have been 'fascinated' or 'overlooked' by the witch, almost always female. Helene Hirsch, in *Schindler's Ark* (Keneally 1982) is accused by Amon Goeth, the camp commandant, of being 'fascinating' in exactly the same way. Aristotle, centuries before, said that the glance of a menstruating woman would tarnish a mirror. Thus, there was little that was new about this misogyny – except in the Middle Ages in Europe the new factor was that the witch was assumed to have made a pact with the Devil. Consequently, witches were punished not for their acts and the damage it did to others but for 'devil-worship' (Thomas 1978: 521).

178

Through this modernizing movement, language (words and sentences) comes to be subject to very detailed analysis. It is unpicked, phoneme by phoneme, and subject to ever closer scrutiny for its true meaning, which resides within the author's intentions. In the business school world, the appeal is to 'the educated ear' of the lecture hall's audience but what speakers are finding is that the organizational reality outside has changed. The business students of the mid-1990s face a world in which they are not going to be perceived as heroic figures but as subjects who are problematic and flawed. Rationality, regularity, science and technology, calculability and predictability – the predicates of the modernist project – did not foresee the onset of 'the world we have lost' and the 'end of organized capitalism'.

Management in retreat

Compared to its high-water mark of the late 1980s management is now in retreat everywhere. In the West it faces delayering, downsizing, automation and besmirching. In Japan, it faces the breakdown of 'the jobs for life' period in *kereitsu* growth as mobility of an inter-company kind becomes conceivable for the first time in a long time for the service class member. In Eastern Europe and Russia, kleptocracy has replaced the service classes' major support system in bureaucracy.

For global capital, the managerial knowledge worker seen just five years ago as the *support* of the world system of economic activity is under threat as *the* problem of the global system. In discussions of the

This new concept was introduced by the Roman Catholic Church, whose intellectuals built up an extensive demonology culminating in the Papal Bull of 1484. The legend of Theophilus, the monk who transferred his allegiance from God to Satan, was well known and led to the Faustian tradition. But the Bull related only to Germany and by 1520, thirteen editions had been printed. In England, it was only in the late Elizabethan period that Protestants embraced such notions. From 1584 continental versions of witchcraft were widely known in English translation, but the predominant view was that it was an activity (hence a craft) and not an heretical belief. There is little mention in trials of the period of the witches' sabbat, of sexual assaults by incubus and succubus, of flying witches and of a reliance on the broomstick. On the continent of Europe, however, these elements were much more common (Thomas 1978: 529).

179

Featherstone is also very keen to build upon Stallybrass and White's (1986) discussion of carnivals, festivals and fairs. In Featherstone's discussion, the carnival and the fair are not fully distinguished. Both are seen as the locus of fattening food, intoxicating drink and sexual promiscuity. But the fair was a *local market* as well as a site of pleasure where 'spectacular imagery, bizarre juxtapositions, confusions of boundaries and an immersion in a mêlée of strange sounds, motions, images, people, animals and things' (Featherstone 1991: 23) met the eye of observer and participant.

Fourth, modernism relies upon linearity in space, linearity in time and linearity in thought. For example, the architectural modernist, Le Corbusier saw the straight line as much superior to the curve. Linearity invades all aspects of the university's self-conception. Essays, theses, examination answers and reports must tell a story, with some development of narrative discernible within them. Argumentation is deemed to be incremental, building up to a conclusion which all must accept if it is sufficiently clear in its argument and expression. Differentiation of fact from value, the sacred from the secular, the ethical from the theoretical, is central to the intellectual movements generated within modernism. Out of these dichotomies comes the appearance of value neutrality, of distanciation from the issues at hand, of a rejection of old theology and an embracing of the modern social sciences. Sawday's book on *The Emblazoned Body* (1995) shows in part how knowledge developed in this way from the anatomizing theatres of Leiden and Oxford.

CHAPTER 8   *Fifth Exhibit: The Pillory*

But in England, executions for witchcraft (whether in the form of devil-worship or in invoking the malfecium) occur for the first time in the 1580s when continental ideas entered England through the medium of the printing press. After 'the invention of printing, witchcraft stood revealed as the greatest crime of all' (Thomas 1978: 542).

Unlike on the continent, there were few commercial reasons for witchcraft to be developed in England. Indeed, trials were an expense some communities could not bear. Yet interest grew apace. What is important is the interest printers had in the scandalous, salacious and newsworthy events of the time (see Thomas 1978: Ch. 15, nn 59, 80) – particularly when patriarchal authority was challenged. Demonologists readily pronounced on the weaknesses of women and their greater susceptibility to satanic advances. Within the *Malleus Maleficarum*, a book which listed the ways in which one was to recognize witchcraft, there is a very strong anti-feminist element. Women were seen as sexually voracious – much more than men. Robert Burton in 1621 spoke of 'women's unnatural, unsatiable lust'.

In England the witches supposedly bore a mark on their body which was impervious to pain and did not bleed. Finding a witch thus involved finding a spot on her body which would not bleed and which did not hurt when pierced! Moreover, since witches had a 'familiar' who took an animal form, including wasp, fly or butterfly, witch-hunters merely had to imprison a woman and wait for some animal to come into her presence. This would be her familiar, by definition. The pain and suffering of the accused included torture, long interrogation and often execution by fire (see however Scarre 1987: 30).

But the techniques of the Inquisition are surely long past – unless one happens to see inside many coercive organizations in the contemporary epoch. Corbett (1994: 13–16) for example uses material from Greece during the reign of the Colonels to describe how torturers

180

required. The expenditure of huge amounts of time to learn how to use them 'correctly' and to spot those who cannot is necessary. Universities are replete with such 'positional' understandings. This has led, Featherstone opines, to a lowering in the barriers of what is termed 'culture' which threatens those university disciplines reliant upon defending High Culture.

CHAPTER 8   *Fifth Exhibit: The Pillory*

are socialized into their tasks. Recruits are introduced gently into the tasks of torturing other human beings. This is the sequence:

1. Recruits act as guards outside torture cell.
2. Recruits carry food into cell.
3. Recruits carry out a brief beating of prisoner.
4. Recruits supervise prisoners during prolonged standing.
5. Recruits participate fully in torture.

This sequencing of the induction process, alongside the many rewards for carrying out these activities for the state, creates a much less squeamish squad of torturers today. As Amnesty International can show, there are literally over 100 states who still use torture in carrying out state business whether in Northern Ireland or northern Iraq. No doubt such practices have also worked for millennia on countless human generations. The utilization of pain within a dolocracy is a form of government known to us all.

Consider Leopold von Sacher Masoch (1836–95). When he was 12, his father was Chief of Police in Prague. As a representative of the Austro-Hungarian Empire, Masoch's father had to suppress the Bohemian uprising in 'The Year of Revolutions'. A plot was discovered in which local women of 'birth' had invited the Austrian army officer corps to a huge ball in the city. At a given moment, marked at some point in the music of a particular dance, these women agreed to strangle each and every one of their partners on the dance floor. A wire

181

Velikovsky's predictions, based as they were on historical and mythological research, were much more accurate, and it was not long before a controversy developed in which his work was totally denigrated. The alternative views which Velikovsky articulated were deemed to be so threatening to the dominant disciplines that he was subjected to appalling professional attacks. Such stories are, perhaps, a natural outcome of modernism within university settings.

Second, the growth of bureaucracy in the modern university has put an end to the relatively Isocratic nature of these organizations. Now it is much more hierarchically organized with clear 'lines' of responsibility being outlined. The McUniversity has attempted to utilize 'management' rather than academic principles of organization (Parker and Jary 1995). Third, there is the tremendous pursuit by individuals within universities of *cultural capital*. High entry barriers into certain prestigious groupings mean that the maintenance of these entry barriers in relation to food, consumer products and high culture is

noose, in the form of a garrotte secreted in their ball gowns, was to be placed around the neck of the officer at the moment designated and the garrotting was to be carried out simultaneously. Here the orchestration of death was meant to strike a blow against the oppressors. Unfortunately, the plot was discovered and the necessary steps taken. Anyway, the officer corps was too busy suppressing the revolt to have attended. Thus, this collective act of murder by strong, vengeful women never took place. But upon the young Masoch's mind, this act of will against the representatives of a patriarchal empire made a great impression. Masoch became obsessed with 'The Heritage of Cain' and wrote a number of novels dealing with powerful women imposing themselves upon suffering men. The most well known of these was *Venus in Furs*. Yet by the end of his life he was placed forcibly into a psychiatric institution to die there at the age of 59. The connections to Nietzsche in time and disease, to Prague in space and to de Sade in (dialectical) thought make Leopold Masoch another figure of some interest. His response to revolutionary activity by the peasantry, artisans and aristocracy of a subservient nation was to see it as a sexual act giving pleasure to the submissive who had formerly been dominant. Power is given up briefly, orgasmically, lustfully but not permanently to the dominatrix. The thought of powerful, subordinate women dominating the armed militia of the empire in quasi-sexual encounters was enough for Masoch to begin to articulate a philosophy of his own which the world came to know as Masochism.

182

Power structures within social science shape the ways in which careers are managed. Those who bow not to discipline are marginalized. The work of Jerry Ravetz here is important (Ravetz 1972). He speaks of the ways in which 'shoddy science' can so easily develop as influential figures within disciplines gain control over publications, easier access to research funding, enhanced sponsorship of young researchers and, most fundamentally, achieve refereeing centrality. In such circumstances, it makes a nonsense to talk of peer assessment. The Velikovsky Controversy in the 1960s highlighted the lengths to which a group of disciplinary leaders would go in order to suppress the work of an outsider in their debates. Commenting on the characteristics of Venus, Velikovsky was totally at odds with conventional astrophysical beliefs. The first few attempts at landing on that planet suggested that 'normal science' view of its origins and composition were unable to withstand the test of predicting the results obtained. Such is shoddy science.

CHAPTER 8 *Fifth Exhibit: The Pillory*

According to Lingis (1989: 6), 'savages' do not belong to a society in the form of persons, individuals or juridic subjects but as organs attached to the full body of the earth. In New Guinea, the hunter-gather societies speak 700 mutually incomprehensible languages. They have no elected or hereditary chiefs. They engage in headhunting, not for the pursuit of politics by other means but so that, on one occasion only, each young man will seek out the bravest and most spectacular warrior on the field to kill and cannibalize his body. Thus is the spirit of the enemy interiorized. Men who kill more than once are regarded as twisted killers. 'Big Men' are deemed to be such by the power of their memories and their ability to tell stories – not by their military skills.

Yet savage societies are 'machines of cruelty' (Lingis 1989: 8). Initiation rites involve the cutting of bare flesh while everyone feasts their eyes upon it. Perforations, incisions, circumcisions and clitoridectomies are all very painful. They are meant to be. There is collective pleasure in the pain of others. Clearly there is also pleasure in the pain of the victim for the victim. The pain of those being initiated in savage societies can be heard, seen, felt by members of that grouping. It is meant to be. With the invention of writing and the coming of 'civilization', pain becomes distant. It can be inflicted by the stroke of a pen at a distance of 5,000 miles and the screams of the

183

We must, it says here in the confession, officer, support a counter-movement which has to be allowed to develop and reclaim the analytical right to use social sciences where they abut the humanities – come what may.

There is a hostility in the ranks of the management teachers towards philosophy and philosophical concerns. One can find this in Operational Research, Accounting, and in Organization Theory. In Industrial Relations it is found in its most virulent form. The lambast in this part of *Pandemonium* is directed against those who are blind to such concerns as much as it is directed against the pursuit of MBA-ism. It may well be, of course, that they are a product of the modern university. High modernism is found in those 'ivory' towers' where long-term inhabitants carry out the key tasks of research and discovery. They stand upon notions such as discipline, totalizing attempts, rationality and truth. They seek to defend innovation, novelty and dynamism (Berman 1982), which is what modernism has stood for since the Enlightenment. Modernism and its institutional expression in the university has created untold misery from this viewpoint.

tortured, however loud, will not travel that far. And we know well that, as Foucault (1977a: 4) says, we are unable to make the eye 'wince' as it moves through the body of the page. But within advanced, organized society with its emphasis on 'action at a distance', savagery is still with us, it is amongst us, it is in us, at our most intimate moments. Deleuze (Broadhurst 1992) in characteristically insightful phrases, claims that 'Both sadism and masochism imply that a quantity of libidinal energy be neutralised, desexualised, displaced and put at the service of Thanatos' (Deleuze 1989: 110) and that 'In sadism and masochism there is no mysterious link between pain and pleasure; the mystery lies in the desexualisation process' (ibid.: 120–1).

The desexualization of pain comes in sadism from acts of cruelty and in masochism from the act of waiting in suspense. And if we ask about the contemporary world, as compared to the worlds of de Sade and Masoch, we must conclude that sadism and masochism are very much with us today not only in our private lives but also publicly, often incarcerated within professional organizations. Listen here to Hunter Thompson (1972).

> 'Did you have fun?' asked the bell captain, as he opened the side door for me.
> 'Are you crazy?' I said. 'I have a serious deadline to meet. We've been at the tattoo parlour all night. It was the only way to do it.'
> 'What?' he said. 'You got yourself tattooed?'

184

DO NOT CROSS THE CENTRAL RESERVATION

What is difficult to overcome is the sense of a lack of intellectual base in the social sciences. The pressure to produce the right answers, to quantify intractable problems, to hand in good case analyses is winning out over the pressure to balance arguments, to develop critiques and to learn about ongoing debates. The direction in which many have moved has been towards quantitative, natural science attitudes and approaches with the comforting certainty this stance often engenders.

CHAPTER 8   *Fifth Exhibit: The Pillory*

'Oh! no,' I told him, 'Not me.'
I pointed to Maria . . . 'She's the one who got the tattoo' . . .
'What do you mean?' he said. 'You made that poor girl get tattooed? Just for a newspaper story?'
'It was the right thing to do,' I said. 'We had no choice. We are, after all, professionals.' (quoted in Blincoe 1992: 90)

Buck Ruxton (1899–1936) was also a professional. He was a medical doctor who practised in Lancaster in the 1930s. He was accused, convicted and executed for the particularly nasty murder of his wife and maid. The evidence against him centred upon pieces of a body that were found under a bridge in Cumberland wrapped in pages from a copy of the Lancaster *Guardian* – a newspaper with a rather limited and highly specific circulation. Whilst he was a popular and inexpensive doctor, the townspeople were shocked at the deed itself – not so much the murder of his wife who was deemed to be regularly unfaithful and therefore not unlikely to be the victim of a *crime passionel* – but at the murder of the poor unfortunate maid. It was assumed that she had witnessed the attack upon Mrs Ruxton and had been killed to prevent her from revealing to the authorities what had taken place (Camp 1982: 140–50).

185

The sympathies expressed in written form around this exhibit are very much in line with a view that locates the business disciplines within the orbit of the social sciences and not the natural sciences. However, under pressure, the affinity of style and problematique has become difficult to sustain. The separation of business subjects from social science, of management from the human and behavioural sciences, of organization theory from sociology, has created a lesion which has virtually lobotomized whole areas of intellectual endeavour. Philosophy, art, literature, history and cultural studies have all become disconnected from the analysis of management. These disciplines are not often classified as social sciences anyway but the contemporary schisms within the social sciences have allowed business teachers to escape without any real sensitivity to the issues raised by the humanities. Of course, there is always economics which, in the rest of Europe, has been seen as very widely constituted indeed. In the UK, the role of economics as a social science is unquestioned but there are tectonic thrusts in that discipline which push it away from the humanities towards measurement, technique and results. What has happened is that the business disciplines have come close to losing their status as disciplines within the social science community – always assuming they possessed one to begin with.

CHAPTER 8   *Fifth Exhibit: The Pillory*

→   Ruxton's surgical skills were then used to dismember the bodies, and in the panic of attempting to dispose of the corpses he had randomly thrown the body parts from his car as he travelled north. Another interpretation, however, is possible.

Ruxton was from Bombay and was a declared Zoroastrian. Within this ancient religion (of which more in a moment), there are strong taboos against lesbianism and extremely severe penalties imposed on those found practising it. They are to be killed. Their bodies are to be quartered and spread to the four winds. In this interpretation, Mrs Ruxton was supposed to have engaged in infrequent lesbian relations with her maid which Dr Ruxton happened to chance upon one evening when he returned home early. His religious beliefs having been flagrantly transgressed, and being totally committed to the code of Zoroastrianism, he took the prescribed action and placed pieces of the two bodies deliberately under bridges up and down the major A6 trunk road.

Despite a dubious confession that appeared in the *Daily Mail*, Ruxton never fully revealed why he had committed the crimes, nor was he called to the witness stand, so the hypothesis of the transgression of the Zoroastrian code is somewhat flimsy. Yet, the Zoroastrian explanation – for he was indeed a committed follower – was later pieced together by a Lancastrian playwright. It de-emphasizes the sadistic and macabre aspects of the case and puts in place a religious (and therefore more acceptable?) motivation for the murderous activity of a professional and popular healer. In the city of Lancaster, Ruxton is still remembered for his good works. It is said, for example, that at one of the local factories a workman had his index finger severed by a machine. Such was the nature of his task that he felt his

186

On balance, however, the business schools have been encouraged to look outwards towards the market and its perceived needs rather than inwards towards the pursuit of intellectual edification. What has happened as a consequence has been a separation of business disciplines from social science. Social science has always been a mélange of competing disciplines anyway, but a common concern for understanding social life and a sympathy for the separation of the *Geistwissenschaften* from the *Naturwissenschaften* has meant that a deep suspicion of the natural sciences has been nurtured at several discernible levels. The business disciplines often involve mathematical expertise and knowledge and a willingness to pursue positivistic approaches is not uncommon. Thus, the placing of business administration within the faculties of social studies in universities has created
←   some tensions which cannot easily be ignored.

CHAPTER 8   *Fifth Exhibit: The Pillory*

skilled job would be lost if it was discovered that his finger had gone. Ruxton, the doctor involved, sewed back the finger – even though it would be useless – at no charge, so that the worker could retain his job. His reputation was that of a good, fair-minded, general practitioner. The idea that he was also devoutly religious, albeit in a non-Christian context, met with local approval and satisfaction.

Zoroaster was a religious prophet and reformer who was born on the Iran–Afghanistan border in or around the seventh century BC. He was very keen indeed to establish a monotheistic religion, which at that time was very unusual. The 'Magi' of the Christmas visit to Bethlehem is a term based upon the Zoroastrian word for priest. But other key concepts have entered Judaism and Christianity from this source. The notions of Satan, Heaven, Hell, life after death, the resurrection of the body and an apocalyptic ending to the world are *all* originally from Zoroastrianism. Thus Christianity and our views about human life, death and mortality owe a tremendous intellectual and theological debt to these Persian historical roots. The Zoroastrians, indeed, encouraged and partially financed the building of the Temple in Jerusalem. In the early Jewish tradition the tribal god, Yahweh, takes on much from Zoroastrianism – including the concept of heavenly and hellish angels and the final judgement. However, Zoroastrianism

Developments in the 1980s towards customer care and the supposed sovereignty of the buyer have partly produced this movement towards provider–customer conceptualizations of the staff–student relationship but the idea that these dimensions are relevant to education has required a rethinking of what education is all about. The commercialization of higher education with its associated focus on universities as income-generating institutions rather than as the suppliers of a socially desirable public service has forced or at least greatly encouraged vice-chancellors to 'market and sell high-demand products which attract a premium price'. In other words, courses which are self-funding and surplus-generating are seen as highly important to corporate survival and growth and there has been much institutional encouragement of their development.

Old saws about 'education for life' versus 'education for livelihood' have been overturned in the desire to find high-demand courses and programmes. MBAs have been *a* if not *the* major vehicle then, for the transmission of this change in institutional dynamics. In some places the degree has been seen as a life-saver.

Now it may well have been that this reorientation in higher education has had its beneficial aspect, not least of which is that academic colleagues have been offered jobs they might not otherwise have seen.

CHAPTER 8   *Fifth Exhibit: The Pillory*

itself was split between those who remained firmly committed to the monotheistic concept and adherents of more modern variants which wished to see good and evil as in an eternal struggle, as represented by co-equal deities (Cohn 1994). We can thus see the importance of the Zoroastrians in the past even though today there are only tiny communities in western India and eastern Iran. Nietzsche in *Thus Spake Zarathustra* (1883–91) brought this set of beliefs into the bright daylight of Western scrutiny.

Its view of women would have been of little interest to Nietzsche, however relevant it was to Mozart in *The Magic Flute*. Friedrich Wilhelm Nietzsche (1844–1900) was gifted in many directions and is widely noted for his rejection of traditional Christian beliefs as well as the concept of the *Übermensch*. However, even his genius did not allow him to escape from gender prejudice viewpoints, yet (or possibly because of this gender blindness) one of the elevated figures in *Pandemonium* has to be Nietzsche.

In 1924, a particularly nasty murder was committed in Chicago. Two second generation immigrants named Leopold and Loeb were arrested for the crime and pleaded guilty, using the clever but doomed justification that they were followers of a Nietzschean philosophy. In a not totally dissimilar way, Ian Brady and Myra Hindley, the so-called Moors Murderers, have articulated their commitment to the ideas of

188

The 4 Rs of relevance, recency, results and redemption have surfaced to significance because of a conjunction of forces which has marked the transformation of the MBA from a student into a customer or at least consumer. The relationship between provider and customer is obviously a complex one but the power of the educator to decide what is provided, how and when, is much greater where the relationship is one of provider–patient or its one time equivalent, provider–student. Today, the swing of power has gone much more to the provision of what the customer wants. In between these two extreme points lie the client–provider and consumer–provider relationships. The former suggests a strongly professional relationship in which the actual needs are defined by the provider, whereas the latter implies that the producer responds to large-scale demand and does not necessarily care to target specific groups for particular attention.

CHAPTER 8   *Fifth Exhibit: The Pillory*

the Marquis de Sade. Before killing one of their victims they photographed and tape-recorded the acts which preceded her death. The recording had been copied twice so that the Moors Murderers could listen to the tapes for their later enjoyment. In court, the tapes were played in evidence and many hardened police officers and judicial officials claimed that listening to them was the most harrowing experience they had ever undergone. The views of de Sade were given in evidence and the Attorney-General read a piece from *Juliette* to the court. But more of de Sade and his links to Nietzsche later.

The 'will to power', a concept developed by Nietzsche, has proved to be one of the most difficult and yet insightful terms available to us in the twentieth century. It was the cardinal concept of Nietzsche's only systematic approach to his philosophy and took him about four years to work out its details and its ramifications. It is a principle which covers all of nature in which a self, or 'centre of power', expands beyond its own boundaries and asserts itself over the Other, attempting to appropriate it in the process. The will to power is not identical to life but it is the way in which humanity, 'the weakest, cleverest thing', becomes master of the Earth.

the emphasis is upon 'making a difference' where human energy, ingenuity and inventiveness have turned disaster into success. Such stories and examples play a key part in elevating human individual action to the pinnacle of overarching assumptions within this framework. Redemption is also a keynote here in at least two senses. On one hand the MBA course must make up for the deficiencies or faults the individual undoubtedly possesses before embarking upon the programme. The material covered must make the person whole and free from weakness. S/he must be complete and flawless in terms of the areas of knowledge in her/his possession. Students must be made whole. The second sense in which redemption is essential to the MBA student is that the programme converts paper money into bullion. Clearly the idea that the paper qualification of the degree can be redeemed after a year or so for much higher rewards is one which motivates many course members. The oft-quoted hike in salary of 60 per cent after graduation is the payback for the investment in training (not education) undertaken by the student. His or her organization, so this view of redemption opines, will be willing to pay for this paper investment in bullion of a kind.

CHAPTER 8   *Fifth Exhibit: The Pillory*

➤   It is the driving force behind cultural, artistic and religious life; it is
the impulse behind the creation, ordering and acquisition of knowledge; it is the supremacy of Being over Becoming. We are motivated,
says Nietzsche, not by the will to truth but by the will to render the
world thinkable. We are part of a world which is the will to power and
nothing else.

If organizational analysts look at the ways in which work is carried
out it is easy to see the force of the Nietzschean argument. In the political arena, the existence of the will to power is clear but it is there in
a very visible form in science too. The famous example of the
Velikovsky Controversy in the 1960s shows how those who are outside
the scientific disciplines are unable to make their voices heard in particular fora (De Grazia et al. 1978). Velikovsky made a much better job
of predicting the characteristics of the planet Venus than specialists in
NASA and the leading universities. His evidence and theory were
drawn from a close reading of ancient Hindu, Jewish and biblical
material which saw the solar system to have been profoundly disturbed around 4000 BC by a cataclysmic event. Providing the evidence
consonant with entry of a new planet into the solar system at this
time Velikovsky maintained that Venus was this new planet and would

190

concern is what employers say about MBA students. Here the evidence is that the output of business schools both in the USA and in the
UK are widely seen as arrogant, over-theoretical and too quantitative
by many recruiters. However, this says more perhaps about the quality
of existing management than it does about new graduates. This is certainly not the negative side which is implied in the comments above.

What is negative about the rise of the business schools centred upon
the MBA is the cycle of reinforcement of a narrow, pragmatic and egocentric view of the world and the individual's place within it. As
teachers, we accept far too readily the constraints put upon us from
students for relevance, recency, results and redemption.

First, there is the myopic concentration upon tasks, material and
outcomes which have a demonstrable and foreshortened link between
their use and the course member becoming a better manager.
Everything must be focused upon the immediate, obvious utility of the
presented material to managerial tasks as they are perceived by the student. Material and anecdotal evidence must be recent, preferably
originating in the year in which the course is being taught and concerned with publicly quoted companies and prestigious chief
executive officers. Courses must demonstrate what managerial actions
◄   alone can achieve. Bottom line figures are not the only part of this, for

exhibit surface features very unlike the ones predicted by those followers of the stable planetary view. His predictions about the surface temperature and atmospheric characteristics of Venus proved to be vastly superior to the reigning astrophysical perspective. Despite (or because of) the fact that he was significantly closer to the real readings taken by the later Viking space probes to the planet (the earlier landings proved to be complete failures as data was unavailable after the first few seconds of entry into the Venusian atmosphere), he was ostracized by the astrophysics community. They berated his work's theoretical basis, yet in terms of predictive criteria it was decidedly better.

The will to power of the scientific disciplines is tremendous and the Velikovsky story is but one in a long line which certainly includes the example of Galileo's rejection of the tyranny of that empirical data believed by the Church. Today the battle for the billions of dollars connected to the presumed discovery of a cure for AIDS has produced a clear example of the will to power. US scientists and medical administrators argue in confrontational ways over the discovery of HIV with French counterparts at the Louis Pasteur Institute. The French use the term SIDA to differentiate themselves from the perfidious Anglophones.

The will to power is in every erotic encounter; it is in the sex act itself; it is in the classroom. All forms of passive response such as decadence, despair and tiredness lead to weakness. Thus the will to power is disease and cure alike. It is a collapse into nihilism and a promise of escape from nihilism at one and the same moment.

Solzhenitsyn in *Cancer Ward* (1971) shows starkly and clearly the

191

against the structures and processes they have engendered in the business schools. Obviously being part of a reaction is easier than being the solitary voice but what is about to be said may well be shocking to those who make a living in management education. It may stick in the craw of colleagues but it needs to be articulated nevertheless.

The lambast here articulated is not against MBA students themselves, for many are bright, hardworking, interesting as individuals and are interested in learning. Nor is it necessarily true that MBA degrees are worthless as credentials of intellectualism, for what is often taught is at the forefront of the discipline and incorporates some of the latest findings by skilled researchers and effective teachers. Nor are institutions which teach such degrees of dubious quality nor motivated solely by the search for cash-cows.

What *is* true, however, is that there are severe institutional pressures which arise when MBAs are taught, which create a flux of forces highly dangerous to the values of many university staff. Of least

→ corrupting power of the police state. Oleg Kostoglotsov, the central character, like Solzhenitsyn himself, went in the 1950s from concentration camp to cancer ward and later recovered. The novel was not published openly until 1989 in the USSR at a time when the nation state it criticized was already collapsing. Shulubin, a fellow sufferer in the ward, was a university lecturer in Moscow, and described events under Stalin thus:

> They were destroying text-books written by great scientists, they were changing the curricula into the stove with all your genetics, leftist aesthetics, ethics, cybernetics, arithmetic! (1971: 470–1)

Oleg also questions the ethical value of teaching children at school through the medium of a poem by Georg Herwegh (1817–75) which was mandatory learning during this period.

> Till death shall part the blade and hand
> They may not separate.
> We've practised loving long enough
> Let's come at last to hate.

Oleg Kostoglotsov says poignantly at this point, 'we wish to love, to hell with your hatred' (ibid.: 473–4). Yet hatred is not only to be found in the police state. It is there, within liberal democracy, in a period known as

192

In the confessional

It has become difficult in Britain in the early 1990s to criticize developments in management education if the livelihood of one's immediate colleagues or oneself is closely implicated in the survival of this area of activity. This has not stopped members of other faculties and cognate departments in universities from indulging in their usual banter and barracking of the management sciences, but within the business schools criticism of the intellectual platform upon which the expansion in management education has taken place has been slow to develop. Certainly, lunchtime conversation and gossip within staff circles relates well to the problems of teaching and managing MBA classes; but in public documentation and in the classroom there is very little room for role-distancing oneself from the enterprise. After all, friends may rely upon such courses for their posts and to criticize heavily is seen as being disloyal and counter-productive.

For many years now these informal injunctions against detailed public critique have prevented the disaffected from denouncing courses and curricula. However, time and the tide may be running ← against such orientations as evidenced on most MBA programmes and

The End of History (Fukuyama 1989). We can see it in right-wing politics with the target being immigrants, we can see it in the misogyny of large numbers of the Church of England, we can see it in the xenophobia of nationalist parties and in the treatment of groups such as the gypsies.

Judith Okely in a number of pieces (1975; 1983; 1994) has looked at gypsies with a view to understanding how they continue to function in a world which finds them so unusual. Travellers in the UK have recently been subjected to one of the periodic 'moral panics' which Britain experiences but this is little compared to the opprobrium heaped upon gypsies over the centuries. In Hitler's Germany, the gypsies were rounded up and imprisoned in concentration camps some time before Jews were arrested. Possibly this is because gypsies are contemptuous of wage-labour and consciously reject it out of hand. It is not that they find it difficult to get work of this kind. They just never seek it. Okely disputes the popular idea that gypsies migrated from India. Rather, she suggests that:

> after the collapse of feudalism, groups of travelling people were formed from landless serfs and indigenous people, as well as from individuals along the oriental trade routes . . . They banded together to exploit occupations which required flexibility in space and time and which were outside the fixed wage-labour system. (Okely 1994: 29)

193

What aspects of your life are so nefarious as to make you deserve a pillorying? The Kafkaesque nature of the questions begins to suggest itself. Of course, you are guilty, of course you deserve punishment. Aren't we all? But what is your *particular* crime, of which you know, yet speak not? What exquisite anxieties do you suffer when you think – hope – fear that someone will discover it?

The author is about to admit his deliciously wicked feelings on the next page. For the exhibits in Chapter 8 I deserve a pillorying.

To confess is such an unburdening of oneself. It allows relief from guilt, it shares the responsibility with someone whom one trusts. Much of the power of the priest, the witch, the psychoanalyst, the personal tutor comes from the intimacy which attends the confessional. However, as we all know, your doctor tells her partner, you tell your children about your personal tutee, the priest tells the bishop and soon your intimate secret is no longer so intimate. Nevertheless, we have before us no Room 101 (Orwell 1954) which contains your worst nightmare but the confessional where you can tell your captors what you have done which is truly wicked.

CHAPTER 8   *Fifth Exhibit: The Pillory*

→ As such, they pose a threat to nation states because of their non-national identities, to employers for their refusal to enter wage-labour, to the police for both the above, and to the general populace for the rejection of the dominant value system. They are widely loathed and detested. They have a very distinctive view of the body in which conventional sedentary views of cleanliness are inverted. They see cats and dogs which lick themselves as unclean. Horses, by the same token, are clean. Non-gypsies are seen as having dirty habits such as washing in a sink. No gypsy caravan has a sink, for these breed dirt and pollution. 'Dirty gyppos' then question dominant values to such an extent that they are very vulnerable to mainstream public and state hostility based on fear.

We can also bear witness to hatred within homophobia. In 1980, the Atlanta Center for Disease Control began to file reports that gay men were being affected by a fatal and unknown disease. Patient Zero, who was supposedly the North American source of AIDS and had brought the disease across the Atlantic from some African source, in that year alone claimed to have had 250 sexual partners. The US Government were very keen not to get involved. Randy Shilts (1988) claimed that 25,000 Americans had died of the disease before Ronald Reagan could bring himself to say 'AIDS'. Financial and political expediency by a large number of organizations interfered in the process. French and US researchers argued about who had discovered what and by what name it should be called. Blood banks refused to trace donors, the media talked openly of a 'gay plague' or of a 'gay-related cancer' and there was a struggle amongst gay community leaders who were keen to hang on to newly won freedoms in the face of a media folk panic.

In the movie *And the Band Played On* (1995), an expert from the Center for Disease Control interviews a young man dying from AIDS-related symptoms. The patient is covered in lesions and painfully

194

There was to be no lambasting of the victim – simply, an open uniformity of effort and economy of labour. Yet you see this area of Pandemonium is called 'The Pillory' – and you know, somehow and in some way, that *you* are the intended victim! If you are in the city because you are in a business school somewhere perhaps you know already.

What could you possibly be guilty of which would mean you should ← be punished?

CHAPTER 8   *Fifth Exhibit: The Pillory*

manages to drag a drip around behind him. He rants about the 'sign of the beast', the number 6 (666), in what appears to be an attempt to explain his predicament. When shown a list of men and asked which of them he has had sex with, all he can see is the number '6' in the telephone numbers or the date on which he met them. He sees AIDS as the Devil's work. Yet it is the organizations surrounding AIDS on behalf of the state and medicine which appeared callous and unfeeling in the 1980s.

Disease

There is a small island off the coast of Scotland which was bombed by a military aircraft one fine morning in 1941. The bombs contained the anthrax bacillus and they have made the island uninhabitable ever since. The bacillus is still to be found in the rocks, flora and water of this barren island. The aircraft and the technology used were not German but British – some might even say English. Callousness again.

The War Ministry, which in a genuflection to Orwell's book *Nineteen Eighty-four* is now called the Ministry of Defence, is an organization devoted to the efficient pursuit of death and pain. This is part of its *raison d'être* and forms the central plank of its activities. Often it cannot utilize humans in its testing of equipment and systems – although it does this in 'peace-time' much more than one might think (see Corbett 1994). However, the flesh of the pig is a very close approximation to human skin and muscle and so weaponry and ammunition are tried out on members of the porcine family standing in for 'the enemy'. The pattern of penetration and wound formation is close to what would happen to the human body were it to be subjected to the same attack.

In its pursuit of death-dealing devices the military everywhere and not just in the UK has experimented with biological weaponry. Sometimes it has *unconsciously* used bacteriological warfare when,

195

Bentham was keen to avoid the subjectivities involved in appointed officers whipping convicted recalcitrants. If the whipper was sympathetic to the whipped, he (for it almost certainly was a he) laid on with less force than was just. If, on the other hand, he felt hate or detestation towards the victim, he would lay on with too much force. To avoid such subjectivity-originated problems, Bentham devised 'the perfect flogging machine'. This wonderful device whipped at a steady even rate with a steady even force. It was a mechanical flogger which allowed emotion to be stripped from the whole business of flaying the flesh off a human being. What was dispensed in a utilitarian heaven of rationality was therefore 'a just measure of pain'.

CHAPTER 8   *Fifth Exhibit: The Pillory*

paradoxically, despite its unplanned nature, it has proved vastly superior to conventional force of arms. The importation of smallpox and influenza into the Americas by the European colonists proved to be much more effective in suppressing the indigenous population than muskets or Gatling guns. The cost in exchange of diseases, of course, is high. It is widely believed that syphilis is a Central American disease in terms of its regional origin but was brought back to Europe in the *longue durée* of the sixteenth century for it to spread, transmute and reach its full epidemiological ripeness in the nineteenth century. In some ways, the discovery of a cure for syphilis in 1907 shows the impact it was having upon life *au fin du siècle* in Western Europe. We have already seen the cost it exacted upon Nietzsche's sanity. But there were hundreds of thousands of others who slipped into death as a result of its tertiary form of development. In some senses, then, syphilis was the AIDS of the Enlightenment.

Of primary importance here is the contemporary fear of AIDS which is very widespread. So it is to be expected that political capital will be made from the high levels of public anxiety. The ways in which Africa – at least its Sub-Saharan parts – have become labelled as the centres of infection is an object lesson in racism. Stories about the eating of infected green monkeys, of bizarre sexual practices, of promiscuity levels unknown in the West have all been part of a blaming strategy in which the African is seen as to blame for Occidental dis-ease.

The foreigner is often said to be diseased and she or he often is – for the host nation has a population which is accustomed to local diseases and many of the indigenous peoples have some level of resistance to major infections. In the same way as victims of AIDS do not die of the infection itself but of the diseases which the body can no longer fight off, and these causes of death differ in different societies, so too we must recognize that globalization of diseases is upon us.

196

In this exhibit hall you discover physical attack upon self. If all is appearance, what worries you is that the distant object which lies ahead is a big sign. At the beginning of the section you are about to enter, throbs a phrase from Jeremy Bentham, later used as a book title by Michael Ignatieff (1978). It says A JUST MEASURE OF PAIN. Unfortunately, the recipient of the 'reality' of this message appears to be you, the reader.

CHAPTER 8   *Fifth Exhibit: The Pillory*

Braudel (1974) in his own inimitable way describes the amazingly rapid spread of syphilis in the *longue durée*. We know that sailors, in particular, by being the most mobile of the citizenry were also the most likely to pick up overseas infections. The Age of Enlightenment makes disease much more portable. It ushers in a period of communicable disease transfer which could not have been imagined.

In the eighteenth century we are told that the 'Golden Triangle' of trade between Europe, West Africa and the New World (meaning the USA and the Caribbean) involved the export of manufactured goods westwards. But hidden cargoes lay alongside what was described in the ships' manifests. Along with manufactured goods going out from Lancaster to the Gambia, with the slaves outbound to the Carolinas, and in the cotton *en route* for Lancashire, there were other passengers. Influenza and smallpox went south, malaria and sickle cell disease went west and syphilis came east – at least to begin with. Soon it was almost impossible to see what came from where. For as we should be aware, these alternative cargoes are very much alive. They learn, mutate, adapt and change, searching for a more effective existence. Globalization of this kind means that they rank alongside the top 100 companies that have benefited from international trade. Ali Maow Maalin was supposedly the last person on earth to die of smallpox after this was diagnosed on 26 October 1977. However, since then the disease has broken out again. Bacterial failure is very, very rare. But humans continue to blame one another for their infections and ask others to take responsibility for their own pain and suffering.

CHAPTER 8

Fifth Exhibit: The Pillory

A pillar of state; deep on his front engraven
Deliberation sat and public care

(Milton, *Paradise Lost*, Bk II, ll. 302–3)

Fear and loathing

In the infamous book by Hunter Thompson entitled *Fear and Loathing in Las Vegas* there is a passage which describes the central two characters developing 'the great fear' in the main rooms of a casino called Circus Circus. This feeling will be well known to colleagues who teach to large MBA classes. The sense of alienation, social and psychological distance and fear is well described by the characters in the novel when as adventurous drug takers they find themselves in a police convention looking at the drug 'problem'. They begin to have severe, disturbing hallucinations, which creates tremendous difficulties for them in negotiating the reality of Circus Circus.

Negotiating organizational reality often involves the fear and the loathing of one's colleagues, one's subordinates and last but by no means least, one's superiors. It is said that Harold Geneen, when he was CEO of ITT, would bring his infrequent board meetings to a close only when at least one of his directors had broken down in tears. He ran the organization at that time on a regime of fear and distrust. These are feelings which have not entirely disappeared in the 1990s! Indeed they are well documented in less graphic language in the following interview transcript.

198

So the robber barons lived in the relentless gaze, not so much of the press or a public who engaged in the politics of envy, but of themselves. Their conspicuousness was due to their efforts to act like the medieval barons in the continent they had left behind, but it also owed much to the gaze to which they subjected themselves. Their sense of individuality and of self, finely honed in the non-collectivist atmosphere of *fin-de-siècle* New York, meant that they saw themselves from without as sole authors of their destiny. As such they were very vulnerable to being forced by themselves into taking sole responsibility for events. The gaze of self upon self is a kind of reflection which carries a heavy price.

CHAPTER 7 *Fourth Exhibit: Panopticon City*

'I get remarks all the time.' 'What about?' [*She paused. Then with an embarrassed laugh*] 'Most men comment on my boobs. They say things about them to each other. I walk past and they're just like that' [*She mimicked someone staring at her chest*]. 'This man' [*she named a senior person*] 'I was talking to him and he was just standing there staring at me. He didn't even look at my face, he was like this the whole time. I just feel like punching them. I get comments all the time. This man' [*she named a different manager*] 'he gets on my nerves. . . . Then all of a sudden I had about six men all over me, all staring. . . . My mum says to me ignore them, don't say anything. But I want to say something. I want to tell them to shut up and go away and leave me alone. I could nearly scream sometimes.' (a woman worker quoted in Cockburn 1991: 140)

199

Such was the identification of self with business (the term 'self-made man' reflects this) that business failure often took the form of self-destruction. The Wall Street crash of 1929 and the number of suicides that it caused to take place from highly visible places up in the skyscrapers represents another form of conspicuous consumption. The most conspicuous form of all is to kill oneself in front of a large and appreciative audience. The death of Bob Maxwell was rather a tame affair in comparison to the high visibility of other robber barons' suicides where nothing was left to the imagination. The successful barons 'know' that business is war and their real death – not some metaphorical disappointment – is at stake. It is at this time in US business history that people start to talk of strategy, for the military analogy takes on a potency that all recognize. Failed leaders expected no golden handshake from shareholders distant in time and space. The market was 'red in tooth and claw' and 'strategy' and 'war' became ways of dealing with the 'opposition'. The corporation, a body made legal, required of the capitalist, a body made in success, to be regal, or in failure, hegiral.

CHAPTER 7   *Fourth Exhibit: Panopticon City*

→   In the eighteenth century a 'logic of exclusion' developed (Battersby 1994: 4), which related not only to the dualisms man/animal, civilized/savage pairing but also to that of genius/woman. Romanticism as an artistic school was very much part of this logic of exclusion. The work of art was different from work produced for popular consumption by the masses. The former was a male province, the latter decidedly female. Whilst the Romantic may have male genital organs, however, his soul was 'feminine' (ibid.: 10). This sexual apartheid was based on a very old mythology of the 'logos spermatikos' – 'the spermatic word'. The poet was seen by the Greeks not as an artist but as a shaman, whilst for the Romans 'genius' meant the begetting figure of the *gens* or male clan – a sexual reference to the male who could testify. Males were seen to be hot and dry; females cold and wet. Since men have externalized sexual organs the male body contains more of the heat required for this outgrowth. For Aristotle, only semen grew. Women merely provided a suitable environment for the growth of the foetus. In Renaissance theory, the liver was the fire upon which the contents of the stomach were heated. In illness, 'vapours' produced by a malfunctioning of the burning process entered the head and produced disturbances of the brain. Women were much more likely to have 'the vapours' than men who were, in turn, more likely to suffer

200

untrammelled corporate capitalism. They were deemed to be robbers because of the way in which they treated their employees, but much more importantly because of the way they treated their equals. All those who stood in the way of the truly successful robber barons were stabbed in the back in the headlong rush to make more and more money. Few rules of conduct existed and the period of meetings in coffee houses and the notion that a gentleman's word was his bond (or that a gentlewoman's was her bond) was soon left behind. The 'giving of one's word' in the European coffee houses had been the basis for trust in the markets of the world. This was always subject to periodic bouts of scandal, of course, but in the main the system of centralized financial markets survived for some time on the word of others. In Britain, industrial capitalism had remained in a fragmented state, based as it was outside of London. New York, however, was both a financial and a manufacturing centre and represented much more of a concentration of industrial output. The financial concentration of industrial capital in the north-east was made possible within Wall Street and its environs because of geographical concentration. Here the
←   robber barons fought for survival.

melancholia – an imbalance which brought on great thoughts. Some of the witch-hunters of the 1600s denied that women had the capacity for melancholia at all. As Jean Bodin said in 1850, it was felt that the coldness and wetness of women shows that their ideas, fantasies and so on come from the Devil and not from melancholia (Battersby 1994: 234). This argument became part of a widely accepted rationale for the mass execution and torture of 'witches', who were predominantly unmarried women and widows. In the years 1600–50, this *gynocide* reached its climax. It corresponds to a period of interest in female lusts and adulterous relationships which troubadours sang about (Battersby 1994: 237).

The view that it was from the penis that great thoughts sprang is graphically demonstrated in Rodin's sculpture of Balzac. The piece caused a scandal when it was first shown. Balzac was portrayed with his whole body sheathed in a dressing gown. His body is thrust back and up and is eight feet long, his hands forming a mound under the front of his dressing gown. The penile dimension to Rodin's sculpture is even more obvious in Michael Joaquim Grey's *Apple* in which a carrot-coloured cast of the sculpture is suspended from the ceiling, base and all, with the head hanging down. Suspended in exhibition it looks as it was meant to look – like a semi-erect penis. By calling it *Apple*, Grey implies that this is the real tree of knowledge.

DO NOT CROSS THE CENTRAL RESERVATION

The bloated plutocrats, made visible in the cartoons of the end of the nineteenth century, were often known by another name: the robber barons. The exaggerated nature of their wealth and the means, often illegal, by which it was acquired were reminiscent to an urban work-force of the *mittel*-European aristocracy that they had just left behind some 4,000 miles away. Carnegie from Scotland, the Roosevelts and Vanderbilts from other parts of north-western Europe, brought with them a taste for the baronial. Lifestyles supplied by this model of extravagance were fuelled by income and wealth provided by an

CHAPTER 7 *Fourth Exhibit: Panopticon City*

Battersby (1994), no doubt, would concur that the process of the gendering of genius is a long tradition, of which this is but one small example. In the same exhibition as *Apple* (Some Went Mad. . . . Some Ran Away: 1994), Kiki Smith's *Virgin Mary* is a standing female figure who appears to have been flayed. The implication is that the cult of the Virgin Mary (which goes back, at least, to the Phoenician Mother Goddess Astarte) has led to a cruel misogyny in which women become seen as the living dead, the walking wounded, condemned, as soon as womanhood asserts itself, to be menstruating meat. Cold and wet menstruating meat.

202

projects as an image become central concerns of the self. In fashion, in dieting and in fitness these become clear but so too are they in 'fateful moments' relating to death and sexuality. 'Self-care' in terms of the physical capital it represents is usually addressed to putting off death and the necrotic and investing instead in the attractiveness of the body to others. As an investment project the body is periodically subjected to audit but also to episodes of consumption in public, conspicuous ways.

Conspicuous consumption, as a term in *The Theory of the Leisure Class* (Veblen 1907), was developed in a way to show how affluence often becomes identified with the body, its feeding and its adornment. In the South Seas, various islands developed cultures which took women's body size, particularly their obesity, to be a sign of attractiveness to the wealthy men who sought them out as partners. Only the wealthy, it was said, could afford to pay for women of such size and the appetites which came with them. Thus the body of the wife was a physical reflection of the wealth of the husband. In Long Island at the turn of this century, the Vanderbilts expressed their wealth in parties, and in housing, personal adornment, food utensils and modes of transport. One party consisted of each of hundreds of guests receiving a meal on a golden platter to be eaten with diamond-encrusted knives and forks. All these items were to be taken away by the guests as a memento of the evening. It was not for nothing that they were called 'bloated plutocrats' for their physical appearance represented their wealth much more even than the sad wave of wearing designer labels was to do in the 1980s.

CHAPTER 7   *Fourth Exhibit: Panopticon City*

On the other hand, witchcraft was a vocabulary, a set of myths which allowed the body to be a focus of attention; it allowed open discussion about sexuality and problems of sexual functioning. Sexuality was communally understood and was not a private affair. Women's bodies, by no means totally free, nevertheless were allowed some scope for self-interpretation in the sixteenth and seventeenth centuries. By the eighteenth century, control of the body surrounding discourses was gathering apace, changed in part by 'the civilizing process' (Elias 1978) as it developed. The view of women moved to being one of passivity – at least in aristocratic and middle-class households. Discussions about sex were curbed, public nudity was suppressed and sexual 'swear' words were seen as impolite. Witchcraft and the traditions of moonlit naked dances in rural spots became targets for treatment. Thus, in publications about the activities of the powerful, their fears and hopes, in the years around 1600, one detects a concern within a society in which patriarchal authority was well established but perceived itself to be under threat from vocal women – 'the Monstrous Regiment' (rule) complained of by John Knox.

The weapons available to those robbed of inheritance or their living were not much, but they did exist. They usually took the form of a curse. Commonly it was a loud curse, something like: 'pox, piles and a heavy vengeance' upon you. But to make it into a weapon of some power, the

6. *Supplication*: Individuals try to get people in positions of influence to be sympathetic or nurturant toward them. Employees might bolster the allegiance their bosses have to them by asking to be mentored or 'taken under their wing'. (Feldman and Klitch 1991: 69)

What this kind of material does is to show the importance to a whole cadre of putative and extant middle managers that how they present themselves – how they appear – is crucial. And this is the type of information for which they tend to be very grateful.

Narcissism, as Christopher Lasch (1979) has shown, develops apace in the modern world – or at least in certain parts of it. The myth of Narcissus, who looks at himself in the mirroring waters, longingly, itself reflects back upon a society in which appearance is seen as being of supreme importance. Narcissism, of course, is not only about what one sees in the mirror; it is about infatuation with what one finds there. Self-reflection is by no means necessarily about self-love and coming to love oneself is not that easy for some individuals. Narcissism is connected to sex and death – as so much is. It is reflective of the self as a 'fragile project' where identity and what the body

curse had to be seen to work. Of course, it is still a weapon of the weak against the strong. It is a substitute for political action yet it can still frighten the powerful. It was commonly the revenge of women on men. Thomas's *Religion and the Decline of Magic*, which has so informed this section, fails to notice the force of this point (*pace* 1978: 678–80).

Witchcraft was not 'organized' in the sense of a social movement against the powerful. It was much more individualized than that. However it was often thought to be collectivized and therefore much more dangerous to powerful elements within the society. It was thought that collectivization should be suppressed and so notions of the 'witch-cult' utilizing covens and expressing itself through the sabbat meeting developed as repressionary rationales. This cult clearly adopted an alternative organizational form to the Church, which made it highly dangerous. But the focus of 'press' and public interest was the control of women; women as 'scolds', women as 'cursers', women as 'unnaturally' violent, were all suspect. The witch-cult issue forced many women to be quieter and more submissive than they might otherwise have been. And, interestingly enough, 'it tended to be the witch who was morally in the right and the victim who was in the wrong' (Thomas 1978: 659).

In Michael Crichton's novel *Disclosure* (1994), about organizational life today he tells us, it may well be that there is fear and loathing but directed against female sexual harassers. It is, he says, based on a true

3. *Self-promotions*: Individuals embellish their accomplishments or make overstated claims about their abilities in order to win the respect and admiration of their supervisors. Individuals may self-promote by strategically displaying certificates or awards, claiming they have outside job offers, and puffing up reports of their accomplishments.
4. *Exemplification*: Individuals create the impression of being selflessly dedicated or self-sacrificing, so that people in positions of influence will feel guilty about this and end up giving them desired rewards or promotions. For example, an individual might always arrive at work early or leave late in order to create the image of dedication to his or her job.
5. *Accounting*: Individuals attempt to distance themselves from negative events in which they have been involved. Among other ways, they may do this by denying personal responsibility for the problem (making excuses such as 'I was merely following orders') or by diminishing the dimensions of the problem (making justifications such as 'It's really not so bad').

CHAPTER 7   *Fourth Exhibit: Panopticon City*

story in what he now calls a neo-Nazi world of political correctness facing men. He claims that corporate women are just as guilty of sexual harassment of their male employees as male bosses are of their women staff. He gives some 'facts' to back this up. He maintains that one in ten claims of harassment in the US are by men claiming harassment against them by women. Evidence presented by Crichton takes the form of an Irish company director who was fined £1000 for forcing a male employee to buy condoms and subjecting him to a sex survey, or of Sabitino Gutierrez who was awarded $1 million damages from his boss for her harassment of him. In the UK, one in two male teachers claimed in 1987 to have been harassed by female pupils and one in three men in a survey said that he had been fondled by female colleagues. Yet these are examples which point to a very minor problem which pales into insignificance compared to the reverse issue of male harassment of females. This is not the stuff of novels and the few sensational cases picked up in the tabloid press. This is an everyday occurrence faced by women in the vast majority of organizational forms. How come then that this feature is the one that Crichton has picked upon? It has been said that the book 'is the latest lob in the tide of women-hating' (Blundy 1994). Perhaps the book and the ideas on

They also note the six impression management techniques which are most commonly used in the creation of a favourable image of self:

1. *Ingratiation*: Individuals use flattery, agreeing with others' opinions, and doing favours to get people with influence and power to like them. For instance, in his successful book, *How to Win Friends and Influence People* (1973) Dale Carnegie identifies figuring out a client's good points and playing them to the hilt as the critical ingredient in getting ahead.
2. *Intimidation*: Individuals convey the image of being potentially dangerous to those who might stand in the way of their advancement. Managers, for example, might use veiled threats of exposure of organizations, problems with supervisors who are trying to block their promotions.

CHAPTER 7   *Fourth Exhibit: Panopticon City*

which it is based are in the same framework as *Iron John* (1990) by Robert Bly. Misogyny, as we have already seen, goes back certainly to the Ancient Greeks and Euripides' treatment of the issue. But we find it in John Knox's cry against 'the Monstrous Regiment of Women' and in the satires of Dean Swift. What is often expurgated from the tale of Gulliver in the land of giants, Brobdingnag, is that he is placed into the cleavage of one of the servants at court: what he discovers there is designed to fill the (male) readership with disgust and provide the antidote to any erotic or even prurient feelings which might otherwise occur.

The history of misogyny patently consists of more than these small examples which clearly demonstrate the fear and loathing which some men have for women. Interestingly enough, Swift's famous satirical piece on the solution to Irish famine being the eating of the babies resonates with the treatment of witches (and their supposed hairy unattractive features) in much of the anti-witchcraft tradition of Christianity of which Swift was a Dean.

5. Dishonest or unethical behaviours are sometimes necessary in order to get promotions to which one feels entitled. However, it is important not to advocate dishonest or unethical behaviour or even acknowledge the existence of such behaviour. Instead, individuals should become adept at inconsistency (Jackall 1988), and develop the ability to hold public positions that are either mutually inconsistent or inconsistent with past public positions.

6. Much of the 'real work' of many jobs cannot be tangibly assessed, nor can relative success on those jobs be easily validated. Thus it is important to construct the illusion of success and power socially through symbols such as dress and office design. These props might include locks on file drawers, positioning visitors so the sun is in their eyes, and having visitors' chairs lower than the office occupant's desk.

CHAPTER 7   *Fourth Exhibit: Panopticon City*

Yet Swift is seen to be a misanthrope more than a misogynist and in the following quotation from those who tower above us humans we get a strong flavour of this: 'I cannot but conclude the bulk of your natives to be the most pernicious race of little odious vermin that nature ever suffered to crawl upon the surface of the earth'.

The recognition that we do crawl upon the face of the Earth is reflective perhaps of a strand of thinking at the end of a very long millennium. The whole concept of the *fin de siècle* has been discussed recently by Stjepan Meštrović (1991). In his book, Meštrović argues that there has been a return in very recent years to the previous *fin-de-siècle* spirit evident in Europe a century ago. In a section entitled 'Back to the Future', he claims the following connections.

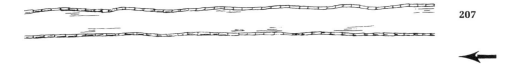

1. Merit alone is insufficient for advancement in organizations. Creating the appearance of being a winner, or looking 'promotable', is as important.
2. In order to advance, it is critical to pursue social relationships with superiors and co-workers. On the surface these relationships should appear to be social in nature, but in reality they are to be used instrumentally for job contacts and insider organizational information.
3. Looking like a 'team player' is central to career advancement. However, individuals should still pursue self-interest at work through what Christopher Lasch (1979) calls 'antagonistic cooperation'; that is appearing co-operative and helpful on the surface while simultaneously seeking information about how to overcome one's competition.
4. In the long run, an individual's career goals will be inconsistent with the interests of any one organization. Therefore, in order to advance, individuals must appear to be loyal and committed to their current employees, while at the same time keeping their résumés circulating and otherwise 'keeping their options open'.

CHAPTER 7   *Fourth Exhibit: Panopticon City*

→ Both then and today there is a common rhetoric of rebellion against the narrative of the Enlightenment. There is a sense of uneasiness, anxiety and excitement. Play, fun and impulse are more valued and a liberal rejection of political 'isms' is supposedly in the ascendancy. Heart is more important than mind and the human beings in both periods live under 'the sign of suicide'. 'Everyone,' says Meštrović, 'has become cynically used to the constant stream of greed, corruption, deceit and other sorts of immorality that pour forth from public and private life' (Meštrović 1991: xiii). Put in a nutshell, the *fin-de-siècle* spirit is one of pessimism, cynicism and ennui; it creates stress, leads to the taking of one's own life and an all-embracing sense of fear.

What you see passing your eyes as we leave this exhibit is the end of the century in which we have lived. Before us is another large square. It is dedicated to Louis Pasteur who did much to usher in a world in which we could dream of the control of disease. You will notice upon the statue the presence of a green mould which has taken hold in the atmosphere of Pandemonium. The square contains traffic originating from all directions and all parts and is somewhat unusually named, given its central statue. It is named

208

The issue here is the development of self-observation and self-surveillance. The concern within modernity for the body and how the presentation of this represents the 'self' and not only one's role or formal social position, has led some writers to focus on *anorexia nervosa* as a defining feature of the modern. It is essentially a representation of self-guilt. As Giddens (1993: 105), very closely following Turner, puts it, anorexia is 'a pathology of reflexive self control'. We are encouraged in the contemporary world to continuously monitor our body and our face. There are over fifty levels of suntan oils available for the sunbather. The vast majority of Westerners think about what they will wear each day and check their appearance in the mirror before leaving the home. The cult of fitness through health clinics and body-building programmes testifies to the importance of appearance, as Lash and Urry (1994) suggest, but also, of course, to the drug 'high' which comes from the release of endorphins in the body of the exerciser. Individually tailored fitness programmes are often designed to maximize this high, and regular exercisers cannot bear to be unable to get their regular fix of endorphins.

The rise of a concern for techniques of impression management is also testament to the interest that the service class have in appearance and impression. Feldman and Klitch (1991), for example, note six key beliefs in the careerist orientation to work which now predominates within the ranks of the service class.

←

The Origin of Species

According to Aristotle there is a ladder of life, a *scala natura*. Particles of matter possessed of an 'active principle' produced, he believed, living organisms when conditions were right. This was the notion of spontaneous generation where in the presence of sunlight, mud and decaying meat one would find life. Such Aristotelian thinking is clear in Frankenstein's monster where spontaneous generation, helped a little by the scientist, is possible. Van Helmont (1577–1644) described an experiment which gave rise to the creation of mice in three weeks. The active agent was human sweat found on a dirty shirt. When placed with a handful of wheat grains in a dark cupboard, the sweaty shirt gave rise to the procreation of mice. It is the same sort of argument which says place a young boy in Eton and seven years later one will find a future leader of Britain.

Experimentation with life began soon after van Helmont's 'experiment' and biogenesis grew in popularity. Experimentation with living species in relatively controlled conditions, as developed by Pasteur in particular from 1860 onwards, influenced contemporary thinking about controlling nature. The impact upon the Parisian population of differing environmental conditions and the effect on wine-growing areas on the other were not deemed to be anomalous. The Parisian underclass became the laboratory of social engineers, whereas the test tubes of Pasteur contained the laboratory of the bio-engineers. The French engineers, trained in the *grandes écoles*, were to see the microcosm of bacterial infection in the same way and in the same light as they saw the proletarian insurrection. They were to be Pasteurized out of sight and out of existence.

The Origin of Species

CHAPTER 6

Third Exhibit:
Satyrsville

Hate stronger, under shew of love well-feigned
The way which to her ruin now I tend

(Milton, *Paradise Lost*, Bk IX, ll. 492–3)

Narcissism and the self-directed gaze

Master of the House:
Servant to the poor,
butler to the great
comforter, philosopher and lifelong mate
everybody's boon companion. . . .

[*self-image of publican*]

Master of the house
isn't worth me spit
comforter, philosopher and lifelong shit
cunning little brain
thinks he's quite a lover but there's not much there. . . .
Comforter, philosopher and lifelong mate?
. . . hypocrite, toady and inebriate.

[*his wife's image*]
(Extracts from *Les Misérables* stage production
See also Byatt 1990: 224)

These extracts show the widely differing conceptualizations of 'self'
which are possible even when one seeks to carefully articulate to oneself what the nature of selfhood actually is.

CHAPTER 7   *Fourth Exhibit: Panopticon City*

Satyriasis

The exhibition hall in which we now find ourselves reflects an organizational phenomenon of central importance. This is satyriasis or 'excessive sexual desire in males'. The term comes from the activities of the woodland deities known as satyrs who in the Greek version possessed a human form but with the added eccentricities of a horse's ears and tail, whilst for the Romans the Satyr was a human with a goat's ears, tail, legs and budding horns (Frazer 1993: 464–5). In the mythology of both cultures they spent many hours copulating with nymphs whom they had wantonly chased through Arcadia. Thus the satyr is a lustful animal yet is in large part human. The satyr is male. He has a grotesquely obvious and persistent erection of the penis as graphic as that seen in Beardsley's drawings of priapism. His prey is women.

As part of this pursuit of sexual gratification the satyr claims that it is the nymph (and see how the usual connotation comes into play here) who has suggested the 'hunt' and penetrative sex at the end of it. Women are blamed for satyriasis. There are in English, we must note, 220 words for a sexually active woman, according to Dale Spender (1982). For a sexually active man, deemed to be much less problematic and more natural somehow, there are only around 20 words. In the Hegelian tradition, to which both the German-speaking Freud and Weber belong, women are noted for their 'holes and slime' in keeping with the long European accusation of responsibility for the Fall. Satyriasis is blamed upon the woman and not the man. Shakespeare's imagery of lust in the words of King Lear is one we should recognize for its misogynist reflections, but in its animalistic imagery we also see both the origins and encouragement of satyriasis.

> 'To hear of pleasure's name;
> The fitchew nor the soiled horse goes to't
> With a more riotous appetite.
> Down from the waist they are Centaurs,
> Though women all above;
> But to the girdle do the Gods inherit,
> Beneath is all the fiends'.
> (*King Lear* IV.vi.124–30)

an I-based eye which, for our purposes, stares back at what it sees. It may not be your 'I' but the writer assumes it could be. I assume your I-based eye is a narcissistic one. If it is not, then apologies – but you *will* look in the mirror more often than you care to admit.

CHAPTER 7   *Fourth Exhibit: Panopticon City*

Lust is seen here through attention to the activities of animals, both real and mystical, in ways which are reminiscent of the Dionysian. In this case, Lear is seeing lust very much as originating in females – but one has to remember the troubles heaped upon his head by his daughters to get some sense of the context of this particular speech. Lear was not the first and by no means the last to accuse young women of expressions of lust when an infirm old man, who is no longer as powerful as in his prime, finds himself unattractive yet gripped by sexual desire. Satyriasis is often the last resort of old, powerful and unattractive males. Their wealth encourages, or at least exaggerates, the descent into an all-embracing excess. Satyriasis then is not only about sex. It is about power. The power of men over women.

Your guide through Pandemonium continues to talk but for a moment you feel uneasy and the unease turns to concern. Is the speaker here not guilty of a crude *androcentricity* much as Foucault is in his later work (Ramazanoglu 1993: 39–48)? Is the discussion turning into a crude example of a male talking about issues which are clear in feminist discourse yet with him acting as if all this is new and insightful? Might it be that this part of Pandemonium is an exemplar of the very thing the guide seeks to criticize? Just as 'despite Foucault's noted disgust with the phallic quality of Greek sexuality, there is also the occasional slippage in that direction in his own discourse' (Ramazanoglu 1993: 41), you might find the area around you in this district of the text to be androcentric and phallocentric. To speak of satyriasis may be to engage in it. Your concern is more than justified. Your guide is red-faced and ill at ease. He avoids looking at the impresa now appearing on the brick walls around you.

In our descent into the excess of this exhibition hall, we have before us the phallus-marked doorways which lead into the homes of the inhabitants. Behind you there is a voice. What is the difference between the penis and the phallus? asks someone of their partner, *sotto voce*. Well, the penis is an organ of excretion and reproduction which is relatively small and squashy and has little to commend itself aesthetically. The phallus, on the other hand, is always erect and full of potency. The former is all too human. The latter is all too omnipotent. For some men, life is a pursuit of the phallus and an escape from the penis.

212

As we are dealing with *Pandemonium* from an Anglophone guide's point of view, however, we must assume that the 'I' of the beholder is a very large component in her or his psyche. The gaze which comes from the mirror when the reader looks into it is not necessarily a Gallic *je*-based eye; nor is it a Germanic *ich*-based eye. It is very much

CHAPTER 7   *Fourth Exhibit: Panopticon City*

Angela Dworkin in *Pornography* (1981: 13–14) argues (if a little inelegantly) that 'The immutable self of the male boils down to an utterly unselfconscious parasitism. The self is the conviction, beyond reason or scrutiny that there is an equation between what one wants and the fact that one is. Going Descartes one better, this conviction might be expressed: I want and I am entitled to have, therefore I am.'

She maintains that men claim the right to name things, to exercise physical power and to utilize the capacity to terrorize. Acts of terror against women by men cover a whole range of behaviours from rape through sexual abuse of children to threats of death. The hidden symbol of power is the penis – meaning of course the phallus (Dworkin 1981: 15). Even the atomic bombs to be dropped on Japan and crushingly defeat the enemy had a decidedly phallic ring to their titles (Easlea 1983). Power of men over women has a monetary component which Dworkin sees as extremely sexual. Men are supposed to hoard sperm as they hoard money. To spend is to ejaculate – to give up the man's most precious natural resource within the spermatic economy. Yet men have the power of sex. The erection is involuntary, it is claimed, so that the man is not responsible for his own penis. It becomes a phallus when presented with woman and she is seen as the cause of its transformation. Whatever he does, it is because of her provocation to do so. Sex is the penis; and virility and all its symbolic importance is achieved through masculine energy. Dworkin analyses a number of items of pornography and argues persuasively that in masculine energy there is a male erotic trinity of sex, violence and death.

213

Do not cross the cultural reservation

Of course, we must note that cultural differences within perceptions of individuality certainly exist. Geert Hofstede's (1992) work on this issue is of major importance. It would be foolish to believe that self-possessed individualism was developed equally across the globe. For if we remember Pascal (1623–62) and his famous dictum 'Verité en deçà des Pyrénées, erreur au delà' (Pascal 1995: 294) (which is usually translated as 'There are truths this side of the Pyrenees that are falsehoods on the other'), then we see that cultural differences are crucial.

CHAPTER 7   *Fourth Exhibit: Panopticon City*

→

Let us consider the case of Rose Keller.

In 1768, Easter Sunday early in the morning, Rose Keller, in her mid-thirties, a German immigrant, a widow, a cotton spinner who had been unemployed for approximately a month, approached [the Marquis de] Sade to beg for alms. He offered her work housecleaning. (Dworkin 1981: 73)

What followed has been the subject of much intensive discussion and debate. According to Dworkin, Keller was subjected to the most brutal forms of sexual abuse. She was locked in a room in his private house where she was tied up, whipped, cut with a knife and had wax rubbed into her wounds. De Sade then ordered her to use brandy on the cuts and locked her in the room making threats of death to her. She escaped using a rope made of bedding and climbed a wall to freedom. Although badly wounded and pursued by de Sade's valet she made her way to the nearby village and found help from other women. Rose Keller brought charges against de Sade and made a long statement about the events of Easter Day. Some eight months later, after de Sade had served time in prison for the attack, Keller accepted money from his mother-in-law and the case was dropped. De Sade was released from jail.

214

Our morality is entirely subordinate to the interests of the class struggle of the proletariat.'

Similarly, the Nazis in the 1930s claimed that 'the only person who is still a private individual in Germany is somebody who is asleep' and Mao, during the Cultural Revolution said that young communists would be 'more concerned about the Party and masses than any private person' (Lyon 1994). In all of these cases, it was only the powerful who were to be allowed privacy. *Plus ça change.* Only the powerful were to be allowed self-identity of a full, sophisticated kind. For the majority, it is no longer face to face relationships which 'count' but the manipulation within some inanimate database of digital symbols. Self-possessing, autonomous individualism (and all the concomitant issues associated with this) is open to fewer and fewer organizational members. 'Personhood' itself is threatened by the 'self' contained in electronic form within numerous electronic systems. The Benthamite 'moral architecture' is meant to be the grave of individual or his/her personalized behaviour.

But self-possessed, personalized behaviours are themselves a product of the Enlightenment and the Cartesian ego. They produce someone who knows how to respond – not to love or charity (*pace* Luhmann 1986) but to the gaze. And the gaze is often coming directly from the highly developed sense of selfhood and is directed at oneself. We subject ourselves to close observation by no other than ourselves.

←

CHAPTER 7   *Fourth Exhibit: Panopticon City*

Commentators have made much of this 'incident'. Simone de Beauvoir opined that 'whipping a few girls . . . is a rather petty feat' but ended the criticism there. Others saw the level of violence in the events of that day only as questionable if Keller were not a liar nor a whore. If she were either, or more usually both, then the incident was unimportant. They tend to play down de Sade's behaviour on the grounds that it was typical of the time anyway or that Keller was in reality a sophisticated blackmailer who played well to the public gallery. The evidence of Keller or any of the other 'girls' is very rarely accepted. So the freedom that de Sade claimed for himself in escaping the religious and moral conventions, norms and mores of society – his right to be a libertine – was almost always at the physical cost of the women who had been procured for his pleasures. And in the writings that he did in prison, it was his procuress whom he blamed for his fate. It was, he claimed, a woman who held responsibility for his actions.

Let us also consider the case of Dora. In Victor Seidler's *Unreasonable Men: Masculinity and Social Theory* (1994), he looks at the ways in which Nietszche, Freud and Wittgenstein all helped in their own way to question modernity. In looking at Freud, Seidler's very interesting discussion of Dora shows how the treatment of this 'hysteric' was predicated upon Freud's refusal to accept that she had been subjected to sexual advances by her father's lover's husband. Her description of propositions made to her are translated by Freud into a deep-seated wish on the young woman's part for this to really happen. Her testimony is seen as an unconscious wish which causes her great anxiety rather than a straightforward description of what she had actually suffered. Freud's own words and analysis show how hard he struggled to find a way of not believing that Dora had been subject to sexual advances by her father's friend. He ruled out this possibility for explaining her 'hysteria', finding it much more appealing to see in her story the repression of female desires rather than the expression of male satyriasis. It is her desire, not his, which explains the problems that the family faced.

215

Thus, the techniques for establishing privacy in the face of systems of state surveillance have been in place for centuries. They involve close control of the membership, systems of exclusion (such as black-balling) and 'punishment' for treachery to the group's aims and objectives. As Lyon (1994: 185–6) shows, often such systems seem eminently reasonable, particularly when faced with those put in place by such as Lenin, who said in 1920, that 'we recognize nothing private.

CHAPTER 7   *Fourth Exhibit: Panopticon City*

Think for a moment about Foucault's discussion of the 'Lapcourt incident'. In Volume 1 of *The History of Sexuality*, Foucault (1979: 31–2) speaks of a simple-minded farm hand from the village of Lapcourt who in 1867 was reported to the mayor for obtaining a 'few caresses from a little girl, just as he had done before and seen done by the village urchins round about him; for, at the edge of the wood, or in the ditch by the road leading to Saint-Nicholas, they would play the familiar game called "curdled milk"'.

Foucault describes this as a petty affair: as inconsequential bucolic pleasures in the life of village sexuality where simple-minded adults and alert children engage in furtive sex. But if we think about this critically can we really assume that the little girl is alert and not terrified; that his behaviour is without moral consequence and is not a use of power by a strong male over a small female; that the fact that the girl reports his action of producing 'curdled milk' is her petty intolerance of a simpleton's natural desires which deserve expression? The phallic concentration of the male academic in this passage pushes into the background the concerns of the female. Despite Foucault's (1979: 344) disgust at the Greek obsession with the virile society and penetration, his own treatment of the Lapcourt incident is itself decidedly phallocentric (Ramazanoglu 1993: 40).

216

In Freemasonry the baring of legs and breasts is designed to 'weed out' women and prevent them from being 'on the level'. The phallic imagery in the Freemasons' enthusiasm for monoliths such as the Canary Wharf Tower and 'Cleopatra's Needle' is also of some significance. The entombing of certain initiates with real skeletons in graves or enclosed spaces again attests to the importance attached to Egyptian artefacts and building techniques within 'the craft'. Any questions from outsiders are dismissed as being out of order because Freemasonry is a 'private' matter and not for public discussion. Incidentally, to reveal anything would also be against the oath which is taken to ensure that there will be absolute secrecy in matters of the craft! The punishment for revealing such secrets is to have one's throat cut. In the early 1980s Lord Hewlett, a leading mason in the northwest of England, was found dead in his home with his throat cut. The open razor lay next to the body: the verdict in the coroner's court was 'suicide'. His Masonic connections were never made fully public in court.

In Nonconformists and Quakers, we see a complete rejection of satyriasis, indeed a rejection of sexual licentiousness altogether. On undertaking strenuous investigations, Josiah Wedgwood found that the manufacturing buildings where his clerks were to be found was 'rather unfavourable to virtue and good order in young men'. Moreover, the head clerk was ill with 'the foul disease' and 'the house-keeper was frolicking with the cashier' (McKendrick 1973: 61). These features, in equal measure to the embezzlement he found, induced Wedgwood to make immediate changes to his 'House in Newport St.' and to his personnel. As Wedgwood's copious notes indicate, a major dynamic for his concerns was his shock at the past and present sexual behaviour of his head clerk and cashier. One had contracted syphilis, the other was engaged in an ongoing liaison within the organization.

The technical development of cost accounting in the Wedgwood factory then has to be seen in parallel to a set of changes aimed at the desexualization of his workforce and the control of the sexual

217

audio surveillance	(e.g. bugs)
visual surveillance	(e.g. video, satellite, night vision)
data surveillance	(e.g. computer networks, software)
sensor technology	(e.g. infra-red, magnetic)
other devices	(e.g. polygraphs, universal personal identifiers (UPI)

(Lyon 1994: 104)

Does it make sense then to speak of a 'surveillance society' (Lyon 1994), the empire of the gaze (Jay 1985) the 'maximum security society' (Marx 1988) or 'the superpanopticon' (Poster 1990)? The answer must surely be 'Yes' – given the developments on all technological and organizational fronts. But as Gouldner (1970: 99) showed, in the face of increasing state surveillance of the populace, a 'possessive, self-protecting individualism' leads to the growth of the concept of privacy. The 'salons' and 'chocolate houses' grew up in Paris and London, during the eighteenth century for example, to be *private* meeting places in which agents of the police and informers were judiciously searched for and forcibly excluded. So whilst Elizabeth Fry and the Quakers were keen to make public what was going on in the prisons of Britain they were also of a mind to hold their own discourse in private surroundings which excluded rude members of the populace. Freemasons had developed techniques for doing so many years earlier and for much the same reasons. In the UK alone, up to 300,000 men in 1994 were estimated to be members of more than 8,000 lodges.

CHAPTER 7   *Fourth Exhibit: Panopticon City*

wantonness of his staff. In this double-edged process Wedgwood was not alone. His condemnation of extravagance and dissipation were echoed throughout eighteenth-century Britain and beyond. In Britain, the Quakers in particular amongst Nonconformists were very keen to use religious precepts to suppress sexuality in a whole range of burgeoning organizational forms, not solely the factory. The prison, the hospital, the workhouse, and so on were all involved. Quaker social conscience was something which went beyond mere religion for it included 'a traditionally Puritan view of the stewardship of talents stressing the value of hard work, lack of waste, the careful organization of resources and personal renunciation, all for the service of others' (Child 1964: 294).

It has been pointed out (Thompson 1968; Sohn-Rethel 1977) that since time-wasting was inimical to efficient capital accumulation the moves towards its calculation and commodification in the eighteenth century were almost inevitable. The time 'spent' in domestic production in the family home during this period was not fully controllable by merchant capital. The 'putting out' system allowed for much responsible autonomy, in that, besides engaging in production, time could be 'spent' by workers in sexual play or in long periods of leisure

218

the surveillance capabilities that are now used to see if very young infants are still breathing in their nurseries is welcomed by anxious parents fearing 'cot deaths'. And the perceived threat of theft of personal items in large office buildings means staff *are* willing to be weighed at the entrance door and to use swipe cards. The cry of 'what have you to object to, if you are not doing anything wrong' is then added to the indication of the positive benefits of a supposed reduction in crime and it becomes difficult to specify one's objections to cameras on the campus.

Yet some of these technologies are worrying, particularly when seen in combination. AT&T recently introduced a 'Universal Card' which combines the functions of a bank card, a credit card and a telephone card. This provides a service but one which empowers AT&T considerably. It empowers AT&T not only in which of its own products it would then be able to sell to 'Universal Card' users but also in that the company could re-sell the information on to willing and eager commercial organizations. Data commands a high price as a commodity.

Outside of consumer-based surveillance, it is possible, as the US Office of Technology Assessment (OTA) has done, to list five categories of surveillance technology:

CHAPTER 7   *Fourth Exhibit: Panopticon City*

activity or in an unrestrained consumption of goods and foodstuffs. Once the workforce were out of the home and into the factory, tighter time discipline was possible. Most employers, though not all, thought that sex had its place (Ignatieff 1978: 50) but not within the expanding walls of the factory nor in the long hours of working time. Almost without exception, entrepreneurs felt that discipline and good order were not improved by sexual activity during work time (Perkin 1979; Gaskell 1836; Factory Commission 1833; Weeks 1981).

Wedgwood is but an early example of this implicit and often explicit relationship in the mind of the early entrepreneur between sexuality and inefficiency. The revelations about the private (sexual) lives of his employees encouraged Wedgwood to dismiss them and to improve his control mechanisms, not only in the area of his costs but in the morality of his workforce too. Elizabeth Fry, another Quaker, was horrified by what she found on her visit to Newgate Prison, where sexual licentiousness was rife. Her suggested reforms of the prison system have to be seen in the light of her wish to control sexuality in organizations as much as her concern for enlightened practices of incarceration. The assumptions of Pacioli's famed invention, double-entry book-keeping with its 'mirror' metaphor and its personification of accounts, found themselves reproduced in a Puritan accountancy which emphasized savings and discouraged consumption. Management control systems were formulated in which the spending of time

219

this technique is increasing. The type of data and the amount of information available to commercial interests can be of staggering proportions. For example, Lyon (1994) claims that some 'feminine hygiene' companies are aware of the expected day of menstruation for thousands of their customers and send free samples to coincide with the individual's cycle.

Robins and Webster (1988) argue that this process of collecting data on the consumer began as part of 'Sloanism' – a much underrated approach to organization design – developed in General Motors in the 1920s by Alfred Sloan. He collected data on the buying habits of his customers by the use of highly sophisticated demographic and socio-economic techniques and encouraged IBM to provide data services for this kind of commercial surveillance.

But, of course, many consumers do not see these processes as a threat. On the contrary, the timely arrival of free tampons or information on cars which appear to fit in with design requirements for your particular 'needs', seems helpful and not at all questionable. Similarly

CHAPTER 7   *Fourth Exhibit: Panopticon City*

and the spending of the body became key focuses of attention. Gradually but generally, sexuality within the organization became a spent force. Yet satyriasis continued to flourish. The theory of desexualization and the pursuit of their own individual practice were kept separate in the minds and bodies of powerful men.

The upper levels of organizations are still replete with satyriasis. In the early days of Hollywood lighting arrangements were primitive but crucial, for wrinkles and facial blemishes showed up in remarkable, attention-arresting detail. There was a strong impetus to employ very young actresses whose skin had not yet begun to show the ravages of time. The highly successful but embittered Betty Grable described her experiences as a 13-year-old Busby Berkeley chorus girl in the following way:

> Those parties were the pits. You'd come out in the early dawn feeling like a piece of meat dogs had been fighting over all night. If my mother hadn't been with me I'd have killed myself a dozen times over. A lot of girls did. It was soul-destroying but everywhere you turned there were stories about how so and so made it that way. The message was you either played it their way or you got out of town. (quoted in Ford 1990: 96)

220

allows for much closer control of their behaviour. Indeed, more important than Big Brother is the fact that 'people are today seduced to conform by the pleasures of consuming the goods that corporate power has to offer' (Shearing and Stenning 1985: 347). Dandeker (1990) shows that the military organization of '3CI' or 'Command, Control, Communication and Intelligence' is becoming very obvious in the realm of consumption. Indeed, the consumer can take on, and is invited to take on, the role of manager. Many academics are familiar with student feedback, done in the form of a satisfaction rating of the service provided, and increasingly these are used in addition to citation indices in which where academics publish counts for as much as 'what' they publish. In another realm, the 'omniscient organization' knows everything that is important about the consumption of their goods and services as well as about the issues concerning production. Thus, the consumer as well as the worker has been targeted for information about themselves and as an object fit for control (Lyon 1994: Chapter 8). Dealing with 'junk mail' has become a way of life for many Western inhabitants. Taft (1995) argues that, in Canada, the average domestic home receives about 60 pounds of advertising material per year. The personalized letters from Reader's Digest Inc. must have some financial impact in the eyes of the company, because the use of

The politics of bodies in the workplace is recognized by Cynthia Cockburn (1991: 27) who sees women's bodies as part of the deal between women workers and their employers. And surely nowhere is this clearer than in the movie business. Here we see sex, violence and death time and time again. The stories of the priapic moguls in Hollywood are legion and some of them even appear to have some basis in truth. The casting couch and the ways in which actresses were expected to behave in order to succeed were associated with the huge sexual appetites of the moguls. Satyriasis is power in action. The cult of the libertine was expressed well by Fatty Arbuckle and Errol Flynn. David Niven's candid memoirs show just how phallocentric were those times where a latter-day libertinism was so obvious.

But what is libertinism? Some young dons at All Souls College in Oxford as early as 1675 attempted to print copies of an explicit sexual manual using the Oxford University presses but were caught in the act by their superiors. Nevertheless, the Restoration provided pornography, the use of four-letter words in explicit published material, the importation of dildoes from Italy and the use of the first condoms for prophylactic rather than contraceptive purposes (Stone 1979: 334). The scene was set for a libertinism which is still discernible today. After the impact of seventeenth-century puritanism had died away, a sexual morality amongst upper-class 'bachelors' developed. In the precepts of Casanova, for example, we can detect an ethical code of sorts – that women of inferior social rank are fair game for sexual exploitation. Similarly, in England, the libertine was expected 'To marry off a former mistress, if possible, before [he] took a new one; to maintain a lady handsomely in her lying in, to provide for the little one if he lived, according to the degree of the mother, if she died' (quoted in Stone 1979: 332).

It was in France, however, that libertinism, merged with anti-Christian ideology, reached its zenith. The erotic writings of Choderlos de Laclos and the Marquis de Sade are the manifestations of this strand of thinking. In England, its more practical outcome was the Hell-Fire

221

against the date in the book's title. The more we can say we are not approaching: 'the exact opposite of the stupid, hedonistic utopias that the old reformers imagined . . . a world which will not grow less but more merciless as it refines itself' (Orwell 1954: 214), the more the time-binding nature of the book is strengthened – not weakened.

Yet it is the parcelled areas of hedonistic utopias – the smile factories – which represent surveillance in more insidious forms. The conversion of citizens into consumers (Shearing and Stenning 1985)

CHAPTER 7 *Fourth Exhibit: Panopticon City*

Club of Sir Francis Dashwood. In the club an emphasis was placed on total disregard for the convention of gentlemanly conduct that men were protective of women's honour from the advances of other men in so far as they saw the woman as likely to be their own property and behaved in a chivalrous way towards women on all occasions. In the Hell-Fire Club women were seen as ripe for abuse, verbal, physical and sexual. Libertinism, as the name suggests, encouraged an escape from the prevailing mores of society and embraced the orientation of 'anything goes' which characterizes the decadents of a century later.

However, it is worth noting here that powerful women often are shown by men to adopt similar forms of behaviour. If one allows for the enmity of jealous male opponents who readily hurl the term 'nymphomaniac' in the direction of female rivals, one can see the following. At the time of de Sade, the relevant term for the same thing was 'uterine frenzy'. Catherine the Great of Russia for example is legendary for her sexual appetite and she commissioned art and furniture decoration which would not find its way readily into today's high street furniture stores. As part of modern myth it is said that she enjoyed sex with horses so much that she had a contraption built which slung a stallion above her in order that she could pleasure herself with the animal. She died, it is said, when the apparatus broke and she was crushed by the falling animal. Back in Hollywood, Tallulah Bankhead enjoyed a reputation for sexual adventureness during her period as one of the industry's leading actresses. As a bisexual female, Bankhead's activities were of interest to the business and she was openly criticized by her contemporaries. Marlon Brando, in his recent memoirs (1995), describes her in very hostile terms, seeking to marginalize her from his life and to portray her in some diabolical way. He shows her to the best of his ability as a pursuer of sexual pleasure and as a heavy drinker. In other words she represents the Dionysian in her life of intermittent passion, whereas his early performances of controlled rationality stand much more for the Apollonian. The predatory male whose conquests are opened up for all to see deems her equally active life to be unacceptable. He presents her as cold and fearful because of the way she threatened *his* virility. She is seen as a threat to the masculine culture of Hollywood.

222

portrayed as an ordinary man with ordinary talents – except in his dedication to the objectives of the state. Such are monuments.

Interestingly, while *Nineteen Eighty-four* envisaged a dystopia in which Big Brother had developed space-binding technology, the success and insight of the book has meant that the text *itself* has become a time-binding technology in which each year can be marked off

CHAPTER 7   *Fourth Exhibit: Panopticon City*

David Noble's book *World without Women* (1994) shows how masculine culture arose with the Latin Church – and almost certainly remains within twentieth-century historians. Early Christian asceticism, male monasticism in the fourth century, the universities growing out of the male cathedral schools, the Inquisition, the Counter-Reformation and modern science were all driven by women. How? They are the presence in the absence; just off-stage, of course, but the play revolves around them. The institutions which dominate the last 500 years are there because of the presence of men in relation to women. Modern industry, as Noble puts it, is a transcendent project through which men can recover from the Fall and restore Eden without Eve. Women are blamed by men for disasters, and the biggest disaster is life itself. Massey (1993) claims that high-technology centres such as the Cambridge Science Park are modern manifestations of the male-centred (phallocentric) monasteries. For they continue the line of exclusion of women from powerful institutions.

represent labyrinths if we so wished, with quiet, unseen corners allowing the non-Stakhanovites to idly hide. Whereas Stakhanov produced an amount of coal one day in 1935 which was fourteen times his minimum quota, in Ashington such heroic feats were often frowned upon. One Charlie Mayes, a gentle and loving man, left North Seaton colliery one day in the same year with a record pay-packet for the fortnight. He was 'the talk of the place' but not all were pleased by his performance. Some were hostile to such levels of output. Thus coal owners saw the need for supervisors to be seen and to see in the midst of the workplace (and the community), the need for straight-line roadways underground, the need for lamps which allowed the miner to see – but also to be seen – the check-weighing of production instead of the observation of work as the measure of output, the pit-head baths and mandatory X-ray screening where the health of the miner could be seen and checked by bath attendant and radiographer. 'Space-binding technologies' as described by Innis in *The Bias of Communication* allow the promulgation of rules over wide geographical distances, even underground. 'Time-binding' technologies, on the other hand, issue commands in tablets of stone which, because of the heaviness of the material, create a certain durability or binding in time. As we shall see later, monumental architecture, which is created to remind the inhabitants of the locale of the name and achievements of individuals, may also be seen as a form of 'time-binding' technology located at a specific point in space. The monument to Stakhanov did not make him out to be exceptionally powerful or blessed with superior skills. He is

CHAPTER 7 *Fourth Exhibit: Panopticon City*

Women, in the main, recognize all too clearly this exclusion and the forms it takes in contemporary organizations, which are often of a hierarchical kind.

The role of the Latin Church in the exclusion of women is foregrounded by Noble for good reason. Extremely ancient customs have survived in Northumberland, that county which lies on the border between Scotland and England. Until the end of the sixteenth century at least, the Northumbrian men 'did not prize the chastity of their women, and women offered their favours freely to strangers, both attitudes which have been observed in several very primitive societies in other parts of the world' (Stone 1979: 383).

Stone is quoting from the journals of an Italian cleric and diplomat who later went on to become Pope Pius II. Travelling northwards through Northumberland, the Italian priest spent the night in a small hamlet, where he had dinner. After the meal, all the men and children withdrew into a fortified 'Peel' tower, leaving the future Pope and the women to take their chance with the Scottish bandits. The Northumbrian men justified this process of excluding on the grounds that rape was the 'worst' fate that would befall the women and this was not a 'crime' within their system of ethics. Since the cleric was an honoured guest, two women offered to 'sleep' with him in his room which, like theirs, contained nothing but straw. The future Pope refused their offer of sex, we are told, only for fear of being murdered by the Scots while in a condition of mortal sin.

224

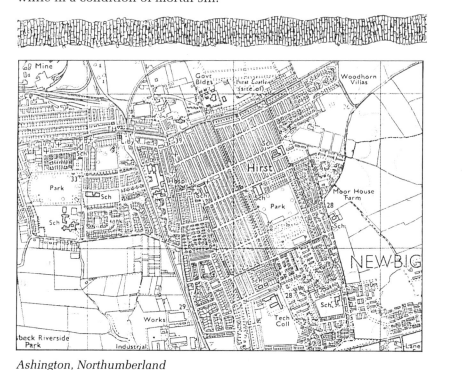

Ashington, Northumberland

Stone describes this as the 'populations habitually casual way' in relation to sex in the medieval period (1979: 383). Notice in passing, however, Stone's sexist and 'racist' biases here in assuming these customs represent 'primitive' forms of behaviour and more importantly that these should be seen from the males' point of view. It is the phallus which speaks, even in academic discourse.

The 'droit de seigneur' was exercised throughout this period and rarely forsaken during the time when other men were encouraged within the Church to organizationally cut themselves off from women. And whilst heterosexuality may have been quietened by these cloisterings, it gives way to the supposed problem of male homosexuality. Here it is important to note that these relationships may not be consensual but subject to violence and threats of death. Satyriasis is not only heterosexual. We have to appreciate that there may well be homosexual priapism too. We need only to appreciate the fact that Luca Pacioli, the 'father' of accounting, was specifically debarred by his superiors from seeing boys to fully appreciate the long pedigree of the role of these sexual drives within the organizational context of the Church.

Following Chatfield (1977), Burchell et al. (1980) maintain that accounting emerged from the management practices of the estate, the trader and the embryonic corporation. What is ignored here is the role of the monastery as a source of inspiration for accounting practices and as a centre for organizational innovation. Luca Pacioli published his fifth book *Summa de Arithmetica* in 1494, many years after becoming a Franciscan monk. In this period, mathematics was seen as a branch of theology, so before a teaching career in this field could begin, young

villages of many industrial societies. The map opposite shows the rationalized approach to planning very clearly indeed. It is panopticism on a very large scale. It transcends the building itself and enters the town as a building programme.

Ashington then, is a surface location which stands for a 'space-binding' technology (Innis 1951: 9) which interestingly reflects the space-binding nature of the underground workings of the collieries upon which it is based. As one can readily grasp, problems of communication underground are very difficult and the darkness creates a world in which non-legitimate activity would be easy to perpetrate since the principles of light (within Newtonian physics, at least) do not allow for obvious underground surveillance. Pits could easily come to

CHAPTER 7 *Fourth Exhibit: Panopticon City*

men were expected to take vows and enter a monastery. Pacioli maintained throughout his life that his views on accounting and mathematics were part of a wider spiritual endeavour which he had learned from the Franciscan friars in his home town of Borgo San Sepulcro (Nakanishi 1979). Without doubt the monastery was a major focus of attention for Pacioli, in both a private and a theoretical sense. Much of the later theoretical development of Pacioli's model and of book-keeping in general derived from a concern to utilize the double-entry system in monasteries. Thus Don Angelo Pietra, a Benedictine monk, and Ludovico Flori, a Jesuit priest, elaborated Pacioli's work in relation to monasterial accounting in ways which persisted for centuries in other organizational forms (Chatfield 1977).

Many orders of monks engaged in trade and commerce at this time. But there were special features of the monasteries of the medieval period which differentiate the monasteries from embryonic corporations. In early Catholicism, a number of doctrinal beliefs stressed that human sexuality was directly derived from the animal kingdom and was therefore best seen as inhuman and bestial in all mature adults. As monasteries developed into bureaucratically organized institutions, these sorts of belief received tremendous support. For example, the Venerable Bede (1907) outlined a whole series of punishments or penitentials for those found engaging in sexual licentiousness. Later the Catholic Bishop of Lincoln, Robert Grosseteste, was also keen to stress

226

The Duke of Portland's final control over the village was his ownership of a railway bridge over the River Wansbeck which he charged the Ashington Coal Company to use. The toll for decades was sixpence per ton of coal moved south to the markets of the world. Trains consisted of thirty wagons carrying 30 tons each and crossed the bridge every 15 minutes or so in a normal working week in the years before the 1950s. Ashington thus represents social architecture emplaced upon a particular location, about 100 years ago. It used contemporary thinking about how to organize, both spatially and functionally, an 'isolated mass' of supposedly refractory industrial workers. The location of supervisors in the 'midst' of the ordinary face workers, the long open streets, the attempted control of social life, the imposition of a bourgeois 'culture' through 'naming' and so on are all features of towns and

CHAPTER 7   *Fourth Exhibit: Panopticon City*

the need to suppress sexuality in the monasteries and convents of the thirteenth century where 'frightful excesses' were in evidence (Cleugh 1963: 87). Throughout the period there were papal calls for 'real' celibacy to be practised. The institutional day was to be filled with work and prayer, prayer and work. Grosseteste himself advocated the careful copying of manuscripts as a useful way of reducing idleness. He was also concerned to test the resilience of nuns to a life of celibacy by enjoining them to sleep naked with young monks on the night before taking final vows (Cleugh 1963: 95). For those caught in acts of sexual abandonment after taking vows of celibacy there was the scourge or castration.

In the militarization of large numbers of monks which also took place at this time, particularly under Pope Gregory VII, the encouragement of male comradeship was evident as a strategy for suppressing hetero-sexual activity. From all this it is clear to see that the medieval Catholic Church spent much time and effort in seeking to eradicate sexuality from the confines of its institutions. The context in which Pacioli was working was supposedly one of celibacy, of work and prayer to reduce the amount of free time available to priests, and of an emphasis on good order, discipline and chastity. It didn't work too well.

227

The community emphasized enhanced social status through exper-tise at football (soccer). The case of the Charlton brothers was held up from the early 1960s for all to see as *the* way forward. They were born and brought up in Juliet Street where their mother could be seen play-ing with them at football in the street. She was a formidable header of the ball, being a close relative of another local hero – Jackie Milburn. The streets teemed with community life of this kind. However, the gridiron system, as Haussmann recognized very well, allowed for much greater social and police control. The police station in Ashington was built in 1891 to bring law and order to the district. Given the lin-ear principles of optics so graphically described by Bentham, an officer of the law standing at the top of Rosalind Street, for example, could see for at least half a mile what was going on in the street. Equipped with bicycles, it was comparatively easy for the police to move from trouble spot to trouble spot. However, Rosalind Street itself was unlikely to be a source of trouble because it was the street of supervisors' houses placed in the midst of 'ordinary' miners. These members of the hier-archy were termed, in classic supervisory parlance, overmen and deputy-overmen. The former were responsible for production, the lat-ter for safety, and their hierarchical positioning indicated clearly for all to see which was deemed to be more important.

CHAPTER 7   *Fourth Exhibit: Panopticon City*

At the time when Pacioli wrote his *Summa* there was a developing sense of the accountability of persons to themselves and each other (Elias 1978). But whilst Pacioli himself was subject to extremely tightly imposed discipline upon his sexuality he nevertheless continued to transgress normal standards of conduct. In his analysis of aristocratic table manners and rules of etiquette, Elias has sought to show that European societies have been characterized by 'a civilizing process' which more or less develops unilinearly, although subject to setback and reversal. Key to this process is the development of social constraint and individual restraint in a wide variety of human relationships. According to Elias, the feeling of shame surrounding human sexual activity increases markedly during the civilizing process. In the Middle Ages, the concealment and segregation of sexuality was relatively slight. Obscenity as a concept came to Europe only at the beginning of the sixteenth century. Prior to this, public nudity was common. Children's books explicitly dealt with sexual matters. But after 1500, the sexual drive outside the monastery and convent was subject to ever stricter control and transformation. Adults were pressurized into privatizing their impulses, silence descended on such matters when children were present, words dealing with sexual acts and bodily parts became highly charged with emotion. Shame and embarrassment developed as recognizable emotional states connected to the individual's own sexuality.

228

of resistance developed. A plethora of Working Men's Clubs grew up to augment the prescribed 'hotels' within the township. At one time there were these three hotels and *fifty-six* drinking clubs, the vast majority of which were larger than all the hotels. Social life for males revolved around the clubs with their restricted membership and specialist cultures. Much emphasis was placed upon a kind of relationship with nature which was not typical of the early nineteenth century. Many miners had 'allotments' of land in which leek growing was encouraged and annual competitions attracted prizes of thousands of pounds. The largest leeks for each year were a source of social status but 'showing' them involved avoidance of sabotage and the use of magical potions to increase length, weight and diameter. Pigeon racing was another source of community interest: many an allotment had a 'cree' or shed where pigeons were kept. The relationship to nature here is one of control, therefore, but not in a crass, destructive sense. It is much more a harnessing of natural forces to encourage nature to channel itself in ways which humans can shape. It is working *with* nature not against it.

CHAPTER 7   *Fourth Exhibit: Panopticon City*

This process of developing self-awareness should not be under-emphasized. The work of Erasmus, in particular, stands as an example of the new 'individualization' where men and women are expected to stand outside of themselves, look at their actions and control their emotions, their language, their behaviour (Elias 1978). The concept of the 'person' presupposes an ability to look at oneself objectively and engage in some self-reflexivity and self-control.

For Hoskin and MacVe (1986), the mirror image of double-entry book-keeping had a primary function, not of balancing the books *per se* but in affording a new measure of control to those who used it. Jacques Lacan demonstrates how the self-concept of individuals, their 'I', is constructed through the image of the body which appears to them in reflections. The mirror stage is crucial in controlling the libidinous desires of human beings for it represents a transformation stage that takes place in individual subjects as they move towards self-awareness and self-control. Thus, Pacioli's *Summa* may be seen as a text within a very specific context. The medieval world in which 'The Method of Venice' developed as a form of accounting was a world in which sexuality was the target for restraint and constraint, particularly within the monasteries. As part of this 'civilizing process', self-identification and self-awareness were stressed. Men and women were encouraged to see themselves as others would see them – as if in a mirror.

usually women (Rosalind, Beatrice, Juliet, etc.) and contained about sixty terraced houses per row. These were called the 'colliery rows' for they were built by the Ashington Coal Company around the turn of the century in an area called 'the Hirst'. Labour was recruited from all over the UK during the 1880s and 1890s, to what was become in this period an industrial boomtown. The land was owned by the teetotal Duke of Portland who insisted that only three public houses were to be allowed to serve the needs of almost 30,000 inhabitants. These were the 'Grand Hotel' located prominently in what was the 'village' centre. It never achieved the status of a town, being therefore the largest mining village in the world. Second came the North Seaton Hotel which was on the fringes of the village and set in green fields . Hence it earned the nickname of 'The White Elephant' and finally the 'Portland Hotel' itself, located in the hierarchically preferred 'west end' of the township.

After some time, schools were built for the population. These were named the Wansbeck, for the older, socially superior west side of the village, and the Hirst East, Hirst North and Hirst South. Rivalry between these locales was encouraged in team sports and community loyalty. In order to escape the limitations upon drinking, a mass form

CHAPTER 7 *Fourth Exhibit: Panopticon City*

The importance of the visual in exciting satyriasis as well as self-control is noteworthy, for language and imagery is often *man*-made (Spender 1982). In the world of advertising, sex and sexual imagery are heavily used. Listen to Dyer (1985) on a Renault automobile advert:

> She is made into a decorative passive object available and controllable like the car. She is moulded in the form that men desire . . .; it invites the signified voyeurism and sexual power and control through the forms of signifiers.

Women are stereotyped in the simplest of terms. Barmaids, nurses and air stewardesses are all presented as sexual objects. Consider the modern airline and its encouragement of masculinism in an overt sexual form in those whom it believes to be powerful: 'Simply by virtue of the phallic shape of planes, flying sets up a male metaphorical structure. This could, however, be offset by the womb-like interior were it not for the connotations of power, hierarchy and chain of command set up by the pervasive symbolism of uniforms and uniformity' (Höpfl 1990). Equally important, says Höpfl, are constant references to clock towers, church spires, skyscrapers, thundering horses and so on in advertising which underline the phallic shape at the expense of the enclosing interior. In itself this male imaginative structure creates difficulties for women, but, argues Höpfl, this is considerably compounded by the reality of the female stewardess figure.

230

A truly remarkable set of claims for architecture but one which allows whole villages to feel its influence over a century later. Soweto, the set of encampments around Johannesburg in South Africa, is named from the fact that it is the constellation of *South Western Townships*. Its name, in classic modernist style, reflects its function and location exactly. Its function is further rationalized by using only its acronymic term. Its identity and place are given to it – imposed upon it – from outside. One hundred years ago, mining villages in the UK were subject to similar forces. Ashington, in Northumberland, for example, was built upon a gridiron system with 'avenues' running east to west for three quarters of a mile being numbered (First Avenue, Second Avenue, etc.) and with streets running north to south of well over a mile in length. These were named after Shakespearean characters,

Her attributes of caring and serving are made to stand in for her complete being. In semiotic terms, she does not provide a metaphor for female caring; it is the caring that provides a realistically plausible link between the stewardess and all women. On board aircraft, almost all that female flyers have to identify with is the symbolism of the female nurturer or sex object, underpinned by a recognition that the pragmatic experience of the stewardess is probably as both these things. At the most powerful level of myth and metaphor, the corporate imagination which so informs airline design is clearly male. It draws all its symbolic reference points from a patriarchal – almost tribal – power structure in which traditionally women have no role. Prime amongst these, says Höpfl, is the cultural baggage which attaches to the military uniforms, particularly those of the navy and the air force which have become a model for airline uniforms. Whilst there are women in the armed forces, in our collective minds, uniformed sailors and flyers are male. More importantly, the uniform signifies a chain of command, dominated at the top by men and this command structure is echoed in the reality of male pilots, who are, of course, given the highly symbolic title of Captain. It is they who speak to us as the deep voice of authority, disembodied and invisible like the Wizard of Oz, from the front of the body of the aircraft.

denounced, individuals were sent to detention centres where they were subject to constant monitoring, including having to share a bed with the observer. It is almost as if the Chinese Government had seen and believed Bentham's claims for his new and great instrument of government – the only effective instrument of reformative management. He makes the following claims for his machine in an early example of advertising blurb.

> Morals reformed – health preserved – industry invigorated – induction diffused – public burdens lightened – economy seated, as it were, up on a rock – the Gordian Knot of the Poor Law not cut, but untied – all by the simple idea on Architecture! (Bentham 1838–43)

CHAPTER 7   *Fourth Exhibit: Panopticon City*

My original intention here was to show how women had been marginalized in discourse (Mills and Tancred 1992) but then it happened that this page itself was at the very outer edge of an early version of *Pandemonium*. Consciously or unconsciously the very phenomenon I wished to criticize had occurred within the text itself. This marginalization revealed itself to me in ways I had not expected. My discussion of marginalization was, in highly graphic form itself indicative of the problem. By accident rather than design, if you believe that there is a difference of any significance between them, female airline staff had been placed at the periphery of the tour of the city. Within this nether world those that fly are out of reach anyway and this is a reason for their positioning, but more seriously this place where we now stand is not the end of *Pandemonium* but is the middle of our journey. In Pandemonium flying women populate all of the city just as they are crucial to visions of Paradise and the medieval imagery attendant upon it. But as in the late Middle Ages, the flying female is bound to a world of earthly limitations. She flies in a circle around powerful and wealthy men, locked into their orbit of meaning systems and subject to their (my?) priapic gaze.

232

Once at our work, we may be subjected to 'profiling' where simply because we share a set of characteristics with other individuals who are thought to have been guilty of some misdemeanour we too are deemed to be high risk and worthy of investigation. The US Internal Revenue Service, for example, operates a red flag system where a simple listing of characteristics which in the past have been found in cases of tax evasion are used to generate close surveillance of anyone who shows similar characteristics. In *Wild Swans* there is a description of post-revolutionary China under Mao in which people were encouraged to complain in the mid-1950s about the regime itself but when this encouragement of openness came to an end, the loyalty of all complainants was investigated. There was a quota in each institution of 5 per cent 'rightists' who had to be denounced and severe penalties were imposed on the head of any institution who could not deliver up this meagre proportion of transgressors. 'Rightists' could be identified by their having any past connections, even of the most tenuous kind, with the Kuomintang regime or by their having visited abroad. Their present loyalty or behaviour was not the issue. What was important was the past. There was tremendous encouragement of reporting of friends, relatives and work colleagues to the authorities. Once

Uniform, says Höpfl, must not be seen to refer only to the clothes worn by staff. Interior décor colours in Executive and Club lounges dip into the same cultural pool, as does the company's overall corporate identity. Beyond the uniform, there is also the idea of 'uniformity' and rigidity for rules, and behind rules a governing order with its patriarchal connotations. Maleness is therefore privileged at the most fundamental level of language and symbolism. Partly this maleness has to do with flying itself for the very shape of the modern plane is suggestive of maleness, and this shape is given precedence over the female symbolism of the aircraft's 'body' with its curves and womb-like interior. As Mills (1995) has shown, British Airways for example, has deliberately chosen gendered images in its advertising campaigns. Throughout airport and interior design the phallic shape of the plane is picked up and then overcoded with a concentrated symbolist use of straight lines and hence rationality. Furniture (which could have been homely or randomly placed) is ordered into right angles; splashes of colour are quickly gathered up and processed into squares. Fabric and carpet patterns are regular, never random – always mathematical. Meanwhile, television advertising stresses the competitive element in business; print and press media focus on the symbolic status and elitism of management structures – and the concentration on time-use places every executive and every company in a kind of gladiatorial arena. If the woman passenger rejects all of these, she is simply an absence – a lack. Which might explain the feeling that some women have that they are 'not quite real' as business travellers. And, indeed, they are not real in any semiotic sense outside the stereotypes discussed above. All they are is two-dimensional photographic images. In the deeper realms of meaning (and therefore of identity), opines Höpfl, women who fly are marginalized and silenced.

→   ## The prisoner of the phallus?

Sigmund Freud wrote 'Anatomy is destiny' thereby suggesting amongst other things that the mind is tyrannized by the body (Freud 1958). Biological capacities do set the potential limits for human activities – and copulation, reproduction, birth and death form common threads to the life of members of the species. Differences in anatomy seem basic, profoundly differentiating and crucial to most if not all societies. The presence or absence of male or female organs is the critical test applied in assigning the gender of children at birth, for to these organs is attributed great social and psychological significance. For example, the level and type of celebration planned, the legal consequence predicted and the economic costs foreseen, frequently differ after parents see which sex organs are present in their child. As Chodorow (1978: 25) puts it 'We live an embodied life: we live with those genital and reproductive organs and capacities; those hormones and chromosomes that locate us physiologically as male and female.'

However, Chodorow goes on immediately to point out that there is nothing self-evident about these biological facts. The presence or absence of particular sex organs do not immediately invest the relevant body with particular behaviour patterns. Despite the atrocious mutilations of eunuchs in both Arab and Chinese societies, the evidence is that 'technical ingenuity took the place of the missing wherewithal' (Gonzalez-Crussi, 1988: 128). Oakley (1981: 53) describes some research work done on male twins who were circumcised by electrocautery at the age of seven months. On one twin the electric current was too strong and his penis was burnt off entirely. He was 'reassigned' as a girl and his genitals were reconstructed to resemble those of a female. His mother later described her 'new daughter' as 'so feminine', showing how gender identity is largely a postnatal and not a perinatal effect. According to Gonzalez-Crussi then, 'the mind is pre-

234

Consider a normal day in the life of a Western employee. As we drive to work, cameras check that we do not cross junctions when the lights are on red or amber. Further cameras on gantries check on the speed at which we are travelling. In the car park of our organization, further electronic surveillance keeps an eye on visitors and the comings and goings of employees. Once at the door the really heavy stuff begins, for as we have seen as we entered Pandemonium, there are now machines which weigh the staff member on entry into and exit from the building and identify him or her through the mandatory use of a swipe card.

←

CHAPTER 7   *Fourth Exhibit: Panopticon City*

eminent over matter (Gonzalez-Crussi 1988: 129) which is the reverse, of course, of Freud's dictum. From psychoanalytic viewpoints, gender is a psychic process not a fixed state or structure. Consider, for example, the conflict between *differing* perceptions of the vagina and penis, those organs seen as fixed, defined and defining by biology. Put simply, Freud viewed the genital difference as crucial to the development of the psychological differences between men and women. At the stage where the girl discovers she has no penis she blames her mother for this fate who, of course, shares her disadvantaged condition. Why mother and daughter should envy possession of a penis is not made clear. The mother is rejected by the girl who turns her affection and attention towards the penile possessor – her father. Later, the girl realizes the futility of seeing her father as a love object and her rejection of her mother gives way again to maternal identification. In this complex set of ways, Freud, by envisaging the female anatomy as inferior, inadequate (the clitoris is an inadequate version of the penis) and lacking, creates an image of women them*selves* and in their entirety as secondary to men. The vagina can also be seen as passive, a receptacle, as an absence waiting for a presence, but it is also viewed by some as all-devouring and barbed – the vagina dentata. Similarly, the clitoris is either the foreshortened penis or seen as the locus of multi-organismic potential. It is perceived to be a profound, disabling lack or the main creative subject of hedonics – the pursuit of pleasure (*Guardian*, 12 February 1992: 5). The penis, of course, is also capable of widely differing interpretations and symbolic utilization (Weeks 1986). Active male sexuality has been characterized by words such as 'penetrative', 'forceful', 'thrusting' and so on and these notions have come to domi-

In the precise period in which we are interested (1580–1630), Maurice of Nassau, Captain-General of Holland and Zeeland, in the face of Spanish threats developed systematic drill of his forces and divided them into small tactical units. Soldiers were taught to systematize their actions and in 42 precise moves developed by Maurice to be capable of constant volleying. Drilled by a cadre of supervising officers who were in constant overview of all activities, this force became quite successful (Lyon 1994). Thus we cannot say that the panopticon was the first surveillance device. What we can say definitely is that it was by no means the last. If we look around us today, the gaze of those who ever more effectively watch over our lives is there for all to see. Indeed that is the point of it!

CHAPTER 7   *Fourth Exhibit: Panopticon City*

nate 'successful' imaginings, so much so that it may be possible to describe many aspects of behaviour in contemporary Western society as phallocentric. There had been some interest of mine in recent years in the re-eroticization of organizations (Burrell 1991; Brewis and Grey 1994) but I now know that there are severe problems with this conceptualization. The way in which it has been expressed is decidedly utopian and it may be time to abandon this notion. Certainly, it fits very well with Anti-Organization Theory and the creation of an alternative set of relationships between men and women. These relations, based on an amorous language (Irigaray 1985) were seen as offering some hope for the future. However, from within the walls of Pandemonium, such ideas now strike me as phallocentric or as a form of priapism. Therefore it is extremely difficult to see how re-eroticization could be progressed. Indeed it is not even clear that it should be progressed. As Brewis and Grey (1994: 81) put it: 'Re-eroticisation theory . . . [treads] the well worn path of quasi-humanistic emancipatory promises through the medium of sexuality.'

The promise of *bonheur*, the good life within 'freedom', is at the root of such middle-aged thinking. It is essentially humanism of a radical kind. It fits within anti-organization theory. As old age creeps up on one, re-eroticization seems like a 'pipe-dream' caused by smoking some opiate or other. Some men claim to be unhappy about the concentration upon the phallic. Let us consider for a moment 'Michael Jackson's Penis' (Fuchs 1995). She argues that the continuing story of his penis is of broad political import. The lasting cultural importance of black genitalia (see Gilman 1985, especially Chapter 4) is reflected in the relevant penis being both a signifier and an absence. It is a 'productive ambivalence', for Jackson is sometimes seen as a transsexual (Fuchs 1995: 16). Yet his choreographed crotch grabbing and rubbing draws attention to the problem of his penis for it seems, perhaps, to go against his physical amorphousness. In the West only one body per gendered subject is 'right'. But Jackson never gets it right.

CHAPTER 7 *Fourth Exhibit: Panopticon City*

Gender benders

The discussion of this phenomenon developed around 1984 with the brief rise to fame of Culture Club and its lead singer 'Boy George'. Boy George deliberately cultivated an ambiguity in gender and sexual preference through pop videos and on-stage appearance. This allowed him and many commentators to talk of the space left by this 'bending' of gender for new identities which deviate from the norm. Whilst he was by no means the first to cultivate a sense of ambiguity about his gender (with David Bowie certainly adopting similar strategies in the late 1970s), Boy George's consummate skill allowed the development of the term at a time when the feminist agenda seemed to be visible and portentous. It created a quickening in the pace of discussions about 'masculinity' and what was meant by this term. In New York in the mid-1980s, Boy George's appearance created 'Boppers Drag' – not an attempt by men to pass themselves off as women but a conscious effort to blur gendered appearances. Men would smear lipstick over their faces or wear dresses with combat boots. The value system of this group did not revolve around transsexuality or cross-dressing, both of which rely heavily upon stereotypical images of the opposite gender.

237

Attempts at panopticism had been made in other places and at other times. The Book of Numbers records how the Israelites kept population records in the fifteenth century BC, whilst in the UK the Doomsday Book was specifically designed to produce a *descriptio* to find out how much wealth there was in the kingdom in order to harness it for the use of the feudal system about to be introduced (Lyon 1994).

In Christ Church, Oxford, there is a 'Watching Loft' where monks in the fifteenth century kept watch on parishioners who, on bringing gifts to the altar, were sometimes in the habit of taking away the offerings of previous visitors when these looked valuable or tempting. At the Rowntree chocolate factory in York there is a gallery for supervisors to walk around to survey the workforce.

CHAPTER 7   *Fourth Exhibit: Panopticon City*

The very concept of 'opposition' was questioned and attempts made to operate on and within the margins of gendered appearance. Full-blown drag has had a long history, and has more than a theatrical significance. In ancient Hinduism and in Greek and Roman society drag had religious connotations whilst in pantomime the artist who ends gender stereotyping has a role to play. Ru Paul Charles, a self-styled drag artist for the 1990s, is recently quoted as saying 'the truth is that I'm a man. The illusion is I look like a woman. But the illusion is truer' (*Cosmopolitan*, February 1992: 33–7). This concentration on appearance rather than biological equipment allows him to say, 'Honey, you're born naked and rest is drag.' In Shakespeare, one also finds that the link between biological equipment and human *character* is open to discussion. A speech by Lady Macbeth, on her desire to escape supposed feminine traits, raises the issue of 'femininity'. She implores

'Come, you spirits that tend on mortal thoughts, unsex me here; and fill me from the crown to the toe top-full of direst cruelty. Make thick my blood, stop up th'access and passage to remorse, that no compunctious visitings of nature shake my fell purpose nor keep peace between th'effect and it. Come to my woman's breasts and take my milk for gall . . .' (*Macbeth*, I.v.41–9)

238

asylums, Foucault showed how the architectural design for a panopticon was seen by some to be the 'perfect managerial tool'. Although the panopticon principle was used in Russian factory design and in the construction of a very small number of American prisons it was unsuccessful in calming the refractory tempers of the inmates for it led to deep psychological problems in those who entered its walls. Its failure in the nineteenth century and late eighteenth century was due not to a concern for the ethics of surveillance but for its pragmatic limitations.

In Miran Bozovic's (1995) edited collection of Bentham's writings on the panopticon, we are able to hear Bentham himself more clearly. This is 'the general idea' of it:

The building is circular.

The apartments of the prisoners occupy the circumference. You may call them if you please the cells. . . .

The apartment of the inspector occupies the centre . . . the inspector's lodge. . . .

To the windows of the lodge there are blinds. . . .

Small lamps, in the outside of each window of the lodge, backed by a reflector . . . throw light into the corresponding cells. . . .

A small tin tube might reach from each cell to the inspector's lodge . . . [so that] the slightest whisper of the one might be heard by the other. (Bozovic 1995: 35–7)

CHAPTER 7 *Fourth Exhibit: Panopticon City*

Lady Macbeth seeks not to embrace supposed male characteristics here but to adopt those attitudes which are thought to be decidedly non-feminine. She asks to be unsexed not resexed. She requires her organs not to be transformed into those of a man but to cease their normal functioning. Thus she does not desire 'masculinity'; she seeks an end to 'femininity'.

Transsexuals and cross-dressers, perhaps, seek to escape from one prison of stereotypical appearance and behaviour only to incarcerate themselves in the other. Gender benders, by operating at the margins, seek to reject their own gender's imprisonment in style, attitude and norms but they do not wish to embrace any other set of constraints, having sought to escape from the first. They desire not to resex themselves but to unsex themselves. Our language here is not helpful because of the deeply embedded nature of our understanding of gender. The word used to describe those undertaking gender bending is 'androgynous' – that is, having both male and female characteristics. But this is inadequate so long as 'male' and 'female' are such constraining terms. Gender bending is about desexing not dual-sexing. It is revolutionary in the sense of transcending categories rather than relying upon them. It is based upon a critical rejection of the implications locked within the linguistic terms themselves. Thus, 'androgyny' will simply not do, for that concept itself relies upon a fusion of tainted concepts. Paradoxical as it may seem, we need desexed or

As Jeremy Bentham and other advocates of management came to know only too well, for many the thought of being observed modifies behaviour. The predominance in the nineteenth century of the small-scale family enterprise based upon entrepreneurial skills brought surveillance to the fore. These entrepreneurs saw no use for 'management' because:

> 'the best instruction,' wrote a German handbook of 1868, 'is by word of mouth. Let it be given by the entrepreneur himself, all seeing, omnipresent and ever available, whose personal orders are reinforced by the personal example which his employees have constantly before their eyes'. (Hobsbawm 1975: 216)

Here then, in the cases cited, we have more examples of the operation of the panopticon.

The interest generated in panopticism by the work of Michel Foucault has led a number of writers to look at forms of surveillance in contemporary organizations. In addressing the concern that Bentham had for the close supervision of the inmates of factories, prisons and

CHAPTER 7 *Fourth Exhibit: Panopticon City*

→ neutral terms in which to continue the debate on gender in the 1990s. Not an easy vocabulary to develop, however.

Yet genetic engineering may provide some movement towards real and linguistic androgyny. Even conventional surgery is a start. Leigh Starr (1991: 46) describes the example of transsexual surgery which, whilst effective, requires candidates for this kind of operation to act as *stereotypical* females. The individual is not allowed to escape being a battlefield of meaning. Surgery also creates the cyborg – the cyber-netic/organic hybrid which fills the celluloid screen with the Six Million Dollar Man and Robocop. But the creation of 'monsters' which transcend normal conceptions relies upon 'the embodiment of that which is exiled from the self' (Leigh Starr 1991: 54). Thus the kind of androgyny which Flaubert appeared to seek (Barnes: 1985) is seen to be as monstrous as his interest in 'natural' animal freaks. An escape from gender stereotyping is an escape from the self and that involves, in part, an escape from the body. Lady Macbeth pronounces 'unsex me here' and in achieving this to some extent she is made capable of mon-strous and murderous acts. She becomes a chimaera at her own behest.

240

DO NOT CROSS THE CENTRAL RESERVATION

viewers on a Saturday early evening in the UK look at other members of the family with a wary eye just to make sure that the 9 million to one chance visitation will not happen tonight.

And in believing, even at the very, very extreme edge of credulity, that it *could* happen, for that one brief moment, anxious viewers behave differently – as *if* they were being watched from a studio in London by someone who, only too willingly, would be a vocal judge of ← their normality.

CHAPTER 7 *Fourth Exhibit: Panopticon City*

The penises which line the walls of much of Pandemonium are like those in Luxor where the Pharaohs painted upon the buildings of the Palace the numbers of dead killed by their armies in battle. The Pharaohs insisted that the penises of their enemies were cut off so that there could be a proper body count of those who had died. Women and children could not provide the organ of necessity so this was a clever accounting practice and measure of military performance. Once presented to the Pharaoh the penises were counted and painted upon the walls. So we can see that the symbolic value of the penis is hugely significant . But so too is that of the phallus. The penis itself is half animal, half human. It is a chimaera. It is penis below and phallus above. It is squashy yet hard, small yet large, ridiculous yet threatening. The penis/phallus is like Magritte's Surrealist masterpiece *Lover's Song* where two lovers look to sea with their legs touching in the attitude of affection. Look at their heads however and one sees that they are chimaeras. Their top halves are those of fish.

As we tour Pandemonium, there is a multiplicity of chimaeras at each and every corner. There are transsexuals, there are hybrid genetic organisms, there are hermaphrodites, centaurs, minotaurs, five-legged sheep and unicorns. Pegasus, Cyclops and Ra look down at us and our limitations. Pandemonium is full of the half-beast and the half-god. This corner of Pandemonium is the kingdom of Priapus but here gender and the role of the phallus is seen as problematic.

241

the street full of friends, relatives and children be told of the reasons for the failure to make connection. Thus, for that week, and for that reason, there was no NTV section on the programme. However, there are tapes of the incident and what was recorded on camera circulating within the BBC (it is alleged) to the merriment of all concerned.

What goes through the mind of the reader at this point? It may well be gendered (or not). Some men (and some women) may think 'There but for the grace of God . . .' Some women (and some men?) may think 'What a disgusting little creep.' But in reality, hidden cameras will always reveal dark secrets. In a sense, that is precisely *what they are designed for*. One could predict, as indeed one imagines the production team did, that sooner or later cameras of this kind, in use on a Saturday evening, will come across sexuality and sexual activity. These activities do occur in the home so surveillance *of* the home will encounter them very rapidly indeed.

As we know very well from *Nineteen Eighty-four*, Orwell's imagineering of Big Brother's technology allowed random entry into people's homes. At the moment, this is not quite possible, but millions of

CHAPTER 7

Fourth Exhibit: Panopticon City

Shame, there sit not, and reproach us as unclean.
So counselled hee, and both together went
Into the thickest wood

(Milton, *Paradise Lost*, Bk IX, ll. 1097–1100)

242

Here we have sex and surveillance, literally hand in hand.

In November 1994 an incident supposedly happened on a BBC television programme entitled *Noel Edmonds's House Party*. There is one section of the show called NTV where a hidden television camera is placed in the home of an unsuspecting viewer and, at a given point in the show, Noel Edmonds looks privately at what can be seen through the hidden camera and indicates to the technicians that it is now possible for them to 'go live' into the observer's home. Suitable party-like arrangements have been made to make the observed a figure of mirth and fun. On this particular occasion what Edmonds allegedly saw was the following. The victim had supposedly been left alone by his family, who were knowledgeable of the plot, and they assumed he would carry on watching BBC1. As soon as they 'left the house', to be joined outside by excited neighbours and friends in the garden who all knew of the surprise, the viewer switched over channels and began watching *Baywatch*. This in itself was enough to prevent the successful operation of this attempt at 'videocy' since Edmonds could not then speak to the victim directly through the screen. But what was worse from Edmonds's point of view was that the victim soon began to masturbate in full view of the hidden TV cameras. Clearly, technicians could not be instructed to go over to the home, for the victim could not be informed of the impending connection by TV link nor could those on site enter the room and tell the householder of his bad luck. Nor could

The connecting streets, which link Satyrsville to Panopticon City have obvious, clichéd names. Three dark alleys named Orwell Passage, Reich Road and Marcuse Mews have been conspicuously bypassed as we made our way to this next exhibit within Pandemonium. Instead, we have been brought along wide boulevards and main thoroughfares which are well lit. Above us, the high cameras, with their infra-red lighting, the better to see us in the darkness, turn in regular sweeps. We have obviously been seen in our exiting of the previous exhibit for they concentrate on our entry. We can hear the whirr of electric motors as the lenses focus upon us specifically.

Some of us had stopped our procession through Pandemonium for a break for our own bodily comfort. In so doing we unknowingly exposed ourselves to the Japanese super-loo. One enters the lavatory by using a swipe card. The toilet knows who you are so is able to identify your excreta. It wishes to know who you are because it has begun the task of analysing your urine and faeces. It needs to identify the owner of the swipe card in case its chemical analysis shows that you are pregnant, or diabetic, or are suffering from some disease of the dietary tract or are taking drugs. It does this regularly. To all those who had interrupted the flow of Pandemonium because of problems of their own bodily flow one would like to ask the following question. Would you like a full chemical analysis of your bodily excreta to be known by your employers? These are not hypothetical toilets. They are sale for $30,000 in 1996.

We feel the need to get off the street and out of the camera's gaze. The doorway into the panopticon which towers above us is a revolving door which allows only one reader at a time to enter into the building. It holds us back a microsecond in order to assess our weight. On

Our guide, the author, may have overestimated the importance of this point but before we can draw breath, having just escaped from lust, he launches in with a reading of a piece from Margaret Atwood's book *The Handmaiden's Tale* (1987).

> Above me, towards the head of the bed, Serena Joy is arranged, out-spread. Her legs are apart, I lie between them, my head on her stomach, her pubic bone under the base of my skull, her thighs on either side of me. She too is fully clothed.
>
> My arms are raised; she holds my hands, each of mine in each of hers. This is supposed to signify that we are one flesh, one being. What it really means is that she is in control, of the process and thus of the product. If any. The rings of her left hand cut into my fingers. It may or may not be revenge.
>
> . . . Below . . . the Commander is fucking. (Atwood 1987: 104)

leaving this particular exhibit, we might guess, our weight will be read again and if it has gone upwards dramatically then a photograph will be taken to ensure that we have nothing large and valuable under our coats. Welcome to the empire of the gaze!

Within the revolving door a handwritten sign says 'THE CONTROL OF SEX-UALITY AND SEXUAL RELATIONS IS ONE OF THE KEY TASKS THE MANAGEMENT OF ALL ORGANIZATIONS HAS SET ITSELF'.

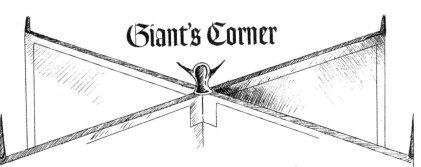

Giant's Corner

244

Consider, if you will, Max Weber. His mother, we are told (Bologh 1990: 28–9), instilled in him the dangers of sex, except for procreation, and an anxiety about his moral and physical health. She would not entrust him as a child to anyone for more than one hour per day and when he contracted meningitis she tended him constantly. He was described by his grandmother as an inwardly vehement person and somewhat reserved. Because he was her eldest child, his mother was pained by his aloofness. As an adolescent he regarded friendships whether close or otherwise as unmanly. Any problems which arose between men could be solved by recourse to the duel. The female terms that he uses are almost always denigratory. He often talks of certain laws being for 'old women' and of pacifism as being for 'ladies of both sexes'. His emphasis on brotherly love seems to exclude passion, yet includes violence. Action belonged to men. Love to women. He advocated ceaseless striving rather than submissive surrender. His passion was for action and not for sexual love. Love is for women in the home and not for men in the public arena. And whilst there is no real sense in which Weber could be described as a satyr given what we know about his 'breakdown' and its aftermath, our conceptualizations of the bureaucratic organizations which he described and analysed so well owe much to his attempts at self-control. The theory of bureaucracy comes from an attempt to control passion and sexuality, not least those of Weber himself. We have been fooled by the ideal type for a half century or more into believing that satyriasis will not be found amongst men who seek greatness. The erotic, the pornographic within associations of human beings to achieve set ends will give way, says Weber, to the onslaught of rationality and the rise of Protestantism.

Giant's Corner